McDougal Littell
Math Course 2

Larson   Boswell   Kanold   Stiff

McDougal Littell
A DIVISION OF HOUGHTON MIFFLIN COMPANY

New Mexico State Reviewers

Suzi Miller
Roosevelt Middle School
Tijeras, New Mexico

Hallie Young
McKinnley Middle School
Albuquerque, New Mexico

Copyright ©2007 by McDougal Littell, a division of Houghton Mifflin Company.
All rights reserved.

Permission is hereby granted to teachers to reprint or photocopy in classroom
quantities the pages or sheets in this work that carry a McDougal Littell copyright
notice. These pages are designed to be reproduced by teachers for use in their
classes with accompanying McDougal Littell material, provided each copy made
shows the copyright notice. Such copies may not be sold and further distribution
is expressly prohibited. Except as authorized above, prior written permission must
be obtained from McDougal Littell, a division of Houghton Mifflin Company, to
reproduce or transmit this work or portions thereof in any other form or by any
other electronic or mechanical means, including any information storage or retrieval
system, unless expressly permitted by federal copyright laws. Address inquiries to
Manager, Rights and Permissions, McDougal Littell, P.O. Box 1667, Evanston,
IL 60201.

ISBN 13: 978-0-618-77442-5

ISBN 10: 0-618-77442-4

2 3 4 5 6 7 8 9—MDO—10 09 08 07

A Note to the
NEW MEXICO STUDENT

Dear Student,

This **New Mexico Notetaking Guide** contains a lesson-by-lesson framework that allows you to take notes and review the main concepts of each lesson in your math textbook. It has been written so that you will have an organized set of **study notes** providing a place to go for review and to prepare for quizzes and tests.

The Notetaking Guide:

- reinforces the goal of each lesson, reviews vocabulary, and provides a place for you to record key concepts.

- provides extra examples to use as a built-in set of practice problems.

- includes checkpoint questions to help reinforce the material that was taught.

The goal of this Notetaking Guide is to present math in a way that you can understand!

Information on the **New Mexico Mathematics Content Standards and Benchmarks** and the **New Mexico Standards Based Assessment (NMSBA)** is covered in the Student Guide and includes:

- an explanation of what the standards mean.

- examples of the types of questions you will encounter on the **NMSBA.**

The **Additional Notetaking Lessons** present supplementary mathematical content. These lessons support state standards and align to the guidelines of the National Council of Teachers of Mathematics.

We wish you success in your math studies as you prepare yourself for a bright future. Think of this as a study guide to help you perform well on the **NMSBA!**

Copyright © by McDougal Littell, a division of Houghton Mifflin Company.

New Mexico Math Course 2
NOTETAKING GUIDE

NM

Table of Contents Preview

This New Mexico Math Course 2 Notetaking Guide includes:

> **A Student Guide to**
>   • **New Mexico Mathematics Content Standards and Benchmarks**
>   • **New Mexico Standards Based Assessment (NMSBA)**

> **Lesson-by-Lesson Notetaking Support**

> **Additional Notetaking Lessons**

Copyright © by McDougal Littell, a division of Houghton Mifflin Company.

Copyright © by McDougal Littell, a division of Houghton Mifflin Company.

Copyright © by McDougal Littell, a division of Houghton Mifflin Company.

12   Surface Area and Volume

13   Probability

Additional Notetaking Lessons

These Additional Lessons have been written to provide enrichment and challenge
opportunities and to support state standards.

Copyright © by McDougal Littell, a division of Houghton Mifflin Company.

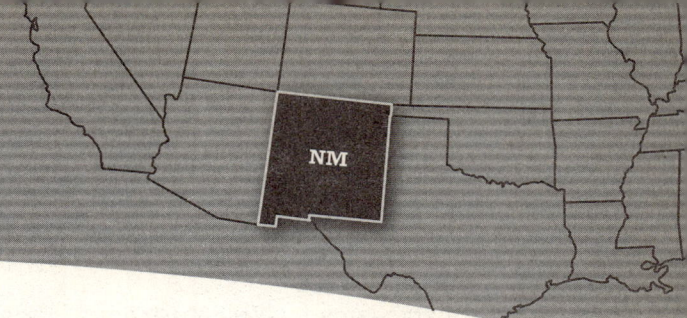

Copyright © by McDougal Littell, a division of Houghton Mifflin Company.

Did you know . . .

. . . that baseball and math standards have some things in common?

. . . and, that your math standards have been written as a commitment to you, the New Mexico student?

So . . .

. . . **"What are Math Standards and what do they have in common with baseball?"**

Compare the standards to a set of rules that must be followed in a sport event. For example, in a baseball game, the batter must move from first base to second base and then third base before proceeding to the home plate to score a run. Learning this rule enables the team to win the game.

Without the knowledge of how a baseball game is played, the team will not have the fundamental concepts to compete.

Math standards, like the rules in baseball, help you focus on a common foundation of mathematical concepts that you will use in everyday life and later in the workplace.

And . . .

. . . How will learning the New Mexico Mathematics Content Standards and Benchmarks make a difference for you, the student?

It is important to learn material that is closely aligned to the math standards because they are what you will be tested on when it comes time to take your state test.

The standards have been written as a commitment to you, the student, to help you focus on the proper content to achieve both depth and understanding of mathematical knowledge.

How Will You Learn the New Mexico Mathematics Content Standards and Benchmarks?

NM

The math standards for **New Mexico** are divided into the following strands:

1. Numbers and Operations
2. Algebra
3. Geometry
4. Measurement
5. Data Analysis and Probability

Each strand is divided into standards and then further broken down into benchmarks and performance standards. This organization guides your teacher through the mathematical content that needs to be covered to help you be successful on the **NMSBA**.

NMSBA stands for the New Mexico Standards Based Assessment. It is given to students in the early spring to evaluate your knowledge of the **New Mexico Content Standards and Benchmarks.** Your teacher will work with you throughout the year to help you prepare and be successful on this test.

> **New Mexico uses a special system to identify the strands, benchmarks, and performance standards. Here is an example of a particular strand, benchmark, and performance standard identifier.**

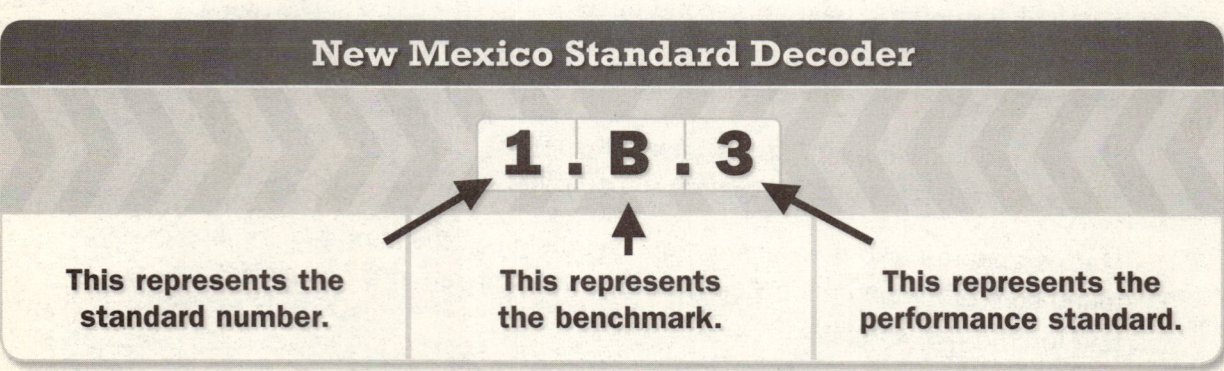

New Mexico Standard Decoder

1 . B . 3

This represents the standard number.

This represents the benchmark.

This represents the performance standard.

So, when you see 1.B.3, you know it belongs to:

Strand 1: Number and Operations

Benchmark B: Understand the meaning of operations and how they relate to one another.

Performance Standard 3: Calculate given percentages of quantities and use them to solve problems (e.g., discounts of sales, interest earned, tips, markups, commission, profit, simple interest).

> **The information that follows highlights the strands, standards, benchmarks, and performance standards, what they mean to you, and examples of what multiple-choice questions might look like on the NMSBA.**

Copyright © by McDougal Littell, a division of Houghton Mifflin Company.

Strand 1: Number and Operations

Standard: Students will understand numerical concepts and mathematical operations.

Benchmarks:

A: Understand numbers, ways of representing numbers, relationships among numbers, and number systems.

B: Understand the meaning of operations and how they relate to one another.

C: Compute fluently and make reasonable estimates.

What It Means To You

Understanding numbers is the basis for all other mathematical concepts. You will learn how to represent and work with very large or very small numbers and determine what number system they belong to.

Here is what a question might look like on the NMSBA:

1.B.3 **Calculate given percentages of quantities and use them to solve problems (e.g., discounts of sales, interest earned, tips, markups, commission, profit, simple interest).**

A store is selling all DVDs at 15% off their original price. What is the sale price of a DVD originally priced at $18?

A $2.70

B $15.30

C $18.00

D $20.70

Solution

Use the following steps to find the sale price of the DVD.

1) Find the amount of the discount.

Discount = 15% of $18

$= 0.15 \times 18 = 2.7$, or $2.70

2) Subtract the discount from the original price.

Sale price = Original price − Discount

$= 18 - 2.70 = 15.30$

The sale price is $15.30. So, the correct answer is B.

Copyright © by McDougal Littell, a division of Houghton Mifflin Company.

Strand 2: Algebra

Standard: Students will understand algebraic concepts and applications.

Benchmarks:

A: Understand patterns, relations, and functions.

B: Represent and analyze mathematical situations and structures using algebraic symbols.

C: Use mathematical models to represent and understand quantitative relationships.

D: Analyze changes in various contexts.

What It Means To You

Algebra is the branch of mathematics in which symbols, usually letters, are used to represent numbers and quantities. Studying this strand will help you recognize and represent patterns and relationships, make generalizations, and analyze how things change.

Here is what a question might look like on the NMSBA:

2.B.2 Use variables and appropriate operations to write an expression, an equation, or an inequality that represents a verbal description.

Belle spends a total of $60\frac{1}{2}$ hours per week at school and at her job. She attends school from 8:15 A.M. until 3:30 P.M., Monday through Friday. Which equation can be used to find t, the maximum number of hours Belle works at her job each week?

A $t = 60\frac{1}{2} - \left(7\frac{1}{4} \times 5\right)$

B $t = 60\frac{1}{2} - \left(7\frac{1}{2} \times 5\right)$

C $t = 60\frac{1}{2} - 7\frac{1}{4}$

D $t = 7\frac{1}{2} \times 5 - 60\frac{1}{2}$

Solution

To determine t, the maximum number of hours that she works at her job each week, subtract the total number of hours she spends at school from the total number of hours she spends at school and at her job.

In one day, Belle attends school for $7\frac{1}{4}$ hours. She attends school 5 days a week. So, in one week, she attends school for $\left(7\frac{1}{4} \times 5\right)$ hours. The maximum number of hours Belle works at her job can be found using the equation

$$t = 60\frac{1}{2} - \left(7\frac{1}{4} \times 5\right)$$

So, the correct answer is A.

Ⓐ   Ⓑ   Ⓒ   Ⓓ

Copyright © by McDougal Littell, a division of Houghton Mifflin Company.

Standard: Students will understand geometric concepts and applications.

Benchmarks:

A: Analyze characteristics and properties of two-and three-dimensional geometric shapes and develop mathematical arguments about geometric relationships.

B: Specify locations and describe spatial relationships using coordinate geometry and other representational systems.

C: Apply transformations and use symmetry to analyze mathematical situations.

D: Use visualization, spatial reasoning, and geometric modeling to solve problems.

What It Means To You

Geometry is the study of points, lines, angles, surfaces, and solids. Studying spatial relationships gives us a visual way to understand properties of geometric shapes.

Here is what a question might look like on the NMSBA:

3.A.5 Use properties to classify solids including pyramids, cones, prisms, and cylinders.

The net shown at the right represents which of the following solids?

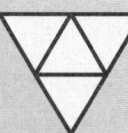

A Triangular prism

B Rectangular prism

C Rectangular pyramid

D Triangular pyramid

Solution

The net represents a solid whose base is a triangle. The other polygons in the net are also triangles, so the net represents a triangular pyramid.

The correct answer is D.

Copyright © by McDougal Littell, a division of Houghton Mifflin Company.

NM

Strand 4: Measurement

Standard: Students will understand measurement systems and applications.

Benchmarks:

A: Understand measurable attributes of objects and the units, systems, and process of measurement.

B: Apply appropriate techniques, tools, and formulas to determine measurements.

What It Means To You

Measurement gives a numerical value to a characteristic of an object, such as the length of a football field. Measurement is important because of all the ways we use it in everyday life.

Here is what questions might look like on the NMSBA:

4.B.3 Solve problems involving scale factors, ratios, and proportions.

Tonya drew a floor plan of her house. She used a scale of 1 inch equals 2 feet. The length of her kitchen is 15 feet. What distance on Tonya's floor plan represents the length of her kitchen?

A 5.5 in.

B 7.5 in.

C 10 in.

D 30 in.

Solution for Question 1

Write and solve a proportion to find the length l of her kitchen on the floor plan.

$$\frac{1}{2} = \frac{l}{15} \quad \longleftarrow \text{inches} \atop \longleftarrow \text{feet}$$

$$1 \cdot 15 = 2 \cdot l$$

$$l = 7.5$$

The length of her kitchen on the floor plan is 7.5 inches, so the correct answer is B.

Ⓐ   Ⓑ   Ⓒ   Ⓓ

2. An athlete on the school swim team can swim 25 yards in 15.2 seconds. During the last swim meet, he swam the 100-yard event at the same rate of speed. About how long did it take him to swim this race?

A 25 sec

B 32 sec

C 61 sec

D 80 sec

Solution for Question 2

Write and solve a proportion to find the amount of time t in seconds that it took the swimmer to finish the race.

$$\frac{15.2}{25} = \frac{t}{100} \quad \longleftarrow \text{time} \atop \longleftarrow \text{yards}$$

$$15.2 \cdot 100 = 25 \cdot t$$

$$t = 60.8$$

It takes the swimmer about 61 seconds to finish the race, so the correct answer is C.

Ⓐ   Ⓑ   Ⓒ   Ⓓ

Copyright © by McDougal Littell, a division of Houghton Mifflin Company.

Standard: Students will understand how to formulate questions, analyze data, and determine probabilities.

Benchmarks:

A: Formulate questions that can be addressed with data and collect, organize, and display relevant data to answer them.

B: Select and use appropriate statistical methods to analyze data.

C: Develop and evaluate inferences and predictions that are based on data.

D: Understand and apply basic concepts of probability.

What It Means To You

Data analysis involves processing information to solve problems that come up in work and in life. Probability is the likelihood that a given event will occur. Studying probability can help you to make predictions.

Here is what a question might look like on the NMSBA:

5.B.2 Know various ways to display data sets (e.g., stem-and-leaf plot, box-and-whisker plot, scatter plots) and use these forms to display a single set of data or to compare two sets of data.

Audrey's science quiz scores are listed below. Which box-and-whisker plot correctly displays the data?

80, 90, 75, 92, 81, 90, 95, 84, 76, 97

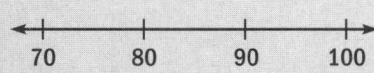

A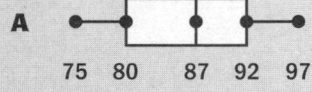

B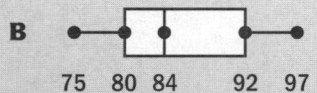

C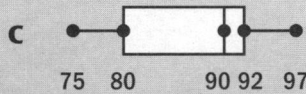

D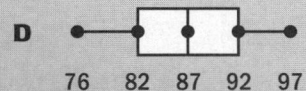

Solution

To make a box-and-whisker plot of the data, first write the data in numerical order.

75 76 80 81 84 90 90 92 95 97

Then find the lower extreme, lower quartile, median, upper quartile, and upper extreme.

The lower extreme is 75.

The lower quartile is 80.

The median is $\frac{84 + 90}{2}$, or 87.

The upper quartile is 92.

The upper extreme is 97.

Identify the box-and-whisker plot that contains these values.

The correct answer is A.

(A)   (B)   (C)   (D)

Copyright © by McDougal Littell, a division of Houghton Mifflin Company.

Describing Patterns

Goal: Describe patterns using whole number operations.

EXAMPLE 1 Recognizing and Extending a Pattern

City Bus Kristen needs to take the city bus to work. She starts work at 5:00 P.M. The bus stops at the bus stop every 30 minutes. If the bus stops at the bus stop at 3:45 P.M., at what times are the next three stops? What time should Kristen take the bus to be to work on time if her bus ride to work is 15 minutes?

To answer the question, start with 3:45 P.M. and repeatedly add [   ] minutes to the time.

Time of first stop: 3:45 P.M.

Time of second stop:

Time of third stop:

Time of fourth stop:

Because 3:45 P.M. and [   ] are too early for Kristen to take the bus and [   ] is too late, she should take the bus at [   ] to be to work on time.

EXAMPLE 2 Extending a Numerical Pattern

> The three dots at the end of a list of numbers mean that the numbers and the pattern continue without end.

Describe the following pattern: 55, 49, 43, 37, ... Then write the next three numbers.

You [   ] the previous number to get the next number in the pattern.

55,   49,   43,   37,   [   ] ,   [   ] ,   [   ] , . . .

EXAMPLE 3 **Extending a Numerical Pattern**

Describe the following pattern: 4, 8, 16, 32, ... Then write the next three numbers.

Need help with whole number operations? See pp. 742–744 of your textbook.

You [   ] to get the next number in the pattern.

4, 8, 16, 32, [ ] , [ ] , [ ] , . . .

Guided Practice Describe the pattern. Then write the next three numbers.

1. 729, 243, 81, . . .	**2.** 40, 33, 26, . . .	**3.** 3, 11, 19, . . .

EXAMPLE 4 **Extending a Visual Pattern**

Quilt A patchwork quilt has squares that follow a pattern. What are the next three squares that the quilter would make?

Solution

Look for a repeated pattern in the quilt squares. Each square has two triangles facing the same direction. Then each square rotates 90° in a counterclockwise direction from the previous square.

Answer:

Guided Practice Describe the pattern. Then draw the next figure.

4. △ □ ⬠

5.
```
        •  •  •
   •  •     •  •  •
•     •  •     •  •  •
```

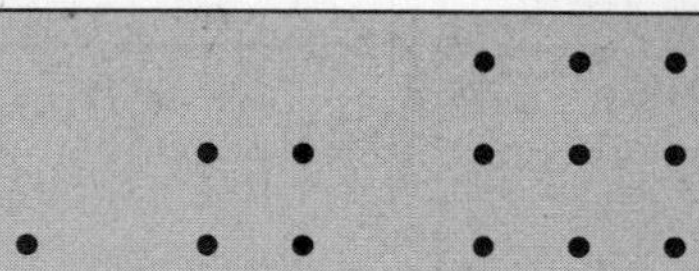

Variables and Expressions

Goal: Evaluate variable expressions.

Vocabulary

Variable:

Variable expression:

Evaluate:

EXAMPLE 1 **Evaluating Variable Expressions**

a. Evaluate $x + 7$ when $x = 4$.   **b.** Evaluate $y - 5$ when $y = 13$.

Solution

a. $x + 7 = $ ⬚   Substitute ⬚ for x.

$= $ ⬚   Add.

b. $y - 5 = $ ⬚   Substitute ⬚ for y.

$= $ ⬚   Subtract.

Guided Practice Evaluate the expression when $d = 3$ and $t = 11$.

1. $6 + d$	**2.** $t - 7$	**3.** $d + 10$

Multiplication and Division Expressions

The expression 2×5 can also be written as ☐ • ☐. There are several different ways you can write multiplication and division expressions.

Multiplication: ☐ is another way of writing $5 \cdot n$.

☐ is another way of writing $a \cdot b$.

☐ is another way of writing $3 \cdot 7$.

Division: ☐/☐ is another way of writing $x \div 4$

EXAMPLE 2 **Evaluating Variable Expressions**

a. Evaluate $6g$ when $g = 5$.　　**b.** Evaluate $\frac{s}{3}$ when $s = 15$.

Solution

a. $6g =$ ☐　　　　Substitute ☐ for g.

$=$ ☐　　　　Multiply.

b. $\frac{s}{3} = \frac{☐}{☐}$　　　Substitute ☐ for s.

$=$ ☐　　　　Divide.

WATCH OUT!
Avoid using the multiplication symbol $\times$ in a variable expression. It could be confused with the variable x.

Guided Practice **Evaluate the expression when $r = 2$ and $z = 9$.**

4. $4r$	**5.** $5z$	**6.** $\frac{z}{3}$

EXAMPLE 3 Evaluating Expressions with Two Variables

Waiter To find the amount of money earned by a waiter at a restaurant, you can evaluate the expression $w + t$, where w is the wages earned and t is the amount of tips left by customers. Find the amount of money earned by a waiter who made $25 in wages and $30 in tips.

Solution

$w + t = \boxed{} + \boxed{}$ Substitute $\boxed{}$ for w and $\boxed{}$ for t.

$ = \boxed{}$ Add.

Answer: The waiter earned $\$\boxed{}$.

Powers and Exponents

Goal: Write repeated multiplication using exponents.

Vocabulary

Power: [   ]

Base: [   ]

Exponent: [   ]

Powers and Exponents

[   ] [   ]

Numbers 4^6 = $4 \cdot 4 \cdot 4 \cdot 4 \cdot 4 \cdot 4$

The power is read
[   ]

[   ] [   ] is a factor [   ] times.

Algebra If n is a nonzero whole number, then:

$a^n = a \cdot a \cdot a \cdot \cdots \cdot a$

[   ] is a factor [   ] times.

The power is read
[   ]

EXAMPLE 1 **Writing Powers**

There were $3 \cdot 3 \cdot 3 \cdot 3 \cdot 3$ fans in attendance at Mica's first football game. What is another way to write the number of fans at Mica's football game?

$3 \cdot 3 \cdot 3 \cdot 3 \cdot 3 =$ [   ]

[   ] is a factor [   ] times.

Answer: There were [   ] fans at Mica's football game.

EXAMPLE 2 **Evaluating Powers**

Evaluate the power.

You can read 5^3 as "5 to the third power" or as "5 cubed." You can read 9^2 as "9 to the second power" or as "9 squared."

a. 5^3 **b.** 9^2 **c.** 2^1

Solution

a. $5^3 = $ [ ]   Write [ ] as a factor [ ] times.

      $= $ [ ]   Multiply.

b. $9^2 = $ [ ]   Write [ ] as a factor [ ] times.

      $= $ [ ]   Multiply.

c. $2^1 = $ [ ]   Write [ ] as a factor [ ] time.

Guided Practice   **Write the product as a power.**

1. $3 \cdot 3 \cdot 3$	**2.** $4 \cdot 4 \cdot 4 \cdot 4 \cdot 4$	**3.** $10 \cdot 10 \cdot 10 \cdot 10$

Evaluate the power.

4. 1^6	**5.** 3^6	**6.** 7^4

EXAMPLE **3** **Evaluating Powers with Variables**

   a. Evaluate y^3 when $y = 4$.   **b.** Evaluate g^2 when $g = 10$.

Solution

   a. $y^3 = $ ☐   Substitute ☐ for y.

   $= $ ☐   Write ☐ as a factor ☐ times.

   $= $ ☐   Multiply.

   b. $g^2 = $ ☐   Substitute ☐ for g.

   $= $ ☐   Write ☐ as a factor ☐ times.

   $= $ ☐   Multiply.

Guided Practice **Complete the following exercises.**

7. Evaluate b^3 when $b = 6$.	**8.** Evaluate p^5 when $p = 2$.

9. To get a result of 1,000,000, you raise 10 to what power?

Order of Operations

LESSON 1.4

Goal: Evaluate expressions involving two or more operations.

Vocabulary

Order of operations:

Order of Operations

1. Evaluate expressions .

2. Evaluate .

3. from left to right.

4. from left to right.

EXAMPLE 1 **Following Order of Operations**

Babysitting You earn spending money by babysitting. You charge $5 per hour plus a flat fee of $2 per child. Find the amount you earned babysitting 1 child for 4 hours.

$2 + 5 \times 4 = $ 　　　　　　First multiply 　 and 　.

$= $ 　　　　　　　　　　　Then add 　 and 　.

Answer: You earned $ 　 .

EXAMPLE 2 **Evaluating a Variable Expression**

Evaluate $a + \dfrac{b^2}{3}$ when $a = 7$ and $b = 6$.

$a + \dfrac{b^2}{3} = $ 　　　　　Substitute 　 for a and 　 for b.

$= 7 + \dfrac{36}{3}$　　　　　　Evaluate the power.

$= $ 　 $= $ 　　　Divide 　 and 　. Then add 　 and 　.

1. $8 + 3 \times 4$	**2.** $32 - 3^3 \div 9$	**3.** $8 \times 4 + 5^2$

4. Evaluate the expression $t - 3v^3$ when $t = 100$ and $v = 2$.

EXAMPLE 3 **Using the Left-to-Right Rule**

a. $15 - 8 + 9 - 3 = $ ☐   Subtract ☐ from ☐.

= ☐   Add ☐ and ☐.

= ☐   Subtract ☐ from ☐.

b. $100 \div 10 \div 2 = $ ☐   Divide ☐ by ☐.

= ☐   Divide ☐ by ☐.

EXAMPLE 4 **Using Grouping Symbols**

Thinking of the letters PEMDAS might help you remember the order of operations:

Parentheses
Exponents
Multiplication
Division
Addition
Subtraction

a. $6(10 - 5) = $ ☐   Subtract ☐ from ☐.

= ☐   Multiply ☐ and ☐.

b. $\dfrac{6 \cdot 6}{8 + 4} = \dfrac{☐}{☐}$ Multiply ☐ and ☐. Add ☐ and ☐.

= ☐   Divide ☐ by ☐.

c. $(4 + 7)^2 - 20 = $ ☐   Add ☐ and ☐.

= ☐   Evaluate the power.

= ☐   Subtract ☐ from ☐.

5. $25 - 10 + 3 - 5$	**6.** $(9 - 4)(5 - 2)^3$	**7.** $\dfrac{9 + 5}{63 \div 9}$

EXAMPLE 5 **Standardized Test Practice**

Basketball The point values for certain baskets in basketball are shown in the table. You make 12 field goals, 5 free throws, and 3 three-point field goals. Your friend makes 15 field goals, 3 free throws, and 4 three-point field goals. How many more points did your friend score than you?

Type of Basket	Points
Three-point field goal	3
Field goal	2
Free throw	1

(A) 2 points   **(B)** 6 points

(C) 7 points   **(D)** 45 points

Solution

You need to evaluate the expression
$(15 \cdot 2 + 3 \cdot 1 + 4 \cdot 3) - (12 \cdot 2 + 5 \cdot 1 + 3 \cdot 3)$.

$(15 \cdot 2 + 3 \cdot 1 + 4 \cdot 3) - (12 \cdot 2 + 5 \cdot 1 + 3 \cdot 3)$

= [_____]   [____] first.

= [____]   Add [__], [__], and [__].

Add [__], [__], and [__].

= [__]   Subtract [__] from [__].

Answer: Your friend scored [__] more points than you. The correct answer

is . **(A)** **(B)** **(C)** **(D)**

LESSON
1.5

Equations and Mental Math

Goal: Use mental math to solve an equation.

Vocabulary

Equation:

Solution:

Solving an equation:

EXAMPLE 1 **Checking Possible Solutions**

Tell whether the value of the variable is a solution to $f + 7 = 13$.

   a. $f = 8$ **b.** $f = 6$

Solution

Symbol	Meaning
$=$	is equal to
$\stackrel{?}{=}$	is equal to?
$\neq$	is not equal to

a. $f + 7 = 13$ Write original equation.

               Substitute ⬚ for f.

               The equation ⬚ true, ⬚.

b. $f + 7 = 13$ Write original equation.

               Substitute ⬚ for f.

               The equation ⬚ true, ⬚.

Guided Practice Tell whether the value of the variable is a solution of the equation.

1. $4t = 20$; $t = 6$	**2.** $17 - p = 12$; $p = 5$	**3.** $12 \div d = 4$; $d = 3$

EXAMPLE **2** **Using Mental Math to Solve Equations**

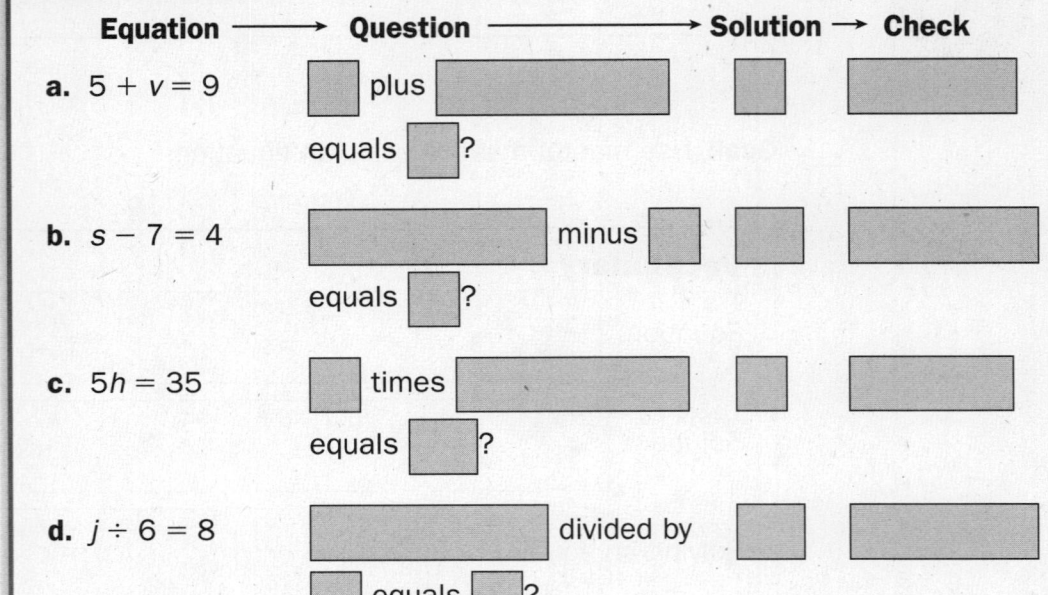

Equation ⟶ Question ⟶ Solution ⟶ Check

a. $5 + v = 9$

☐ plus ☐ equals ☐ ?

b. $s - 7 = 4$

☐ minus ☐ ☐ equals ☐ ?

c. $5h = 35$

☐ times ☐ ☐ equals ☐ ?

d. $j \div 6 = 8$

☐ divided by ☐ ☐ equals ☐ ?

Guided Practice Solve the equation using mental math.

4. $2n = 18$	**5.** $22 = k - 8$	**6.** $4 + r = 17$	**7.** $56 \div w = 8$

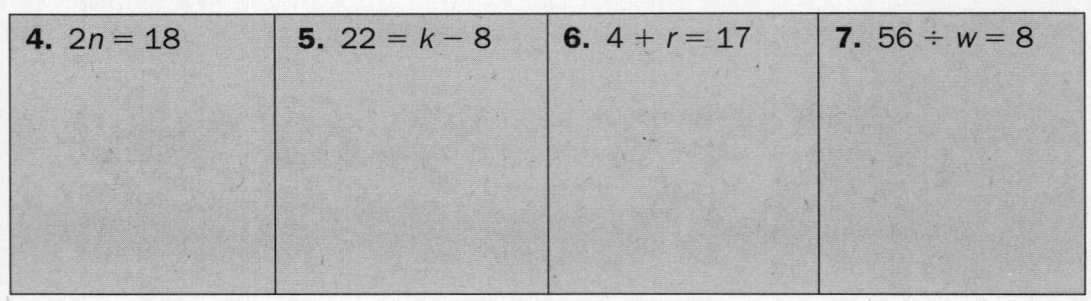

Distance, Speed, and Time

Words Distance traveled is equal to the ☐ (rate of travel) times the ☐ .

Algebra $d =$ ☐

Numbers distance = 2 feet per second · 30 seconds = ☐

EXAMPLE 3 **Using Mental Math to Solve an Equation**

Race Walker A race walker travels at a speed of 5 miles per hour. She tallies her training schedule and finds that she walked 100 miles this month. How much time did she spend walking this month?

Solution

☐	Write formula for distance.
☐ = ☐	Substitute the values you know.
☐ = ☐	Use mental math to solve the equation.

Answer: She walked ☐ hours this month.

Guided Practice **Solve the following problem.**

8. A high speed passenger commuter ferry is advertised as being able to make a 16 mile crossing between land and an island in only 48 minutes. How many minutes does it take the ferry to travel 1 mile?

Perimeter and Area

Goal: Use formulas to find perimeter and area.

Vocabulary

Perimeter:

Area:

Perimeter and Area

Rectangle

width w

length ℓ

Square

side length s

Perimeter P $P =$ $P =$

Area A $A =$ $A =$

EXAMPLE 1   **Finding Perimeter**

If you forget the formula for the perimeter of a rectangle, you could draw and label a diagram of a rectangle. Then just add the lengths of the sides.

Find the perimeter of the rectangle or square with the given dimensions.

a. $\ell = 6$ feet, $w = 3$ feet   **b.** $s = 5$ centimeters

Solution

a. $P =$ **b.** $P =$

$=$ $=$

$=$ $=$ $=$

Answer: The perimeter is   feet.

Answer: The perimeter is   centimeters.

Find the perimeter of the rectangle or square.

1.

2 m

5 m

2.

7 ft

7 ft

EXAMPLE 2 **Finding Area**

Find the area of the rectangle or square with the given dimensions.

a. $\ell = 10$ feet, $w = 4$ feet

b. $s = 12$ centimeters

Solution

a. $A = $ [ ]

$= $ [ ]

$= $ [ ]

Answer: The area is
[ ] square feet.

b. $A = $ [ ]

$= $ [ ]

$= $ [ ]

Answer: The area is
[ ] square centimeters.

Guided Practice Find the area of the rectangle or square.

3.

5 m

6 m

4.

10 ft

10 ft

5. Find the perimeter and the area of a rectangle that has a length of 12 inches and a width of 9 inches.

EXAMPLE 3 **Using Perimeter and Area**

Garden A rectangular garden has a length of 20 meters and a width of 15 meters. Find the perimeter and the area of the garden.

$P = $ ⬚

$= $ ⬚

$= $ ⬚

$= $ ⬚

$A = $ ⬚

$= $ ⬚

$= $ ⬚

Answer: The perimeter is ⬚, and the area is ⬚.

EXAMPLE 4 **Standardized Test Practice**

Painting Mark is planning to paint one wall of his living room, as shown. One can of paint can cover 60 square feet. How many cans of paint does Mark need?

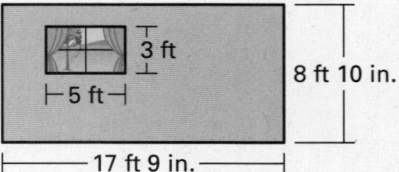

3 ft

5 ft

8 ft 10 in.

17 ft 9 in.

Ⓐ 1 can Ⓑ 2 cans Ⓒ 3 cans Ⓓ 5 cans

1. Estimate the wall's area, including the window, using $\ell = $ ⬚ feet and $w = $ ⬚ feet.

$A = \text{length} \times \text{width} = $ ⬚ (⬚) $= $ ⬚ ft^2

2. Calculate the window's area.

$A = \text{length} \times \text{width} = $ ⬚ (⬚) $= $ ⬚ ft^2

3. Subtract to find the area that will be painted.

⬚ $-$ ⬚ $= $ ⬚ ft^2

4. Divide the area that will be painted by ⬚ to find the number of cans of paint needed.

⬚ $\div$ ⬚ $= $ ⬚ R ⬚

Answer: Mark needs ⬚ cans of paint. The correct answer is ⬚.

Ⓐ Ⓑ Ⓒ Ⓓ

A Problem Solving Plan

Goal: Use a 4-step plan to solve many kinds of problems.

EXAMPLE 1 **Understanding and Planning**

Commercials A programmer at a television station has exactly 160 seconds of time to fill with commercials. The programmer must choose 3 commercials from the table, and one of the commercials must be the station's commercial. What commercials can the programmer use?

Commercial	Time (seconds)
Station Commercial	45
A	30
B	55
C	80
D	60

To solve this problem, you need to make sure you understand the problem. Then make a plan for solving the problem.

Read and Understand
What do you Know?

The programmer must fill [   ] of commercial time.

The programmer must choose [ ] commercials.

[   ] must be included.

What do you want to find out?

[   ]

Make a Plan
How can you relate what you know to what you want to find out?

[   ]

1. How many seconds long is the station commercial?

2. How many seconds does this leave for the remaining two commercials?

EXAMPLE 2 **Solving and Looking Back**

To solve the television commercial problem from the previous page, you need to carry out the plan from Example 1 and then check the answer.

Solve the Problem

Because of the station commercial requirement, there are ☐ − ☐ = ☐ seconds for playing the other two commercials. Make a list of all the combinations of the other two commercials and the time it takes to play them.

> Notice the pattern of commercial pairings in the table:
>
> A B C D
>
> A B C D
>
> A B C D
>
> Using a pattern like this guarantees that you don't forget any commercial pairings.

Commercials	Total Time (seconds)
A: 30 sec, B: 55 sec	☐
A: 30 sec, C: 80 sec	☐
A: 30 sec, D: 60 sec	☐
B: 55 sec, C: 80 sec	☐
B: 55 sec, D: 60 sec	☐
C: 80 sec, D: 60 sec	☐

Answer: The programmer must play the station commercial and commercials ☐ and ☐.

Look Back

The answer lists exactly 3 commercials, one of which is the station commercial, totaling to ☐ seconds + ☐ seconds = ☐ seconds.

3. Suppose the station commercial was 50 seconds long. Now what commercials would the programmer need to play?

Problem Solving Plan

1. [   ] Read the problem carefully. Identify the question and any important information.

2. [   ] Decide on a problem solving strategy.

3. [   ] Use the problem solving strategy to answer the question.

4. [   ] Check that your answer is reasonable.

Words to Review

Give an example of the vocabulary word.

Variable

Variable expression

Evaluate

Power

Base

Exponent

Order of operations

Equation

Solution

Solving an equation

Perimeter

Area

Review your notes and Chapter 1 by using the Chapter Review on pages 43–46 of your textbook.

Comparing, Ordering, and Rounding Decimals

LESSON 2.1

Goal: Compare, order, and round decimals.

Vocabulary

Decimal:

Decimals and Place Value

hundred thousands	ten thousands	thousands	hundreds	tens	ones	tenths	hundredths	thousandths	ten-thousandths	hundred-thousandths

fifteen and two tenths

fifteen and eight hundredths

EXAMPLE 1 Comparing Decimals

Baby Weights At Jason's 6-month checkup, he weighed 15.2 pounds. At Ali's 6-month checkup, she weighed 15.08 pounds. Compare the weights of the babies to determine who weighed more.

The [　] and [　] digits are the same.

15.**2**0 ← Write a [　] as a placeholder.

15.**0**8

The [　] digits are different. [　], so [　].

Answer: Because 15.2 [　] 15.08, [　] weighed more.

Guided Practice Copy and complete the statement using <, >, or =.

1. 15.3 _?_ 15.09	**2.** 6.3 _?_ 6.30	**3.** 9.238 _?_ 9.36

EXAMPLE 2 **Ordering Decimals**

Remember that numbers on a number line increase from left to right.

Order 6.14, 6.3, 6.07, 6, and 6.27 from least to greatest.

On a number line, mark tenths between [   ]. Mark

hundredths by dividing each tenth into [   ] equal parts. Then

graph each number.

From least to greatest, the numbers are [   ].

Rounding Decimals

To round a decimal to a given place value, look at the digit in the place

to the [   ].

- If the digit is less than [   ], round down.
- If the digit is [   ] or greater, round up.

EXAMPLE 3 **Rounding a Decimal**

Round 8.548 to the nearest tenth.

You want to round to the nearest [   ].

8.**5**48   Because the hundredths' digit is less than [   ],

round [   ] and drop the remaining digits.

Answer: The decimal 8.548 rounded to the nearest tenth is [   ].

Guided Practice **Order the numbers from least to greatest.**

4. 7.59, 8.2, 8.15, 7.95, 7.85	**5.** 1.36, 1.4, 1.59, 1.92, 1.5

6. Round 61.0962 to the nearest hundredth.

Adding and Subtracting Decimals

Goal: Add and subtract decimals.

Vocabulary

Front-end estimation:

EXAMPLE 1 **Adding and Subtracting Decimals**

a. 2.149 + 1.32

$$
\begin{array}{r}
2.149 \\
+\ 1.320 \\
\hline
\end{array}
$$

← Write ☐ as a placeholder.

b. 5 − 3.18

$$
\begin{array}{r}
5.00 \\
-\ 3.18 \\
\hline
\end{array}
$$

← Write ☐ as placeholders.

Guided Practice **Find the sum or difference.**

1. 42.9 + 26.5	**2.** 4.62 + 3.4	**3.** 2.859 + 3.48
4. 2.5 − 0.9	**5.** 8.43 − 6.21	**6.** 1 − 0.16

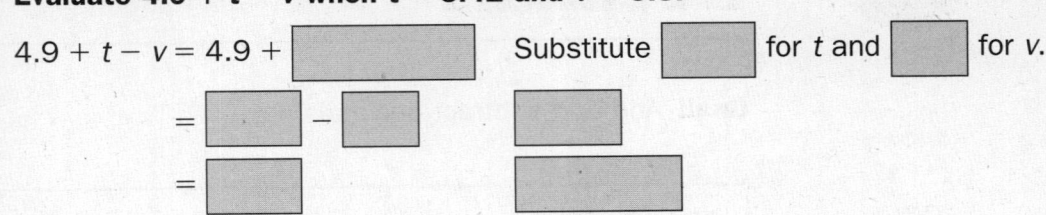

EXAMPLE 2 Evaluating a Variable Expression

WATCH OUT!
Don't forget to add
and subtract from left
to right.

Evaluate 4.9 + t − v when t = 3.42 and v = 3.8.

4.9 + t − v = 4.9 + ⬚   Substitute ⬚ for t and ⬚ for v.

= ⬚ − ⬚   ⬚

= ⬚   ⬚

Guided Practice Evaluate the expression when d = 5.82 and f = 4.9.

7. d + f	8. d − f	9. 11 − f − d

EXAMPLE 3 Estimating a Sum

Lunch Joel and Manny are eating lunch at a deli. Joel's lunch costs
$6.75, and Manny's lunch costs $5.40. They want to order two
chocolate shakes, which will cost an additional $3.89. They have
$15.00 to pay the bill. Can they buy the milkshakes?

Solution

1. Add the front-end
digits: the dollars.

$**6**.75

$**5**.40

+ $**3**.89

⬚

2. Estimate the sum
of the remaining
digits: the cents.

$6.**75**

$5.**40** → ⬚

+ $3.**89** ⬚

3. Add the results.

⬚

+ ⬚

⬚

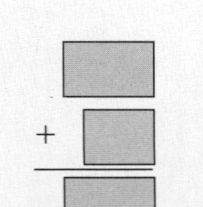

Answer: The estimated sum is ⬚ than $15, so they ⬚ buy
the milkshakes.

Multiplying Decimals

Goal: Multiply decimals.

Vocabulary

Leading digit:

Multiplying Decimals

Words Multiply decimals as you would [   ]. Then place the [   ] in the product. The number of decimal places in the product is equal to [   ] [   ].

Numbers $0.7 \times 0.3 =$ [   ]

EXAMPLE 1 **Multiplying Decimals**

$$
\begin{array}{r}
2.56 \\
\times\ 0.43 \\
\hline
768 \\
1024 \\
\hline
1.1008
\end{array}
$$

[   ] decimal places

+ [   ] decimal places

[   ] decimal places

EXAMPLE 2 **Multiplying Decimals**

a. 0.55   ☐ decimal places

   × 12   + ☐ decimal places

   ☐

   ☐

   ☐   ☐ decimal places

> After you place the decimal point, you can ☐ any zeros at the end of an answer.

Answer: 0.55 × 12 = ☐

✓ **Check** Because $\frac{1}{2}$ of 12 is ☐ , the product is reasonable.

b.   1.168   ☐ decimal places

   × 0.07   + ☐ decimal places

   ☐   ☐ decimal places

> Write a ☐ before the 8 as a placeholder so that the number has five decimal places.

Answer: 1.168 × 0.07 = ☐

✓ **Check** Because 1 × 0.07 = ☐ , the product is reasonable.

Guided Practice **Find the product. Then check that your answer is reasonable.**

1. 2.5 × 3.9	**2.** 0.43 × 0.16	**3.** 5.103 × 2.9

EXAMPLE 3 **Multiplying Decimals to Find Area**

Table Top Alonzo is building a table to hold his model train. The table top is going to be 4.75 feet long and 3.5 feet wide. What is the area of the table top?

Solution

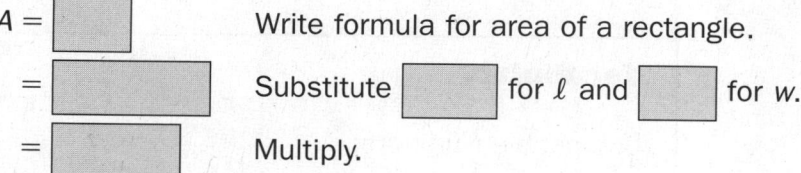

$A = \boxed{}$ Write formula for area of a rectangle.

$= \boxed{}$ Substitute $\boxed{}$ for ℓ and $\boxed{}$ for w.

$= \boxed{}$ Multiply.

Answer: The area of the table top is $\boxed{}$.

Guided Practice Find the area of the rectangle.

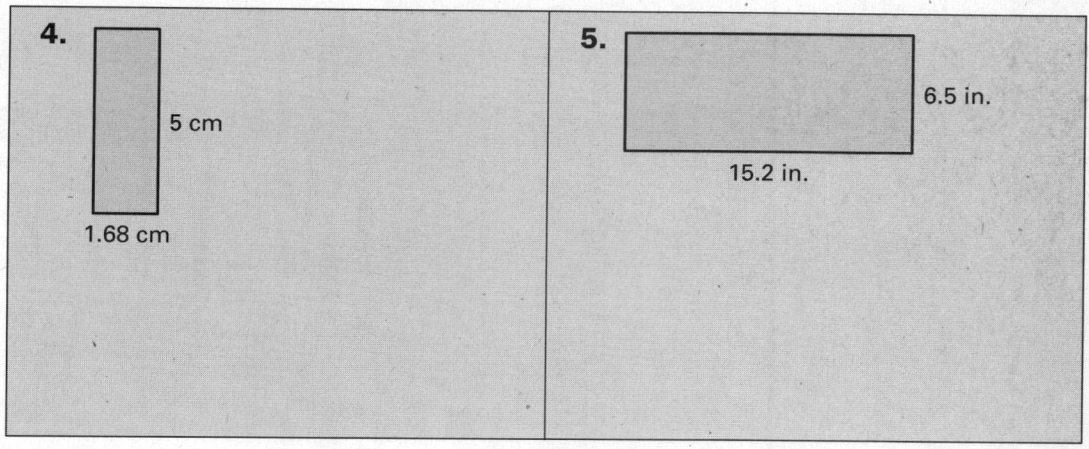

4.

5 cm

1.68 cm

5.

6.5 in.

15.2 in.

Dividing Decimals

Goal: Divide decimals.

Vocabulary

Compatible Numbers:

EXAMPLE 1 **Dividing a Decimal by a Whole Number**

Gift Joy and her three cousins spent $21.40 on a gift for their grandfather. Each cousin contributed the same amount of money. How much did each cousin spend?

⬛
⬛)21.40

⬛

⬛

⬛

⬛

⬛

⬛

Divide as you would with ⬛.

Line up decimal point in ⬛ with decimal point in ⬛.

Stop dividing when you get a ⬛ remainder.

Answer: Each cousin spent ⬛

Guided Practice Find the quotient. Then check your answer.

1. 253.4 ÷ 7	**2.** 14.76 ÷ 3	**3.** 91.8 ÷ 9

Dividing by a Decimal

Words When you divide by a decimal, multiply both the divisor and the dividend by a [_____] that will make the divisor a [_____].

Numbers $12.5\overline{)8.75}$ ⟶ $[\ \ ]\overline{)87.5}$ with 0.7

EXAMPLE 2 **Dividing Decimals**

Divide: **a.** $6.826 \div 0.002$ **b.** $12 \div 2.4$ **c.** $0.028 \div 0.5$

Solution

a. $0.002\overline{)6.826}$ To multiply divisor and dividend by [____], move both decimal points [__] place(s) to the right.

$$
\begin{array}{r}
3413 \\
2\overline{)6826} \\
\underline{6} \\
8 \\
\underline{8} \\
2 \\
\underline{2} \\
6 \\
\underline{6} \\
0
\end{array}
$$

b. $2.4\overline{)12.0}$ To multiply divisor and dividend by [____], move both decimal points [__] place(s) to the right. Write [__] as a placeholder.

$$
\begin{array}{r}
5 \\
24\overline{)120} \\
\underline{120} \\
0
\end{array}
$$

c. $0.5\overline{)0.028}$ To multiply divisor and dividend by 10, move both decimal points [__] place(s) to the right.

$$
\begin{array}{r}
0.056 \\
5\overline{)0.28} \\
\underline{25} \\
30 \\
\underline{30} \\
0
\end{array}
$$

— Line up [_____].

WATCH OUT!
Don't forget to write zeros as placeholders in the quotient.

Find the quotient. Then check your answer.

4. 19.6 ÷ 0.5	**5.** 48.45 ÷ 5.7	**6.** 0.495 ÷ 8.25
7. 16.0125 ÷ 9.15	**8.** 75 ÷ 3.2	**9.** 9.6 ÷ 4

EXAMPLE 3 **Rounding a Quotient**

Socks A pack of six pairs of socks costs $9.75. Find the price of one pair of socks. Round to the nearest cent.

In Example 3, you are rounding to the nearest cent, or hundredth. Divide only until the quotient reaches the thousandths' place. Then round.

Solution

1. Divide $9.75 by 6.

```
     1.625
  6)9.750
    6
    37
    36
    15
    12
     30
     30
      0
```

Write and bring down [ ] as a placeholder.

Stop dividing when the quotient reaches the
[ ] place.

2. Round the quotient to the nearest cent. $1.625 ⟶ [ ]

Answer: The price of each pair of socks is [ ].

Scientific Notation

Goal: Read and write numbers using scientific notation.

Vocabulary

Scientific notation: [_____]

Using Scientific Notation

A number is written in scientific notation if it has the form $c \times 10^n$ where c is [_____] 1 and less than 10 and n is [_____].

Standard form	Product form	Scientific notation
2,860,000	$2.86 \times$ [____]	[____] $\times 10^{[\ ]}$

EXAMPLE 1 Writing Numbers in Scientific Notation

Budget The budget to support the national parks in the United States was $64,500,000 in 1998. To write 64,500,000 in scientific notation, use powers of 10.

Standard form	Product form	Scientific notation
64,500,000	[____] $\times$ [____]	[____] $\times 10^{[\ ]}$

Answer: The budget for national parks in the United States was $ [_____] in 1998.

Powers of ten:
$10^1 = 10$
$10^2 = 100$
$10^3 = 1000$
$10^4 = 10,000$
$10^5 = 100,000$
$10^6 = 1,000,000$

EXAMPLE 2 **Writing Numbers in Standard Form**

Write the number in standard form.

a. 3×10^5 **b.** 6.702×10^9

> You read 3×10^5 as "three times ten to the fifth power."

Solution

Scientific notation	Product form	Standard form
a. 3×10^5	$3 \times$ [ ]	[ ]
b. 6.702×10^9	[ ] $\times$ [ ]	[ ]

Guided Practice Write the number in scientific notation.

1. 27,500,000	2. 10,200,000,000	3. 3,600,000

Write the number in standard form.

4. 6.37×10^4	5. 2.09×10^7	6. 1×10^1

36 | Chapter 2   Notetaking Guide

EXAMPLE 3 **Comparing Numbers in Scientific Notation**

Population The population of Alaska was about 6.35×10^5 in 2001. The population of Nebraska was about 1.71×10^6 in 2001. Which state had the greater population?

Solution

To compare numbers written in scientific notation, first compare the

[   ]. If the exponents are [   ], then compare the

[   ].

Alaska: 6.35×10^5 Exponent is [   ].

Nebraska: 1.71×10^6 Exponent is [   ].

Because 5 [ ] 6, 6.35×10^5 [ ] 1.71×10^6.

Answer: [   ] had the greater population.

✓ **Check** Write the numbers in [   ] and compare.

$6.35 \times 10^5 = $ [   ]

$1.71 \times 10^6 = $ [   ]

So, 6.35×10^5 [ ] 1.71×10^6.

Guided Practice Copy and complete the statement using <, >, or =.

7. 3.4×10^{30} _?_ 2.05×10^{32}	8. 2.59×10^{15} _?_ 2.06×10^{15}

Lesson 2.5   Scientific Notation | **37**

Measuring in Metric Units

Goal: Measure and estimate using metric units.

Vocabulary

Metric system:

Metric units of length:

Mass:

Metric units of mass:

Capacity:

Metric units of capacity:

Benchmarks

1 millimeter is about the thickness of a dime.

1 centimeter is about the width of a large paper clip.

1 meter is about the height of the back of a chair.

1 kilometer is about the combined length of 9 football fields.

1 milligram is about the mass of a grain of sugar.

1 gram is about the mass of a small paper clip.

1 kilogram is about the mass of a textbook.

1 millimeter is about the capacity of an eyedropper.

1 liter is about the capacity of a large water bottle.

1 kiloliter is about the capacity of 8 large trash cans.

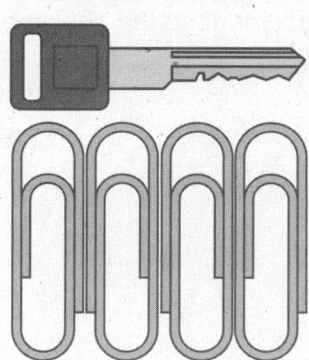

EXAMPLE 1 — Using Metric Units of Length

Estimate the length of a key by imagining paper clips laid next to it. Then measure the key with a metric ruler to check your estimate.

WATCH OUT!

A typical metric ruler allows you to measure only to the nearest tenth of a centimeter.

Solution

1. About [ ] large paper clips fit next to the key, so it is about [ ] long.

2. Measure using a ruler.

cm   1   2   3   4

Each centimeter is divided into [ ], so the key is [ ] long.

EXAMPLE 2 — Measuring Mass

Find the mass of the plastic model of bananas.

Each gram is divided into [ ], so the mass of the model is [ ].

17 g   18   19 g

EXAMPLE 3 — Using Metric Units of Mass

Copy and complete the statement using the appropriate metric unit:
The mass of a computer monitor is 5 _?_ .

The mass of a computer monitor is [ ] than 5 grains of sugar $\left(5\ \boxed{}\right)$, and is also [ ] than the mass of 5 paper clips $\left(5\ \boxed{}\right)$.

Because a good estimate for the mass of a computer monitor is 5 [ ], the appropriate metric unit is [ ].

Answer: The mass of a computer monitor is 5 [ ].

Guided Practice Complete the following exercise.

1. Estimate the length of a video cassette in centimeters. Then use a metric ruler to check your estimate.

Copy and complete the statement using the appropriate metric unit.

2. The mass of a cat is 4 _?_ .

3. The mass of a rubber band is 175 _?_ .

EXAMPLE 4 **Measuring a Liquid Amount**

Find the amount of liquid in the measuring cup.

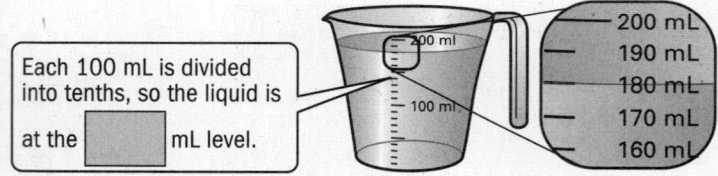

Each 100 mL is divided into tenths, so the liquid is at the [   ] mL level.

200 mL
190 mL
180 mL
170 mL
160 mL

Answer: The measuring cup contains [   ] milliliters of liquid.

EXAMPLE 5 **Standardized Test Practice**

What is the most reasonable capacity of a bucket?

(A) 6 L   (B) 65 mL   (C) 75 L   (D) 2 kL

Solution

Both [   ] ([   ] large water bottles) and [   ] ([   ] large trash cans) would overfill a bucket. Using [   ] ([   ] eyedroppers) would be too little. That leaves [   ] ([   ] large water bottles), which seems reasonable.

Answer: The most reasonable capacity of a bucket is [   ]. The correct answer is [   ]. (A) (B) (C) (D)

Match the object with the appropriate capacity.

1. Spoon	**2.** Hot tub	**3.** Drinking glass
A. 1.3 kL	**A.** 1.3 kL	**A.** 1.3 kL
B. 250 mL	**B.** 250 mL	**B.** 250 mL
C. 2 mL	**C.** 2 mL	**C.** 2 mL

Converting Metric Units

LESSON 2.7

Goal: Convert between metric units.

The metric system is a [_____]. Metric prefixes are associated with decimal place values.

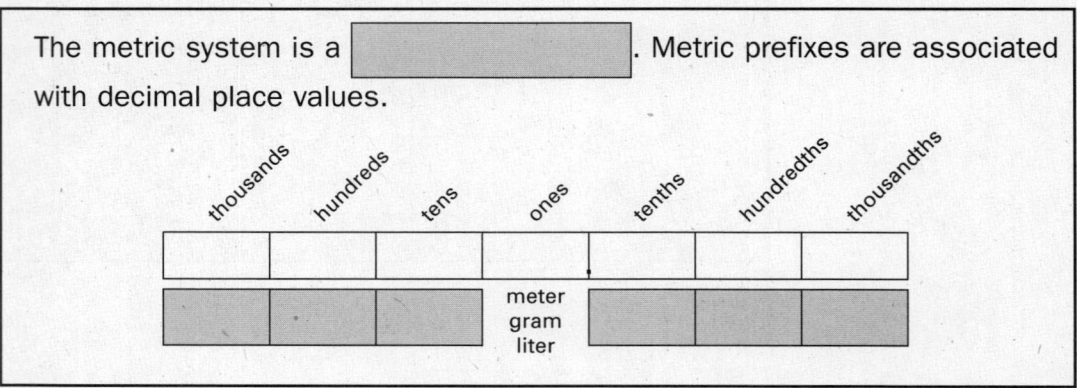

thousands | hundreds | tens | ones | tenths | hundredths | thousandths

meter
gram
liter

To convert between metric units n decimal places apart, [_____] or [_____] as follows.

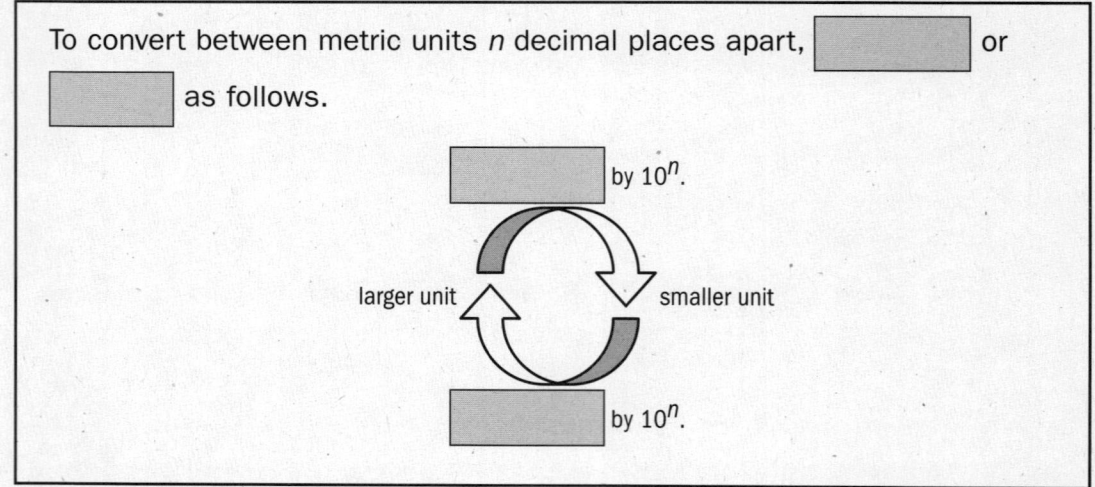

[_____] by 10^n.

larger unit ⟳ smaller unit

[_____] by 10^n.

EXAMPLE 1 Converting Metric Units of Length

The height of a chain-link fence is 137 centimeters. How many meters tall is the fence?

Solution

You are converting from a smaller unit ([   ]) to a larger unit

([   ]), so [   ] by a power of 10.

From [   ] to [   ], the decimal point is moved

[   ], so divide by [   ], or [   ].

137 ÷ [   ] = [   ]

137 centimeters = [   ] meters

Answer: The fence is [   ] tall.

EXAMPLE 2 Converting Units of Mass and Capacity

Copy and complete the statement.

    a. 4620 g = _?_ kg   **b.** 27 L = _?_ mL

Solution

    a. To convert from grams to kilograms, [   ].

        4620 ÷ [   ] = [   ], so 4620 g = [   ] kg.

    b. To convert from liters to milliliters, [   ].

        27 × [   ] = [   ], so 27 L = [   ] mL.

Copy and complete the statement.

1. 5600 m = __?__ km	**2.** 68 m = __?__ mm	**3.** 275 cm = __?__ m
4. 382 mm = __?__ cm	**5.** 500 g = __?__ kg	**6.** 1.75 kL = __?__ L

EXAMPLE 3 Comparing Metric Measures

Copy and complete the statement using <, >, or =.

    a. 650 cm __?__ 6 m   **b.** 1.6 kg __?__ 1525 g

Solution

> To compare two measurements that have different units, convert one of the measures so that both have the same units.

a. 650 cm __?__ 6 m   Strategy: Convert meters to ☐.

650 cm __?__ ☐ cm   6 × ☐ = ☐, so 6 m = ☐ cm.

650 cm ☐ ☐ cm   Compare.

Answer: 650 cm ☐ 6 m

b. 1.6 kg __?__ 1525 g   Strategy: Convert kilograms to ☐.

☐ g __?__ 1525 g   1.6 × ☐ = ☐,

                               so 1.6 kg = ☐ g.

☐ g ☐ 1525 g   Compare.

Answer: 1.6 kg ☐ 1525 g

Copy and complete the statement using <, >, or =.

1. 6.8 kL __?__ 6725 L	**2.** 2.1 g __?__ 2100 mg	**3.** 7.3 mm __?__ 73 cm

EXAMPLE 4 **Standardized Test Practice**

Garden Beds Hank is planting a garden in his yard that is 8.5 meters long. Suppose the garden is divided into smaller beds that each measure 212.5 centimeters in length. How many small garden beds would there be?

Ⓐ 2.5   **Ⓑ** 4   **Ⓒ** 25   **Ⓓ** 40

Solution

1. Convert 8.5 meters to [ ] by multiplying by [ ].

8.5 × [ ] = [ ], so 8.5 m = [ ].

2. To find the number of gardens, divide the [ ]

by [ ].

[ ] cm ÷ [ ] cm = [ ]

Answer: The garden would be divided into [ ] smaller beds.

The correct answer is [ ].

Words to Review

Give an example of the vocabulary word.

Decimal

Front-end estimation

Leading digits

Compatible numbers

Scientific notation

Metric system

Meter

Millimeter

Centimeter

Kilometer

Mass

Gram

Milligram

Kilogram

Capacity

Liter

Milliliter

Kiloliter

Review your notes and Chapter 2 by using the Chapter Review on pages 97–100 of your textbook.

LESSON
3.1

Mean, Median, and Mode

Goal: Describe data using mean, median, and mode.

Vocabulary

Mean: The sum of the values divided by the number of values.

Median: The middle value when the values are written in numerical order. If the set has two middle numbers the median is the mean of the two.

Mode: The value that occurs most frequently in a set of data. There can be one or more modes in a set of data

Range: Difference between the largest value and the smallest value.

EXAMPLE 1 Finding a Mean

Heights The students in Ms. Whitney's class practice measuring by finding each other's heights. The results are shown below. Find the mean height.

1.6 m	1.8 m	1.5 m	1.3 m	1.9 m
1.4 m	1.6 m	1.5 m	1.8 m	1.6 m

$$\text{Mean} = \frac{1.6+1.4+1.8+1.6+1.5+1.5+1.3+1.8+1.9+1.6}{10}$$

$$= \frac{16}{10}$$

$$= 1.6$$

Answer: The mean height of the students is $\boxed{1.6\,m}$.

EXAMPLE **2** **Finding Median, Mode, and Range**

Find the median, mode(s), and range of the numbers below.

54 58 51 48 63 59 57 52 54 58

Write the numbers in order from | least to greatest |.

| 48, 51, 52, 54, 54, 57, 58, 58, 59, 63 |

Median: Because there is an even number of data values, the median

is the | mean of the two middle values |

$$\text{Median} = \frac{\boxed{54+57}}{\boxed{2}} = \frac{\boxed{111}}{\boxed{2}} = \boxed{55.5}$$

Modes: The numbers that occur most often are $\boxed{54}$ and $\boxed{58}$.

Range: Find the difference between the greatest and the least values.

$$\text{Range} = \boxed{63 - 48} = \boxed{15}$$

Need help ordering whole numbers? See page 736 of your textbook.

Guided Practice Find the mean, median, mode(s), and range.

1. 6, 2, 7, 11, 2, 10, 5, 3, 8	**2.** 27, 63, 49, 34, 70, 58, 55, 68
2, 2, 3, 5, ⑥ 7, 8, 10, 11 median = 6 mean = 6 mode = 2 range = 9 (2-11)	

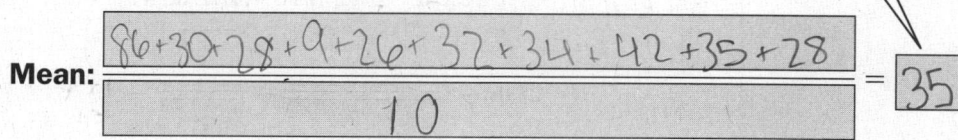

EXAMPLE 3 **Choosing the Best Average**

School Play The numbers of tickets sold for the upcoming school play are listed below.

86   30   28   9   26   32   34   42   35   28

Which average best represents the number of tickets sold?

Solution

Compare the mean, median, and mode.

> The mean suggests that the numbers of tickets sold are greater than they actually are.

Mean: $\dfrac{86+30+28+9+26+32+34+42+35+28}{10} = \boxed{35}$

Median: 9   26   28   28   **30**   **32**   34   35   42   86

$\dfrac{30+32}{2} = \boxed{31}$

The median is $\boxed{31}$.

> The mode suggests that the numbers of tickets sold are less than they actually are.

Mode: The number of tickets most often sold is $\boxed{28}$.

Answer: The $\boxed{\text{median}}$ best represents the number of tickets sold.

EXAMPLE 4 **Standardized Test Practice**

Shirts You pay $38 for 3 shirts. A few weeks later, you buy 2 more shirts for a total of $20. What is the mean cost of all the shirts?

(A) $7.60   (B) $11.60   (C) $19.33   (D) $58

Solution

To find the mean cost of all the shirts, divide the sum of the costs by the number of shirts purchased.

$$\text{Mean} = \frac{\boxed{} + \boxed{}}{\boxed{}} = \frac{\boxed{}}{\boxed{}} = \boxed{}$$

Answer: The mean cost of all the shirts is $\boxed{}$. The correct answer

is $\boxed{}$.   (A)   (B)   (C)   (D)

Bar Graphs and Line Graphs

Goal: Make and interpret bar graphs and line graphs.

Vocabulary

Bar graph: A graph in which the length of bars are used to represent and compare data.

Line graph: A graph in which points that represent data pairs are plotted using a horizontal number line and a verticle number line. The points are connected using line segments to show a change of data over time.

Horizontal axis: The horizontal number line on a graph.

Vertical axis: The verticle number line on a graph.

EXAMPLE 1 **Making a Bar Graph**

Use a bar graph to represent the data in the table.

School Population				
School	**Smith**	**Hall**	**Greenman**	**Carlson**
Students	651	703	528	639

1. Choose a scale.

The largest data value is 703. So, start the scale at 0 and extend it

to a value greater than 703, such as 800. Use increments of 100.

2. Draw and label the graph.

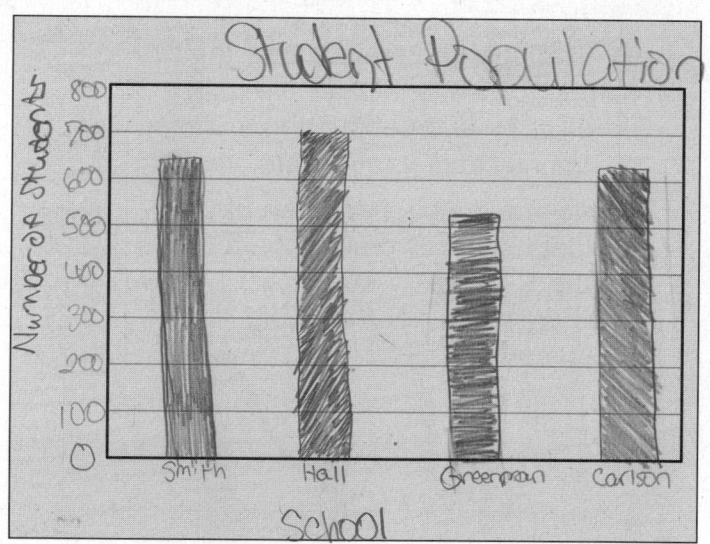

Use the scale to determine the length of the bars.

Include horizontal gridlines.

All of the bars should have the same width.

Guided Practice **Make a bar graph of the data.**

1.

Football Players	
Grade Level	**Number of Players**
9th	3
10th	8
11th	23
12th	28

EXAMPLE **2** **Making a Double Bar Graph**

TV Stations The table shows the number of stations available to Satellite TV and Cable TV in a community during four years.

To make a double bar graph of the data, start by drawing bars for the Satellite TV stations. Then draw bars for the Cable TV stations.

Year	Satellite	Cable
1998	50	37
1999	84	52
2000	100	75
2001	125	130

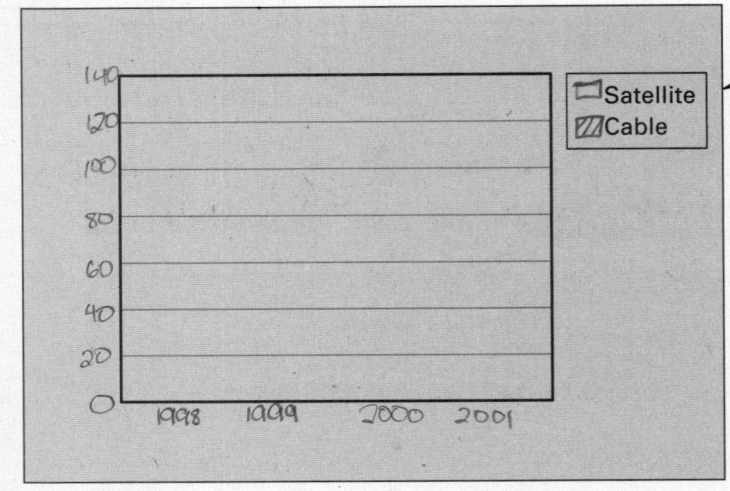

A legend tells you what each bar represents.

☐Satellite
▨Cable

EXAMPLE **3** **Interpreting a Line Graph**

Ice Skating School The line graph shows the enrollment at the Kids on Ice Skating School from 1995 through 2000. What conclusion can you make about the line graph?

In the line graph, the break in the vertical axis allows you to focus on the values between 125 and 185.

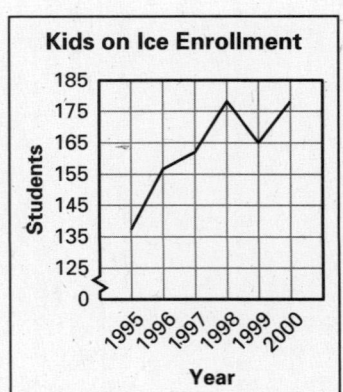

Answer: The line graph shows that the enrollment ⬚ between

⬚ and ⬚ , but there was a ⬚ from ⬚ to ⬚ .

From ⬚ to ⬚ , the enrollment ⬚ .

EXAMPLE 4 Making a Line Graph

Bike Riders Use the table to make a line graph of the number of students riding their bikes to a certain school from 1995 through 2000.

1. Choose the horizontal and vertical axes. Years from 1995 through 2000 will be shown on the [   ] axis. The greatest number of bike riders is 36. So, start the [   ] axis at 0 and end with 40, using increments of 5.

Year	Bike Riders
1995	12
1996	15
1997	21
1998	33
1999	36
2000	31

2. Draw and label the graph.

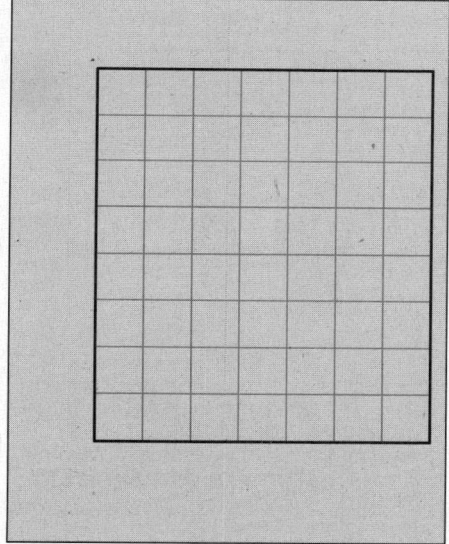

Plot a point for each year. Then connect the points with line segments.

Include evenly spaced horizontal and vertical gridlines.

2. Make a double bar graph of the data collected by a car dealership in one month.

Types of Vehicles People Bought					
Vehicle	Sedan	SUV	Station Wagon	Truck	Van
Male	12	18	2	15	3
Female	10	15	6	11	5

Male
Female

3. What conclusions can you make about the line graph in Example 4?

4. Make a line graph of the data collected by a customer service call center.

Customers Are On Hold					
Time	8 A.M.	10 A.M.	Noon	2 P.M.	4 P.M.
Average Hold Time (in minutes)	1	3	7	5	2

Stem-and-Leaf Plots

Goal: Display data using stem-and-leaf plots.

Vocabulary

Stem-and-leaf plot:

EXAMPLE 1 **Making a Stem-and-Leaf Plot**

The table shows the number of phone calls received by a telethon each hour for ten hours. Display the numbers of phone calls on a stem-and-leaf plot.

Hour	Number of Calls Received	Hour	Number of Calls Received
1	15	6	27
2	21	7	53
3	36	8	52
4	31	9	39
5	38	10	20

Solution

1. The numbers range from [ ] to [ ], so let the [ ] be the tens' digits from [ ] to [ ]. Let the [ ] be the ones' digits.

2. Write the [ ] first. Draw a [ ] next to the stems. Then record each number of phone calls by writing its [ ] on the same line as the corresponding [ ].

3. Make an ordered stem-and-leaf plot.

Unordered Plot

In the ordered plot, the leaves for each stem are listed in order from least to greatest.

Ordered Plot

Include a key to show what the stems and leaves represent.

Key: ☐ | ☐ = ☐

Key: ☐ | ☐ = ☐

EXAMPLE **2** **Interpreting a Stem-and-Leaf Plot**

100-Meter Hurdles Sophia runs the 100-meter hurdles for her track team. Her race times (in seconds) are listed below. Use a stem-and-leaf plot to order the data. Then make a conclusion about the data.

18.5   21.3   19.0   19.6   17.8   22.4   21.6   19.3   18.9   22.8   21.3

Solution

Begin by making an unordered stem-and-leaf plot. Because the race times range from ☐ to ☐ , the stems are the digits in the ☐ places. The leaves are the digits in the ☐ place.

Then make an ordered stem-and-leaf plot.

Unordered Plot

Ordered Plot

Key: ☐ | ☐ = ☐

Key: ☐ | ☐ = ☐

Answer: Sophia runs ☐ races under 20 seconds than ☐ 20 seconds.

1. The number of customers visiting Tyrone's book shop each day are listed below. Make an ordered stem-and-leaf plot of the numbers.

18 12 20 32 15 45 53 18 23 24 39 27 19 26 17 20

2. Use the stem-and-leaf plot from Exercise 1 to determine the number of customers greater than 32.

3. Use the stem-and-leaf plot from Exercise 1 to make a conclusion about the daily number of customers in Tyrone's store.

Box-and-Whisker Plots

Goal: Display data using box-and-whisker plots.

Vocabulary

Box-and-whisker plot:

Lower quartile:

Upper quartile:

Lower extreme:

Upper extreme:

Interquartile range:

EXAMPLE 1 Making a Box-and-Whisker Plot

Ages The ages of the skaters at the Aurora Skating Rink are listed below. How can the data be displayed so that it is divided into quarters?

6, 8, 9, 12, 13, 14, 14, 15, 15, 16,
16, 18, 18, 19, 25, 27, 28, 32, 42, 56

Solution

1. Find the median, the quartiles, and the extremes.

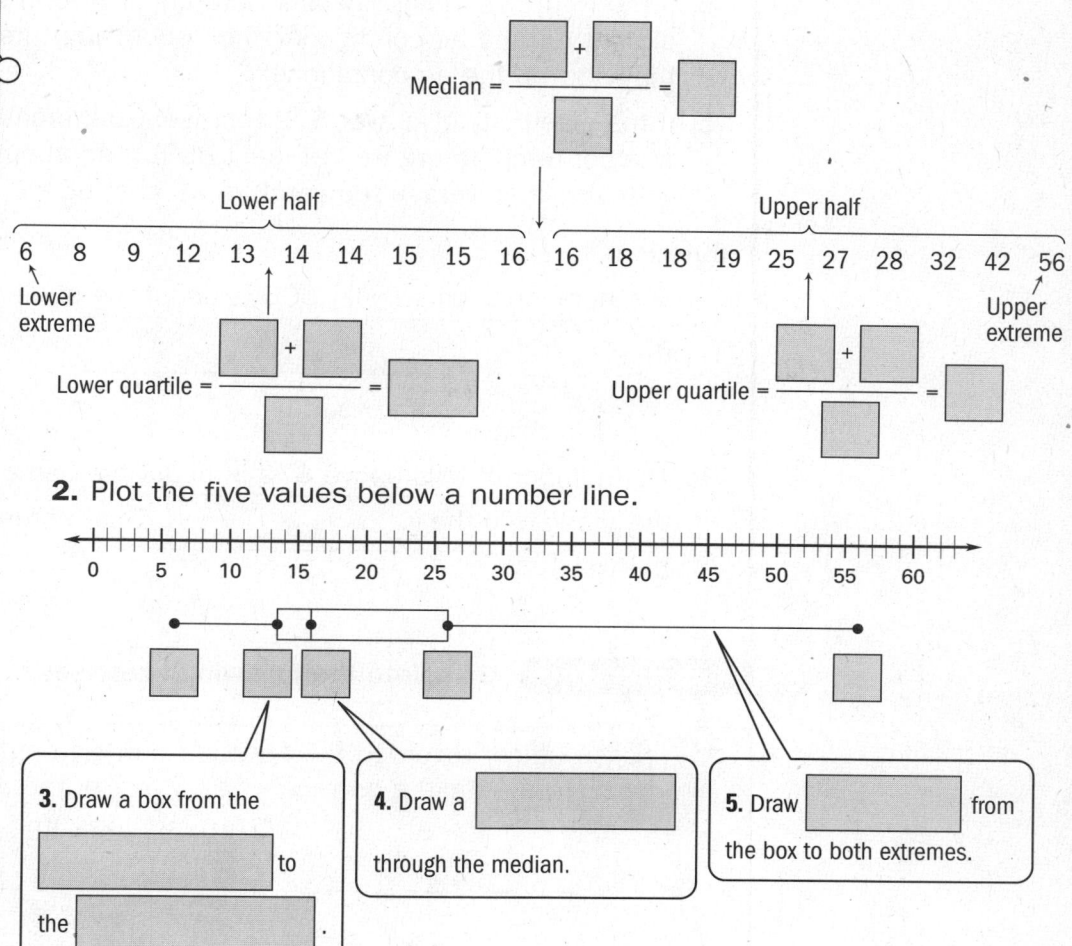

If a data set has an odd number of values, the median value is not included in either the lower half or the upper half.

2. Plot the five values below a number line.

3. Draw a box from the _____ to the _____ .

4. Draw a _____ through the median.

5. Draw _____ from the box to both extremes.

EXAMPLE 2 **Interpreting a Box-and-Whisker Plot**

Electric Bills The amounts of the electricity bills in the Nguyen's home in a year are displayed in the box-and-whisker plot below.

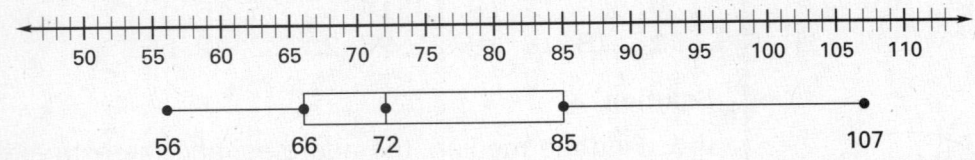

a. If the Nguyen's electricity bills were under $66 in the months that they did not run the air conditioner, then about what fraction of the year did they not run the air conditioner?

b. If the electricity bills over $72 represent the months where the average outdoor temperature was at least 85°F, then about what fraction of the year was the average temperature at least 85°F?

Solution

a. The number of bills under $66 is about the same on the number line as _____ , which represents about

_____ of the year.

b. The number of bills above $72 is about the same as the number from the median to the _____ . This represents about _____ of the year.

Guided Practice **Complete the following exercises.**

1. A police officer recorded the speeds (in miles per hour) of cars traveling on a highway. Make a box-and-whisker plot of the data listed below.

56 48 37 49 55 50 57 60 59 47 59 57 55 58 54 48

2. Use the box-and-whisker plot from Exercise 1 to make a conclusion about the data.

3. In Example 2, is the number of electricity bills between $66 and $72 necessarily less than the number of bills between $72 and $85?

EXAMPLE 3 **Comparing Box-and-Whisker Plots**

DVDs The box-and-whisker plots below represent the prices of DVDs at two different stores. What conclusions can you draw about the data?

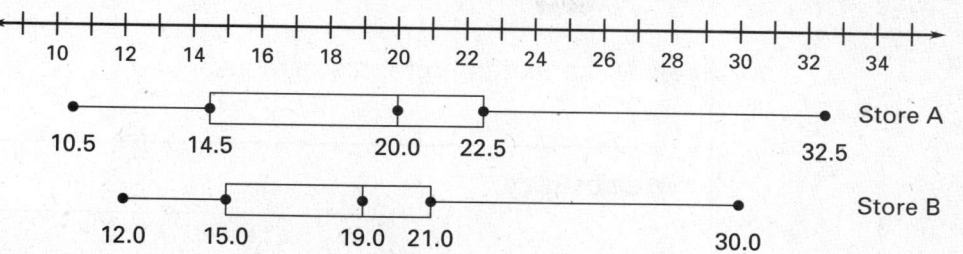

Solution

In general, Store A has a ▢ range of prices. ▢ has the most expensive DVD, but also has the least expensive DVD. The median price of Store B's DVDs is ▢ than the median price of Store A's DVDs.

Histograms

Goal: Make and interpret histograms.

Vocabulary

Frequency table:

Frequency:

Histogram:

EXAMPLE 1 **Making a Frequency Table**

Auction The sellers on an Internet auction site tracked how many people viewed the auction each day. The data are listed below. Make a frequency table of the data.

15, 28, 36, 16, 18, 27, 40, 39, 25, 19, 36, 19, 42, 39, 27, 30, 49, 6, 27, 38, 0, 42, 37, 26, 17, 16, 25, 31, 29, 8, 10, 28, 34, 16, 9, 40, 32

Solution

1. Choose intervals of ▢ that cover all the data values, which range from ▢ to ▢. In the table, each interval covers ▢ whole numbers. The first interval is ▢ and the last interval is ▢.

2. Make a ▢ next to the interval containing a given number of viewers of the auction.

3. Write the frequency for each interval by ▢ of tally marks for the interval.

Viewers	Tally	Frequency
▢	▢	▢
10–19	▢	▢
20–29	▢	▢
30–39	▢	▢
▢	▢	▢

EXAMPLE **2** **Making a Histogram**

Phone Calls A business kept track of how many phone solicitors called them. The table shows the number of phone calls received each day. Make a histogram of the data.

Phone Calls	Tally	Frequency
0–4		8
5–9		0
10–14		12
15–19		18
20–24		9

Solution

1. Draw and label the [____] and [____] axes.

   List each interval from the frequency table on the [____].

   The greatest frequency is [____]. So, start the vertical axis at [____] and end it at [____], using increments of 2.

2. Draw a bar for [____]. The bars should have [____] width.

   Include [____] grid lines.

   Bars that are next to each other should [____] gap between them.

WATCH OUT!
Make sure that your histogram includes all of the intervals in the table, even the intervals that have a frequency of 0.

1. The runs scored by the school baseball team in each game are listed below. Make a frequency table of the data.

2, 8, 0, 3, 5, 10, 2, 1, 3, 1, 0, 14, 2, 3, 5, 0, 6, 2, 12, 4, 8, 2

2. Make a histogram of the data in Exercise 1.

EXAMPLE 3 **Standardized Test Practice**

Traffic Patterns City officials are looking at traffic patterns at a major intersection. They have tracked the average number of cars backed up at the stoplight between 5 A.M. and 6:59 P.M.

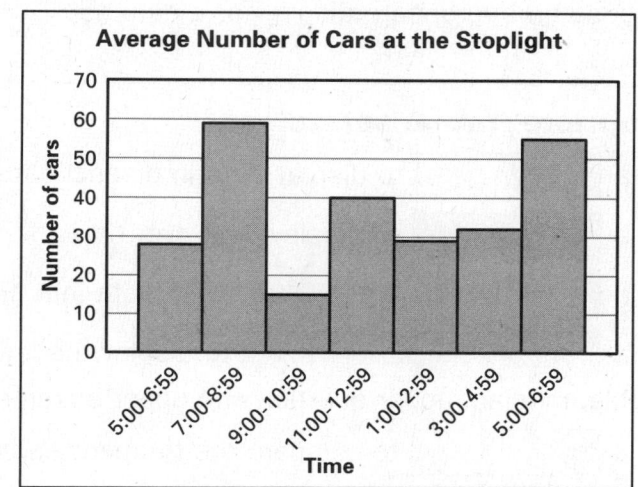

Which statement is *not* supported by these data?

(A) More cars are backed up at the stoplight between 5:00 A.M. and 8:59 A.M. than between 1:00 P.M. and 4:59 P.M.

(B) The number of cars backed up at the stoplight between 5:00 P.M. and 6:59 P.M. is about half the number of cars backed up at the stoplight between 5:00 A.M. and 6:59 A.M.

(C) The number of cars backed up at the stoplight is greatest during the times people would be traveling to and from work, and eating out for lunch.

(D) The number of cars backed up at the stoplight between 9:00 A.M. and 10:59 A.M. is about half the number of cars backed up at the stoplight between 3:00 P.M. and 4:59 P.M.

Solution

The number of cars backed up at the stoplight between 5:00 P.M. and

6:59 P.M. is about ▢ . The number of cars backed up at the stoplight

between 5:00 A.M. and 6:59 A.M. is about ▢ .

Answer: The number of cars backed up at the stoplight between 5:00 P.M.

and 6:59 P.M. is about ▢ the number of cars backed up at the

stoplight between 5:00 A.M. and 6:59 A.M. The correct answer is ▢ .

(A) **(B)** **(C)** **(D)**

Appropriate Data Displays

Goal: Choose an appropriate display for a data set.

Appropriate Data Displays

• Use a [＿＿＿＿] to display data in distinct categories.

• Use a [＿＿＿＿] to display data over time.

• Use a [＿＿＿＿＿＿] to group data into ordered lists.

• Use a [＿＿＿＿＿＿] to display the lower extreme, lower quartile, median, upper quartile, and upper extreme of a data set.

• Use a [＿＿＿＿] to compare the frequencies of data that fall in equal intervals.

EXAMPLE 1 **Choosing an Appropriate Data Display**

A movie theater manager wants to display the attendances to the movies shown in the theaters. What data display(s) should she use to see how the data are distributed, without displaying the individual data?

Answer: Either a [＿＿＿＿] or a [＿＿＿＿] will show how the data are distributed without showing individual data.

EXAMPLE 2 **Identifying Misleading Data Displays**

Is the graph potentially misleading? Explain.

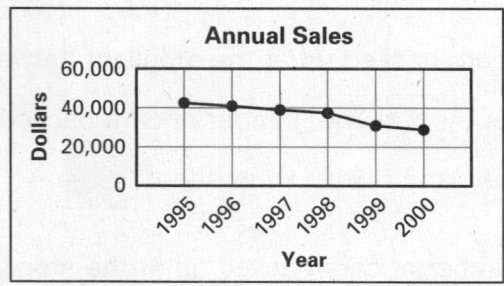

Solution

The graph could be misleading because the vertical scale uses [＿＿＿＿＿＿＿]. The graph indicates a [＿＿＿＿] change in sales. If the vertical scale had [＿＿＿＿] increments, the change in sales would look more significant.

1. A bookstore sells eight different types of books. Which data display(s) should be used to compare the number of each type of book in stock?

2. Redraw the line graph in Example 2 with smaller increments on the vertical scale. Compare the two graphs. What do you notice?

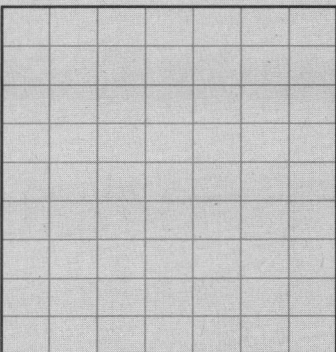

Words to Review

Give an example of the vocabulary word.

Mean

Median

Mode

Range

Bar graph

Line graph

Horizontal axis

Vertical axis

Stem-and-leaf plot

Box-and-whisker plot

Lower quartile

Upper quartile

Lower extreme

Upper extreme

Interquartile range

Frequency table

Frequency

Histogram

Review your notes and Chapter 3 by using the Chapter Review on pages 151–154 of your textbook.

Prime Factorization

Goal: Write a number as a product of prime numbers.

Vocabulary

Prime number: a whole number greater than one, whose only factors are 1 and itself.

Composite number: a whole number greater than 1 that is not prime.

Prime factorization: Expressing a whole number as a product of prime numbers.

Factor tree: A diagram used to write prime factorization of a number.

EXAMPLE 1 Writing Factors of a Number

Gardening Mrs. Gilbert bought 48 plants to put in her garden. She wants to break the plants up into groups that are the same size. Find the possible group sizes by writing all the factors of 48.

$48 = 1 \times \boxed{48}$

$= 2 \times \boxed{24}$

$= 3 \times \boxed{16}$

$= 4 \times \boxed{12}$ 48 isn't divisible by $\boxed{5}$. Skip to $\boxed{6}$.

$= 6 \times \boxed{8}$ 48 isn't divisible by $\boxed{7}$. Skip to $\boxed{8}$.

$= 8 \times \boxed{6}$ Stop when the factors $\boxed{\text{repeat}}$.

Answer: The factors of 48 are _____.

Need help with divisibility rules? See page 739 of your textbook.

EXAMPLE 2 Identifying Prime and Composite Numbers

Tell whether the number is *prime* or *composite*.

a. 52

b. 17

Solution

a. The factors of 52 are

[   ] .

So, 52 is [   ] .

b. The factors of 17 are

[   ] . So, 17 is [   ] .

EXAMPLE 3 Using a Factor Tree

Use a factor tree to write the prime factorization of 36.

To *factor* a number means to write the number as a product of its factors.

One possible factor tree:

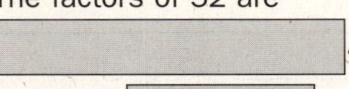

Write original number.

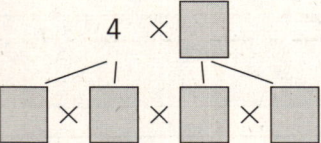

Factor 36 as 4 × [ ].

Factor 4 as [ ] × [ ] and [ ] as [ ] × [ ].

Another possible factor tree:

36
/ \
3 × 12

Write original number.

Factor 36 as 3 × 12.

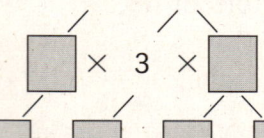

Factor 12 as 3 × [ ].

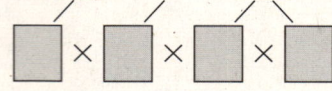

Factor [ ] as [ ] × [ ].

Both trees give the same result: 36 = [   ] .

Answer: The prime factorization of 36 is [   ] .

Guided Practice Use a factor tree to write the prime factorization of the number.

1. 20	**2.** 32	**3.** 52	**4.** 68

Greatest Common Factor

LESSON 4.2

Goal: Find the greatest common factor of two or more numbers.

Vocabulary

Common factor:

Greatest common factor (GCF):

Relatively prime:

EXAMPLE 1 **Making a List to Find the GCF**

Flower Arranging A florist is making bouquets from 32 poppies, 40 irises, and 56 gerbera daisies. What is the greatest number of bouquets that the florist can make using the same number of each flower in the bouquets? How many poppies, irises, and gerbera daisies will be in each bouquet?

Factors of 32:

Factors of 40:

Factors of 56:

The common factors are

. The GCF is .

Answer: The greatest common factor of 32, 40, and 56 is . So, the greatest number of bouquets that can be made is . Then each bouquet will have poppies, irises, and gerbera daisies.

Find the greatest common factor of the numbers by listing the factors.

1. 20, 35	**2.** 28, 49	**3.** 45, 60
4. 10, 24, 36	**5.** 15, 40, 50	**6.** 54, 72, 99

EXAMPLE 2 **Using Prime Factorization to Find the GCF**

Find the greatest common factor of 120 and 165 using prime factorization.

Large numbers may have many factors, and it may be difficult to list all the factors. It may be easier to use prime factorization to find the greatest common factor of large numbers.

Begin by writing the prime factorization of each number.

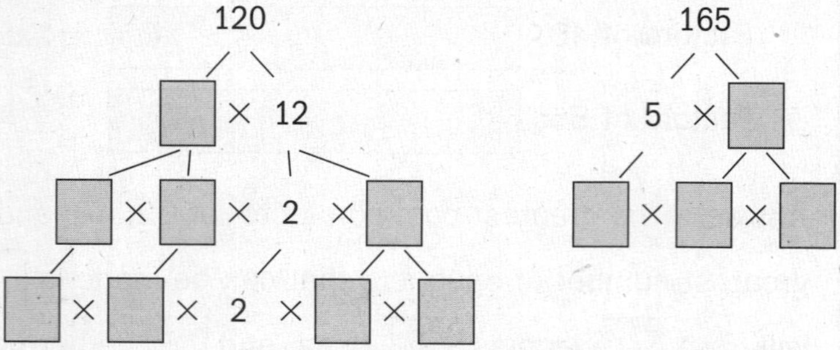

120

☐ × 12

☐ × ☐ × 2 × ☐

☐ × ☐ × 2 × ☐ × ☐

165

5 × ☐

☐ × ☐ × ☐

120: ▭

165: ▭

Answer: The common prime factors of 120 and 165 are ☐ and ☐.

So, the greatest common factor is ☐ × ☐ = ☐.

Find the greatest common factor of the numbers using prime factorization.

7. 100, 140	**8.** 96, 160
9. 108, 172	**10.** 200, 280

EXAMPLE 3 **Identifying Relatively Prime Numbers**

Tell whether the numbers are relatively prime.

   a. 16, 25

       Factors of 16: _____   The GCF is ___.

       Factors of 25: _____

   Answer: Because the GCF is ___, 16 and 25 are _____.

   b. 21, 54

       Factors of 21: _____   The GCF is ___.

       Factors of 54: _____

   Answer: Because the GCF is ___, 21 and 54 are

       _____.

Equivalent Fractions

Goal: Write equivalent fractions.

Vocabulary

Fraction:

Numerator:

Denominator:

Equivalent fractions:

Simplest form:

EXAMPLE 1 **Identifying Equivalent Fractions**

Radio There are 12 songs played in one hour on a local radio station. Three of the songs are new releases. What *fraction* of the songs played in an hour are new releases?

The songs in the problem are arranged in the diagram. Using the diagram, you can write two equivalent fractions.

$$\frac{\text{Number of new releases}}{\text{Number of songs}} =$$

$$\frac{\text{Number of groups of 3 new releases}}{\text{Number of groups of 3 songs}} =$$

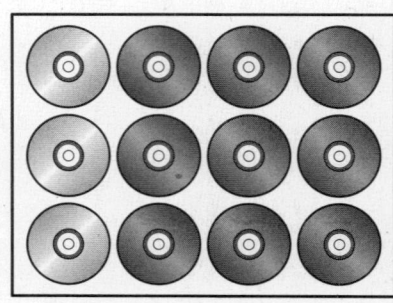

The fractions [ ] and [ ] are equivalent equivalent fractions because they represent the same part-to-whole relationship.

For any fraction, if you tried to list all the equivalent fractions, the list would continue without end. This is because you can multiply the numerator and denominator by *any* nonzero number.

EXAMPLE 2 **Writing Equivalent Fractions**

Write two fractions that are equivalent to $\frac{3}{9}$.

Multiply or divide the numerator and denominator by the same nonzero number to find an equivalent fraction.

$\frac{3}{9} = \dfrac{\boxed{} \times \boxed{}}{\boxed{} \times \boxed{}} = \frac{6}{18}$ Multiply numerator and denominator by 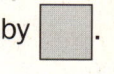.

$\frac{3}{9} = \dfrac{\boxed{} \div \boxed{}}{\boxed{} \div \boxed{}} = \frac{1}{3}$ Divide numerator and denominator by $\boxed{}$, a common factor of $\boxed{}$ and $\boxed{}$.

EXAMPLE 3 **Simplifying Fractions**

Write the fraction in simplest form.

a. $\frac{10}{32}$ **b.** $\frac{9}{14}$

Solution

a. $\frac{10}{32} = \dfrac{\boxed{} \cdot \boxed{}}{\boxed{} \cdot \boxed{}}$ The GCF of $\boxed{}$ and $\boxed{}$ is $\boxed{}$.

$= \boxed{}$

b. $\frac{9}{14}$ The GCF of $\boxed{}$ and $\boxed{}$ is $\boxed{}$.

The fraction is in simplest form.

Guided Practice Write two fractions that are equivalent to the given fraction.

1. $\frac{1}{5}$	**2.** $\frac{7}{15}$	**3.** $\frac{10}{12}$	**4.** $\frac{20}{25}$

Write the fraction in simplest form.

5. $\frac{12}{18}$	6. $\frac{20}{36}$	7. $\frac{15}{60}$	8. $\frac{24}{40}$

EXAMPLE 4 **Using Fractions in Simplest Form**

Student Council Janet and Bob are both running for Student Council Representative in their homerooms. Janet received 18 out of 30 votes in her homeroom. Bob received 15 out of 25 votes in his homeroom. Write the fraction of votes received by each candidate in simplest form. Are the fractions equivalent?

Janet

$$\frac{\text{Votes received}}{\text{Total votes in the homeroom}} = \frac{18}{30} = \frac{\boxed{} \div \boxed{}}{\boxed{} \div \boxed{}} = \boxed{}$$

Bob

$$\frac{\text{Votes received}}{\text{Total votes in the homeroom}} = \frac{15}{25} = \frac{\boxed{} \div \boxed{}}{\boxed{} \div \boxed{}} = \boxed{}$$

Answer: $\boxed{}$, $\frac{18}{30}$ and $\frac{15}{25}$ $\boxed{}$ equivalent fractions.

Least Common Multiple

Goal: Find the LCM of two or more numbers.

Vocabulary

Multiple:

Common multiple:

Least common multiple:

EXAMPLE 1 **Using the Least Common Multiple**

Commercials One TV station shows commercials every 6 minutes. Another station shows commercials every 8 minutes. For the shows that air at 7:00 A.M., at what time will both stations first play a commercial?

You can determine when both stations will first play a commercial by finding the least common multiple of 6 and 8. Begin by writing the multiples of 6 and 8. Then identify any common multiples.

Multiples of 6:

Multiples of 8:

and are common multiples. The LCM is .

Answer: The television stations will first both show a commercial in minutes, or at A.M.

EXAMPLE 2 **Finding the Least Common Multiple**

Find the least common multiple of 5 and 9.

Multiples of 5:

Multiples of 9:

Answer: The least common multiple of 5 and 9 is .

EXAMPLE **3** **Using Prime Factorization to Find the LCM**

Find the LCM of 95 and 240 using prime factorization.

> Use the prime factorization method to find the least common multiple of large numbers.

1. Begin by writing the prime factorization of each number.

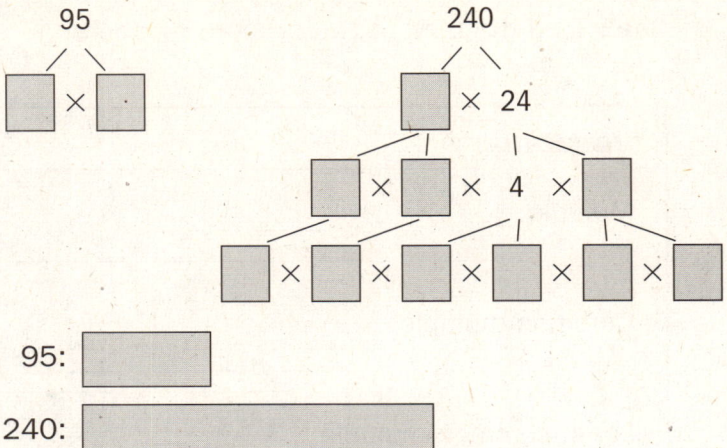

95: ▭

240: ▭

2. Circle the common factor. Then multiply the common factor and all the uncircled factors.

▭ = ▭

Answer: The least common multiple of 95 and 240 is ▭.

Guided Practice **Find the LCM of the numbers by listing the multiples.**

1. 4, 7	**2.** 10, 15
3. 3, 8, 12	**4.** 2, 6, 10

Find the LCM of the numbers using prime factorization.

5. 42, 70	**6.** 18, 27
7. 15, 20, 40	**8.** 45, 60, 72

EXAMPLE 4 **Using the Least Common Multiple**

Fitness Center All classes at the fitness center start at 6 A.M. The water aerobics class repeats every 60 minutes. The power yoga class repeats every 45 minutes. The circuit training class repeats every 90 minutes. What is the next time that all three classes start at the same time?

Solution

Find the least common multiple of 60, 45, and 90.

60 = [ ]   45 = [ ]   90 = [ ]

The least common multiple is [ ] = [ ].

Answer: The classes start at the same time again in [ ] minutes, or [ ] hours, after 6 A.M., which is [ ] A.M.

Comparing and Ordering Fractions

LESSON 4.5

Goal: Compare and order fractions.

Vocabulary

Least common denominator:

Comparing Two or More Fractions

1. Find the [ ] of the fractions.

2. Use the [ ] to write [ ] fractions.

3. Compare the [ ].

EXAMPLE 1 **Comparing Fractions Using the LCD**

Sewing Tara is sewing a red shirt and a blue shirt. The pattern for the red shirt calls for $\frac{5}{8}$ yard of fabric. The pattern for the blue shirt calls for $\frac{7}{12}$ yard of fabric. Which shirt is made from more fabric?

Solution

1. Find the [ ] of the fractions.

Because the LCM of 8 and 12 is [ ], the [ ] is [ ].

2. Use the [ ] to write equivalent fractions.

Red: $\frac{5}{8} = \frac{\quad}{\quad} = \boxed{}$ Blue: $\frac{7}{12} = \frac{\quad}{\quad} = \boxed{}$

3. Compare the numerators: [ ], so $\frac{5}{8}$ [ ] $\frac{7}{12}$.

Answer: The [ ] shirt is made from more fabric.

EXAMPLE **2** **Standardized Test Practice**

Which list shows $\frac{1}{4}$, $\frac{2}{5}$, $\frac{3}{10}$, and $\frac{5}{6}$ in order from least to greatest?

(A) $\frac{1}{4}$, $\frac{2}{5}$, $\frac{5}{6}$, $\frac{3}{10}$

(B) $\frac{5}{6}$, $\frac{1}{4}$, $\frac{2}{5}$, $\frac{3}{10}$

(C) $\frac{1}{4}$, $\frac{3}{10}$, $\frac{2}{5}$, $\frac{5}{6}$

(D) $\frac{3}{10}$, $\frac{5}{6}$, $\frac{2}{5}$, $\frac{1}{4}$

Solution

1. Find the LCD of the fractions.

Because the LCM of 4, 5, 10, and 6 is ⬚ , the LCD is ⬚ .

2. Use the LCD to write equivalent fractions.

$$\frac{1}{4} = \frac{\boxed{}}{\boxed{}} = \boxed{}$$

$$\frac{2}{5} = \frac{\boxed{}}{\boxed{}} = \boxed{}$$

$$\frac{3}{10} = \frac{\boxed{}}{\boxed{}} = \boxed{}$$

$$\frac{5}{6} = \frac{\boxed{}}{\boxed{}} = \boxed{}$$

3. Compare the numerators: , so ⬚

Answer: The order of the fractions from least to greatest, is

⬚ . The correct answer is ⬚ .   **(A)**   **(B)**   **(C)**   **(D)**

Guided Practice   **Copy and complete the statement using <, >, or =.**

1. $\frac{3}{5}$? $\frac{8}{13}$

2. $\frac{7}{8}$? $\frac{11}{12}$

3. $\frac{3}{7}$? $\frac{4}{11}$

Order the fractions from least to greatest.

4. $\frac{5}{6}$, $\frac{3}{4}$, $\frac{1}{2}$, $\frac{7}{12}$

5. $\frac{2}{9}$, $\frac{1}{6}$, $\frac{2}{3}$, $\frac{7}{18}$

6. $\frac{4}{5}$, $\frac{19}{20}$, $\frac{3}{4}$, $\frac{7}{10}$

EXAMPLE 3 **Comparing Fractions Using Approximation**

Use approximation to tell which fraction is greater, $\frac{15}{32}$ or $\frac{23}{42}$.

Notice that $\frac{15}{32}$ and $\frac{23}{42}$ are both approximately equal to ☐ because the

numerator of each fraction is about ☐ the denominator.

Because $\frac{1}{2} = \frac{\boxed{}}{32}$, you know that $\frac{15}{32}$ ☐ $\frac{1}{2}$.

Because $\frac{1}{2} = \frac{\boxed{}}{42}$, you know that $\frac{23}{42}$ ☐ $\frac{1}{2}$.

Answer: So, $\frac{15}{32}$ ☐ $\frac{23}{42}$.

Mixed Numbers and Improper Fractions

Goal: Compare and order fractions and mixed numbers.

Vocabulary

Mixed number:

Proper fraction:

Improper fraction:

Writing Mixed Numbers as Improper Fractions

Words To write a mixed number as an improper fraction, multiply the

[ ] and the [ ], add the

[ ], and write the sum [ ] the denominator.

The mixed number $2\frac{5}{6}$ is read "two and five sixths."

Numbers $2\frac{5}{6} = \dfrac{\boxed{} + \boxed{}}{\boxed{}} = \boxed{}$

EXAMPLE 1 Writing Improper Fractions

Write (a) $4\frac{2}{5}$ and (b) $3\frac{1}{9}$ as improper fractions.

a. $4\frac{2}{5} = \dfrac{\boxed{} + \boxed{}}{\boxed{}} = \boxed{}$

b. $3\frac{1}{9} = \dfrac{\boxed{} + \boxed{}}{\boxed{}} = \boxed{}$

Writing Improper Fractions as Mixed Numbers

Words To write an improper fraction as a mixed number, divide the [ ] by the [ ] and write any remainder as a [ ].

Numbers $\frac{17}{5} \rightarrow 17 \div \boxed{} = \boxed{}$, or $\boxed{}$

EXAMPLE 2 **Writing Mixed Numbers**

Need help with dividing whole numbers? See page 744 of your textbook.

Write $\frac{34}{5}$ as a mixed number.

$\boxed{}$, or $\boxed{}$

$5\overline{)34}$

$\boxed{}$

$\boxed{}$

You can write a remainder as a fraction:

$\boxed{}$
_____

Answer: $\frac{34}{5} = \boxed{}$

Guided Practice Write the number as an improper fraction.

1. $2\frac{1}{3}$	2. 7	3. $3\frac{3}{4}$	4. $5\frac{2}{5}$

Write the improper fraction as a mixed number.

5. $\frac{17}{11}$	6. $\frac{19}{5}$	7. $\frac{22}{4}$	8. $\frac{27}{8}$

EXAMPLE **3** **Comparing Mixed Numbers and Fractions**

Compare $\frac{23}{8}$ and $2\frac{2}{3}$.

1. Write $2\frac{2}{3}$ as an improper fraction: $2\frac{2}{3} = $ ▢ .

2. Rewrite $\frac{23}{8}$ and $\frac{8}{3}$ using the least common denominator of ▢ .

$\frac{23}{8} = \frac{}{} = $ ▢ $\frac{8}{3} = \frac{}{} = $ ▢

3. Compare the fractions: ▢ , so $\frac{23}{8}$ ▢ $2\frac{2}{3}$.

EXAMPLE 4 **Ordering Mixed Numbers and Fractions**

County Fair The county fair holds a pie eating contest. Participants are to eat as many pies as they can in 10 minutes. Joe ate $4\frac{1}{4}$ pies, Conan ate 5 pies, David ate $\frac{22}{5}$ pies, and Jonathan ate $4\frac{1}{2}$ pies. Order the amounts of pie the contestants ate from least to greatest.

Solution

The denominators are 4, 1 $\left(\text{because } 5 = \boxed{} \right)$, 5, and 2. Write the

numbers as improper fractions using the least common denominator of ▢ .

$4\frac{1}{4} = $ ▢ $= \frac{}{} = $ ▢ $5 = $ ▢ $= \frac{}{} = $ ▢

$\frac{22}{5} = \frac{}{} = $ ▢ $4\frac{1}{2} = $ ▢ $= \frac{}{} = $ ▢

Answer: From least to greatest, the amounts of pie the contestants ate are

▢ .

Fractions and Decimals

Goal: Write fractions as decimals and decimals as fractions.

Vocabulary

Terminating decimal:

Repeating decimal:

EXAMPLE 1 **Writing Fractions as Decimals**

Write (a) $\frac{5}{8}$ and (b) $2\frac{3}{5}$ as decimals.

> Need help with dividing decimals? See page 71 of your textbook.

Solution

a.

$8\overline{)5.000}$ ← Write zeros in dividend as placeholders.

← Remainder is [ ].

Answer: $\frac{5}{8} =$ [ ]

b.

$5\overline{)3.0}$ ← Write a zero in dividend as a placeholder.

← Remainder is [ ].

Answer: $2\frac{3}{5} =$ [ ] + [ ] = [ ]

Write the fraction or mixed number as a decimal.

1. $\frac{7}{10}$	2. $\frac{25}{400}$	3. $4\frac{3}{4}$	4. $3\frac{1}{8}$

EXAMPLE 2 **Writing Fractions as Repeating Decimals**

Write (a) $\frac{11}{6}$ and (b) $\frac{14}{15}$ as decimals.

Solution

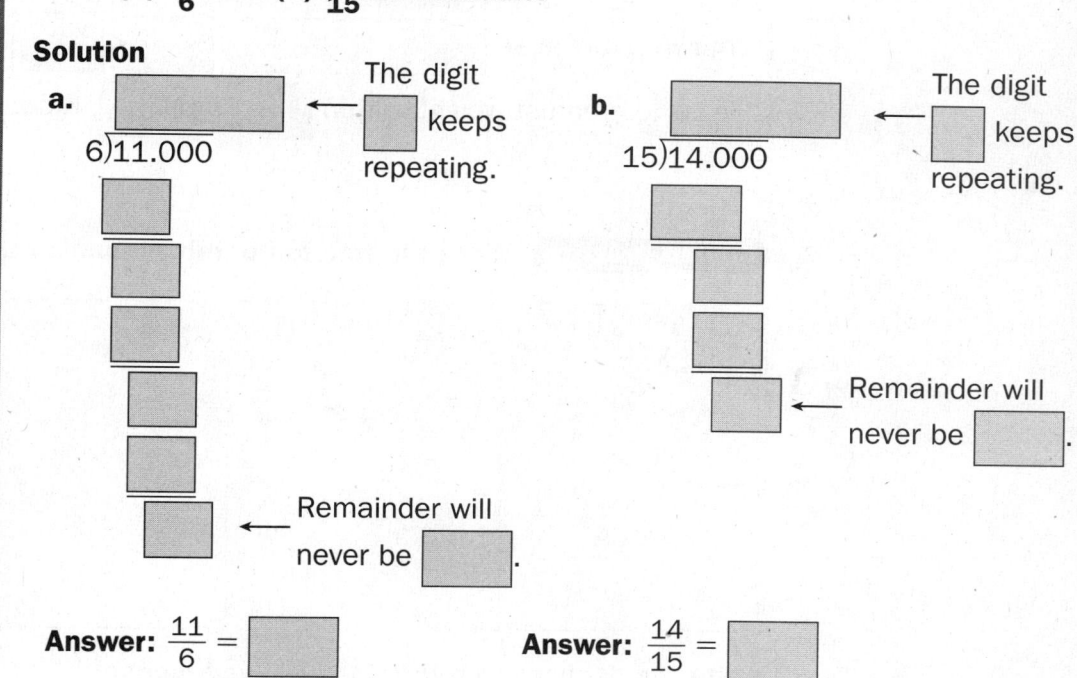

a. The digit [ ] keeps repeating.

$6\overline{)11.000}$

Remainder will never be [ ].

b. The digit [ ] keeps repeating.

$15\overline{)14.000}$

Remainder will never be [ ].

Answer: $\frac{11}{6} =$ [ ]   **Answer:** $\frac{14}{15} =$ [ ]

EXAMPLE 3 **Writing Decimals as Fractions**

Write (a) 0.72 and (b) 3.875 as a fraction or mixed number.

Need help with place value? See page 56 of your textbook.

Solution

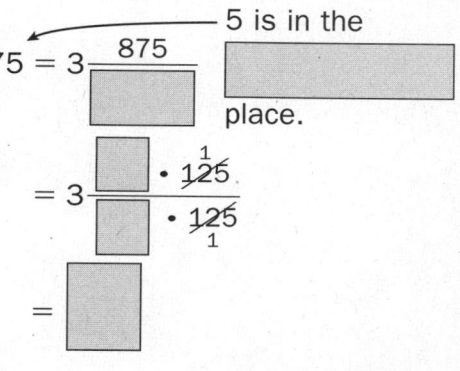

a. $0.72 = \dfrac{72}{\boxed{}}$ 2 is in the [ ] place.

$= \dfrac{\overset{1}{\cancel{4}} \cdot }{\underset{1}{\cancel{4}} \cdot }$

$=$ [ ]

b. $3.875 = 3\dfrac{875}{\boxed{}}$ 5 is in the [ ] place.

$= 3\dfrac{\overset{1}{\cancel{125}} \cdot }{\underset{1}{\cancel{125}} \cdot }$

$=$ [ ]

EXAMPLE **4** **Ordering Numbers**

Veterinarian Jorja's cat gave birth to a litter of kittens. She took the kittens to the veterinarian for a check-up. The kitten's weights were recorded for their medical records. What is the order of the kittens from least to greatest weight?

Only the digit(s) under the bar should be repeated. In Example 4, Kitten 1's weight written as a decimal is $0.8\overline{3} = 0.8333...$, not 0.838383....

Kitten 1: $\dfrac{5}{6}$ pound = ⬚ pound

Kitten 2: $\dfrac{2}{5}$ pound = ⬚ pound

Kitten 3: $\dfrac{1}{4}$ pound = ⬚ pound

Kitten 4: $\dfrac{3}{8}$ pound = ⬚ pound

Answer: Because ⬚ < ⬚ < ⬚ < ⬚, the kittens are, from least to greatest weight, Kitten ⬚, Kitten ⬚, Kitten ⬚, and Kitten ⬚.

Guided Practice Write the fraction or mixed number as a decimal.

5. $\dfrac{5}{12}$	**6.** $\dfrac{17}{8}$	**7.** $3\dfrac{2}{9}$	**8.** $6\dfrac{7}{16}$

Write the decimal as a fraction or mixed number.

9. 0.8	**10.** 3.35	**11.** 0.625	**12.** 1.175

Words to Review

Give an example of the vocabulary word.

Prime number

Composite number

Prime factorization

Factor tree

Common factor

Greatest common factor

Relatively prime

Fraction

Numerator

Denominator

Equivalent fractions

Simplest form

Multiple

Common multiple

Least common multiple

Least common denominator

Mixed number

Proper fraction

Improper fraction

Terminating decimal

Repeating decimal

Review your notes and Chapter 4 by using the Chapter Review on pages 207–210 of your textbook.

Adding and Subtracting Fractions

Goal: Add and subtract fractions.

Fractions with Common Denominators

Words To add or subtract two fractions with a common denominator, write the [____] or [____] of the numerators over the [____].

Numbers $\dfrac{1}{5} + \dfrac{2}{5} = $ [____]

$\dfrac{4}{7} - \dfrac{1}{7} = $ [____]

Algebra $\dfrac{a}{c} + \dfrac{b}{c} = $ [____] $(c \neq 0)$

$\dfrac{a}{c} - \dfrac{b}{c} = $ [____] $(c \neq 0)$

EXAMPLE 1 Adding Fractions

$\dfrac{2}{7} + \dfrac{3}{7} = $ [____] Add numerators.

$= $ [____] Simplify numerator.

EXAMPLE 2 Subtracting Fractions

$\dfrac{4}{9} - \dfrac{1}{9} = $ [____] Subtract numerators.

$= $ [____] Simplify numerator.

$= $ [____] Simplify fraction.

Need help with simplifying fractions? See page 177 of your textbook.

Guided Practice Add or subtract. Simplify if possible.

1. $\frac{3}{10} + \frac{1}{10}$	2. $\frac{2}{11} + \frac{8}{11}$	3. $\frac{6}{7} - \frac{4}{7}$	4. $\frac{8}{15} - \frac{3}{15}$

Fractions with Different Denominators

1. Rewrite the fractions using the [   ].

2. Add or subtract the [   ].

3. Write the result over the [   ].

4. [   ] if possible.

EXAMPLE 3 Adding Fractions

$\frac{3}{4} + \frac{4}{5} =$ [   ]   Rewrite the fractions using the LCD of $\frac{3}{4}$ and $\frac{4}{5}$.

$=$ [   ]   Add numerators.

$=$ [   ], or [   ]   Simplify.

Need help with writing improper fractions as mixed numbers? See page 195 of your textbook.

✓ **Check** You can use estimation to check that your answer is reasonable. Because $\frac{3}{4}$ is [   ] $\frac{1}{2}$ and $\frac{4}{5}$ is [   ] $\frac{1}{2}$, the sum of $\frac{3}{4}$ and $\frac{4}{5}$ should be [   ] than 1.

EXAMPLE 4 — Standardized Test Practice

Travel The usual flight from Houston to Dallas takes $\frac{5}{6}$ hour. Due to favorable weather conditions, today's flight only takes $\frac{3}{4}$ hour. How much faster was today's flight than usual?

A $\frac{1}{12}$ hour   **B** $\frac{1}{6}$ hour   **C** 1 hour   **D** $1\frac{7}{12}$ hours

Solution

To find how much faster today's flight was, subtract $\frac{3}{4}$ from $\frac{5}{6}$.

$\frac{5}{6} - \frac{3}{4} = $    Rewrite $\frac{5}{6}$ and $\frac{3}{4}$ using the LCD of the fractions.

$= $ 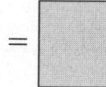   Subtract numerators.

$= $ Simplify numerator.

Answer: Today's flight was   hour faster. The correct answer is   .

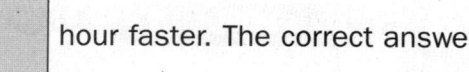

(A) **(B)** **(C)** **(D)**

Guided Practice **Add or subtract. Simplify if possible.**

5. $\frac{1}{3} + \frac{4}{15}$	**6.** $\frac{5}{8} + \frac{11}{12}$	**7.** $\frac{5}{6} - \frac{2}{3}$	**8.** $\frac{7}{10} - \frac{1}{4}$

Adding and Subtracting Mixed Numbers

Goal: Add and subtract mixed numbers.

Adding and Subtracting Mixed Numbers

1. Find the [   ] of the fractions, if necessary.

2. [   ] the fractions, if necessary. Then add or subtract the fractions.

3. Add or subtract the [   ].

4. [   ] if possible.

EXAMPLE 1 **Adding with a Common Denominator**

Garden Javier bought $23\frac{1}{5}$ yards of humus to build a vegetable garden. He topped the garden with $25\frac{2}{5}$ yards of mulch. How much garden material did he put in the vegetable garden?

To solve the problem, you need to find the sum of $23\frac{1}{5}$ and $25\frac{2}{5}$.

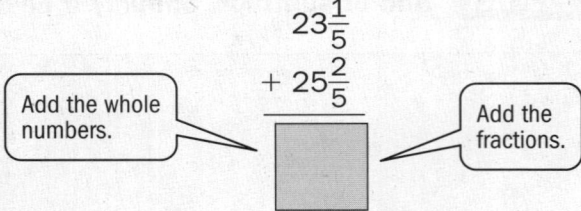

$$23\frac{1}{5}$$
$$+\ 25\frac{2}{5}$$

Add the whole numbers.   Add the fractions.

Answer: Javier put [   ] yards of garden material in the vegetable garden.

EXAMPLE 2 **Subtracting with a Common Denominator**

$$4\frac{5}{8} - 2\frac{1}{8} = \boxed{}$$ Subtract fractions and whole numbers.

$$= \boxed{}$$ Simplify.

Guided Practice Add or subtract. Simplify if possible.

1. $5\frac{3}{10} + 2\frac{1}{10}$	**2.** $6\frac{1}{6} + 1\frac{2}{6}$	**3.** $7\frac{4}{9} - 3\frac{1}{9}$	**4.** $15\frac{7}{8} - 7\frac{7}{8}$

In Example 3, you can estimate the answer by rounding each mixed number to the nearest whole number. By doing so, you have $4 + 6 = 10$, so your answer is reasonable.

EXAMPLE 3 **Adding with Different Denominators**

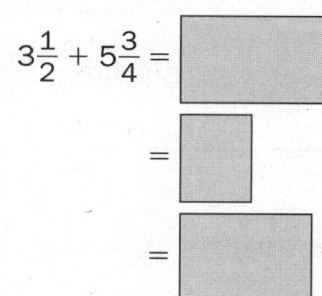

$3\frac{1}{2} + 5\frac{3}{4} = $ ☐ Rewrite fractions using the LCD of ☐ and ☐.

$= $ ☐ Add fractions and whole numbers.

$= $ ☐ Write ☐ as a mixed number.

$= $ ☐ Add whole numbers.

EXAMPLE 4 **Renaming to Subtract Mixed Numbers**

$8\frac{1}{10} - 5\frac{3}{5} = $ ☐ Rewrite fractions using the LCD of ☐ and, ☐.

$= $ ☐ Rename ☐ as ☐.

$= $ ☐ Subtract fractions and whole numbers.

$= $ ☐ Simplify.

Guided Practice Add or subtract. Simplify if possible.

5. $3\frac{1}{6} + 1\frac{2}{3}$	**6.** $7\frac{1}{2} + 2\frac{2}{3}$	**7.** $10 - 3\frac{2}{5}$	**8.** $7\frac{1}{5} - 6\frac{5}{6}$

Multiplying Fractions and Mixed Numbers

Goal: Multiply fractions and mixed numbers.

Multiplying Fractions

Words The product of two or more fractions is equal to the product of the [_____] over the product of the [_____].

Numbers $\dfrac{2}{9} \cdot \dfrac{4}{5} =$ [____] **Algebra** $\dfrac{a}{b} \cdot \dfrac{c}{d} =$ [____] $(b, d \neq 0)$

EXAMPLE 1 Multiplying Fractions

Baking Eva's bread recipe calls for $\frac{1}{4}$ cup of olive oil. She only wants to make half of the recipe. How much olive oil does Eva need?

$\dfrac{1}{2} \cdot \dfrac{1}{4} =$ [____]   Use rule for multiplying fractions.

$=$ [____]   Multiply.

Answer: Eva needs [____] cup of olive oil for half of the bread recipe.

✓ **Check:** Use a model to find the product.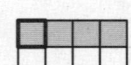

Guided Practice Find the product. Simplify if possible.

1. $\dfrac{3}{4} \cdot \dfrac{1}{2}$	2. $\dfrac{7}{10} \cdot \dfrac{1}{3}$	3. $\dfrac{2}{5} \cdot \dfrac{5}{8}$	4. $\dfrac{2}{3} \cdot \dfrac{3}{4}$

EXAMPLE 2 Multiplying Whole Numbers and Fractions

Bus At Jefferson Middle School, $\frac{2}{5}$ of the students ride the bus to and from school. If 750 students attend Jefferson Middle School, how many students take the bus to and from school?

Solution

$\frac{2}{5} \times 750 = $ ◻   Write 750 as $\frac{750}{1}$.

$= $ ◻   Use rule for multiplying fractions.
         Divide out the GCF of ◻ and ◻.

$= $ ◻ , or ◻   Multiply.

Answer: There are ◻ students who take the bus to and from school.

If you don't understand the process of dividing out common factors, write a question down in your notebook and discuss the question with a friend or teacher. Then write down what you learn.

EXAMPLE 3 Multiplying Mixed Numbers

$2\frac{4}{5} \times 2\frac{1}{12} = $ ◻   Write ◻ and ◻ as improper fractions.

$= $ ◻   Use rule for multiplying fractions. Divide out GCF of ◻ and ◻ and GCF of ◻ and ◻.

$= $ ◻   Multiply.

$= $ ◻   Write as a mixed number.

Guided Practice Find the product. Simplify if possible.

5. $6 \times \frac{1}{4}$	**6.** $\frac{2}{3} \times 10$	**7.** $3\frac{9}{10} \times 2\frac{2}{3}$	**8.** $2\frac{1}{2} \times 7\frac{4}{15}$

Dividing Fractions and Mixed Numbers

Goal: Divide fractions and mixed numbers.

Vocabulary

Reciprocal:

Using Reciprocals to Divide

Words To divide by any nonzero number, multiply by its [ ].

Numbers $\dfrac{3}{4} \div \dfrac{2}{3} = $ [ ] $= $ [ ]

Algebra $\dfrac{a}{b} \div \dfrac{c}{d} = $ [ ] $= $ [ ] $(b, c, d \neq 0)$

EXAMPLE 1 **Dividing a Fraction by a Fraction**

$\dfrac{3}{5} \div \dfrac{9}{10} = $ [ ]   Multiply by reciprocal.

$= $ [ ]   Use rule for multiplying fractions. Divide out common factors.

$= $ [ ]   Multiply.

In Example 2, you can check your answer by multiplying the quotient and the divisor and comparing the result with the dividend: $\dfrac{1}{16} \times 6 = \dfrac{1}{16} \times \dfrac{6}{1} = \dfrac{3}{8}.$

EXAMPLE 2 **Dividing a Fraction by a Whole Number**

$\dfrac{3}{8} \div 6 = $ [ ]   Multiply by reciprocal.

$= $ [ ]   Use rule for multiplying fractions. Divide out common factor.

$= $ [ ]   Multiply.

1. $\frac{5}{12} \div \frac{1}{10}$	2. $\frac{8}{3} \div \frac{4}{9}$	3. $\frac{3}{4} \div 9$	4. $\frac{2}{5} \div 8$

EXAMPLE 3 **Standardized Test Practice**

Craft Fair Organizers of a craft show have to place a cone on the sidewalk every $2\frac{1}{2}$ yards to mark where the craft vendors can set up their booths. One sidewalk that will be used in the craft show is 20 yards long. How many cones must be placed along this sidewalk?

  Ⓐ 6 cones   Ⓑ 7 cones   Ⓒ 8 cones   Ⓓ 9 cones

Solution

Method 1 Draw a diagram on graph paper. Make the sidewalk 20 boxes long.

Draw a point to mark off the location of a cone every $2\frac{1}{2}$ grid boxes.

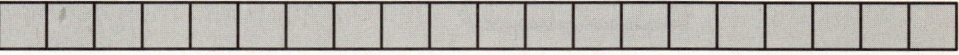

Method 2 Use division.

$20 \div 2\frac{1}{2} = $ ▢   Write ▢ as an improper fraction.

$= $ ▢   Multiply by reciprocal.

$= $ ▢   Use rule for multiplying fractions. Divide out common factor.

$= $ ▢   Multiply.

The quotient ▢ gives you the number of *spaces*, not the

number of *cones*. Subtract ▢ to get the number of cones.

▢ $= $ ▢

Answer: ▢ cones must be placed along this sidewalk. The correct answer

is ▢.   Ⓐ   Ⓑ   Ⓒ   Ⓓ

EXAMPLE 4 Dividing Two Mixed Numbers

Divide $7\frac{1}{3}$ by $1\frac{8}{9}$.

$7\frac{1}{3} \div 1\frac{8}{9} =$ 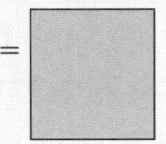   Write ▢ and ▢ as improper fractions.

$=$ ▢   Multiply by reciprocal.

$=$ ▢   Use rule for multiplying fractions.
Divide out common factor.

$=$ ▢ , or ▢   Multiply.

✓ **Check:** Estimate the quotient by rounding each mixed number to the nearest whole number.

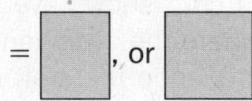
$7\frac{1}{3} \div 1\frac{8}{9} \approx 7 \div 2 = 3.5$ ✓

Guided Practice Find the quotient. Then estimate to check the answer.

5. $5 \div \frac{10}{11}$	6. $8 \div 4\frac{4}{5}$	7. $3\frac{3}{5} \div \frac{1}{4}$	8. $1\frac{1}{6} \div 1\frac{1}{3}$

Measuring in Customary Units

Goal: Measure and estimate using customary units.

Vocabulary

U.S. customary system:

Inch:

Foot:

Yard:

Mile:

Ounce:

Pound:

Ton:

Fluid Ounce:

Cup:

Pint:

Quart:

Gallon:

EXAMPLE 1 Using Customary Units of Length

To estimate the length of a playing card, think of small paper clips laid next to it. Then measure the playing card with a ruler to check your estimate.

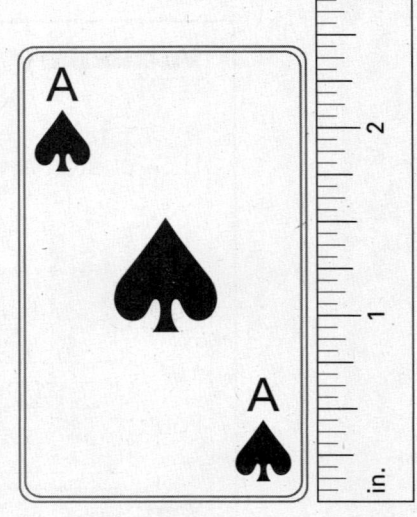

About [ ] paper clips fit alongside the card, so it is about [ ] inches long.

The ruler shows [ ] of an inch, so the playing card is [ ] inches long.

Be careful to distinguish between mass and weight. Your mass is the same wherever you are, but your weight depends on gravity. On the moon, for instance, you would weigh about $\frac{1}{6}$ of what you weigh on Earth.

EXAMPLE 2 Measuring Weight

Find the weight of the cantaloupe.

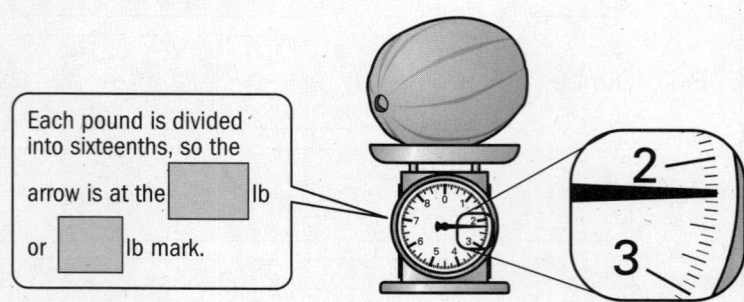

Each pound is divided into sixteenths, so the arrow is at the [ ] lb or [ ] lb mark.

EXAMPLE 3 **Using Customary Units of Weight**

Copy and complete the statement with the appropriate customary unit:
The weight of a television is 56 __?__ .

The weight of a television is greater than ▢▢▢▢▢▢ (56 ▢),

and it is certainly less than the weight of ▢▢▢▢▢ (56 ▢).

Because a good estimate for the weight of a television is the weight of
▢▢▢▢▢▢ , the appropriate customary unit is ▢▢▢▢ .

Answer: The weight of a television is 56 ▢▢▢▢ .

Guided Practice Complete the following exercises.

1. Estimate the length of a CD case. Then use a ruler to check
the estimate.

2. The weight of a kitchen chair is 15 __?__ .

EXAMPLE 4 Measuring a Liquid Amount

WATCH OUT!
A fluid ounce is not the same as an ounce. Fluid ounces are a measure of the capacity of a container holding liquid, while an ounce measures the weight of the container.

Find the amount of liquid in the measuring cup.

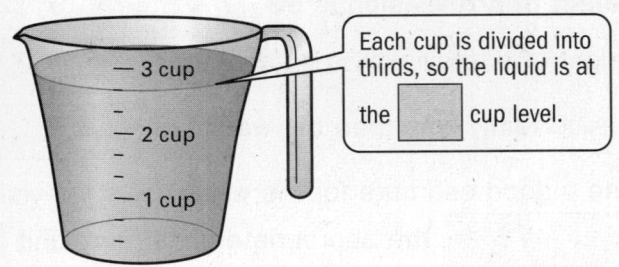

Each cup is divided into thirds, so the liquid is at the ☐ cup level.

Answer: There are about ☐ cups of liquid in the measuring cup.

EXAMPLE 5 Standardized Test Practice

What is the most reasonable capacity of a soup bowl?

Ⓐ 2 fl oz   Ⓑ 2 qt   Ⓒ 20 gal   Ⓓ 2 c

Solution

Both ☐ of water and ☐ of water are too much to fill the soup bowl. A soup bowl holds more than ☐ of water, so that capacity is too small. That leaves ☐ of water, which seems an appropriate capacity.

Answer: The most reasonable capacity of a soup bowl is ☐. The correct answer is ☐. Ⓐ Ⓑ Ⓒ Ⓓ

Guided Practice Match the object with the appropriate capacity.

3. Large watering can	4. Spoon	5. Ladle
A. $\frac{3}{4}$ fl oz	**A.** $\frac{3}{4}$ fl oz	**A.** $\frac{3}{4}$ fl oz
B. 1 cup	**B.** 1 cup	**B.** 1 cup
C. $2\frac{1}{2}$ gal	**C.** $2\frac{1}{2}$ gal	**C.** $2\frac{1}{2}$ gal

Converting Customary Units

Goal: Convert between customary units.

Converting Units of Measure

Length

1 ft = ☐ in.

1 yd = ☐ ft = ☐ in.

1 mi = ☐ yd = ☐ ft

Weight

1 lb = ☐ oz

1 T = ☐ lb

Capacity

1 c = ☐ fl oz

1 pt = ☐ c

1 qt = ☐ pt

1 gal = ☐ qt

EXAMPLE 1 **Converting Customary Units of Length**

Farming The corn field on the Walters farm is made of 36 rows of the same length. Each row is 129 feet long. How many yards long is one row of corn?

Solution

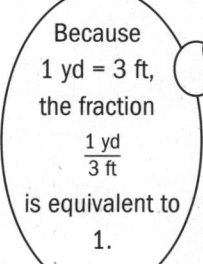

Because 1 yd = 3 ft, the fraction $\frac{1 \text{ yd}}{3 \text{ ft}}$ is equivalent to 1.

$129 \text{ ft} \times \dfrac{1 \text{ yd}}{3 \text{ ft}} = $ ☐   Use rule for multiplying fractions. Divide out common factor and unit.

$= $ ☐   Multiply.

Answer: A row of corn is ☐ yards long.

EXAMPLE **2** **Converting Customary Units of Weight**

African Elephants The weight of an average African elephant is 6 tons. How many pounds is this?

Solution

Use the fact that 1 T = 2000 lb.

$$6\ T \times \frac{2000\ lb}{1\ T} = \boxed{}$$ Write 6 T as $\boxed{}$.

$$= \boxed{}$$ Use rule for multiplying fractions. Divide out common unit.

$$= \boxed{}$$ Multiply.

Answer: The weight of an average African elephant is $\boxed{}$ pounds.

EXAMPLE **3** **Converting Customary Units of Capacity**

Convert 36 fluid ounces to pints. Use the fact that 1 c = 8 fl oz and 1 pt = 2 c.

$$36\ fl\ oz \times \frac{1\ c}{8\ fl\ oz} \times \frac{1\ pt}{2\ c} = \boxed{}$$ Use rule for multiplying fractions. Divide out common factors and units.

$$= \boxed{}\ , or\ \boxed{}$$ Multiply.

Guided Practice **Copy and complete the statement.**

1. 2500 lb = __?__ T	**2.** 12 yd = __?__ in.	**3.** 9 c = __?__ fl oz

EXAMPLE 4 Writing Measurements in Mixed Units

Convert 30 fluid ounces to cups and fluid ounces.

1. Convert 30 fluid ounces to cups.

$$30 \text{ fl oz} \times \frac{1 \text{ c}}{8 \text{ fl oz}} = \boxed{}$$

$$= \boxed{} \text{, or } \boxed{}$$

2. Convert the fractional part from cups to fluid ounces.

$$\boxed{} = \boxed{}$$

$$= \boxed{}$$

Answer: So, 30 fl oz = $\boxed{}$ c $\boxed{}$ fl oz.

Guided Practice Copy and complete the statement.

4. 19 oz = __?__ lb __?__ oz

5. 9 pt = __?__ qt __?__ pt

EXAMPLE 5 Adding and Subtracting with Mixed Units

Animals Two puppies are in the veterinarian's office. The terrier weighs 18 pounds 9 ounces. The poodle weighs 12 pounds 13 ounces.

a. Find the sum of the weights.　　**b.** Find the difference of the weights.

Solution

a. Add. Then rename the sum.

```
  18 lb     9 oz
+ 12 lb    13 oz
_____
   [ ] lb  [ ] oz
```

$\boxed{}$ lb $\boxed{}$ oz = $\boxed{}$ lb $\boxed{}$ oz

Answer: $\boxed{}$ lb $\boxed{}$ oz

b. Rename. Then subtract.

```
  18 lb   9 oz          [ ] lb [ ] oz
- 12 lb  13 oz        - [ ] lb [ ] oz
_____          _____
                         [ ] lb [ ] oz
```

Answer: $\boxed{}$ lb $\boxed{}$ oz

Words to Review

Give an example of the vocabulary word.

Reciprocal

U.S. customary system

Inch

Foot

Yard

Mile

Ounce

Pound

Ton

Fluid ounce

Cup

Pint

Quart

Gallon

Review your notes and Chapter 5 by using the Chapter Review on pages 257–260 of your textbook.

Comparing and Ordering Integers

Goal: Compare and order integers.

Vocabulary

Integer:

Negative integer:

Positive integer:

Opposite:

Integers and Their Opposites

Zero

Negative integers | Positive integers

−4 −3 −2 −1 0 1 2 3 4

The integer −4 is read "negative four." A number other than 0 that has no sign is considered to be positive, so the integer 4 is read "positive four" or "four."

Two numbers are **opposites** if they are the [   ] from zero on a number line but are on [   ] of zero. For example, −3 is the opposite of [   ]. The opposite of 0 is [   ].

EXAMPLE 1 **Writing Integers**

Temperatures The temperature increased 12 degrees between 7 A.M. and 7 P.M. The temperature decreased 14 degrees between 7 P.M. and 7 A.M. You can use integers to represent the increase and decrease in the temperature.

Solution

12 degree increase: [   ]   14 degree decrease: [   ]

Guided Practice Write the opposite of the integer.

1. −17	**2.** 3	**3.** 41	**4.** −215

EXAMPLE 2 **Comparing Integers Using a Number Line**

> **WATCH OUT!**
> Don't confuse a negative sign with a subtraction sign. A negative sign indicates a direction on a number line, not an operation.

a. Compare −1 and −4.

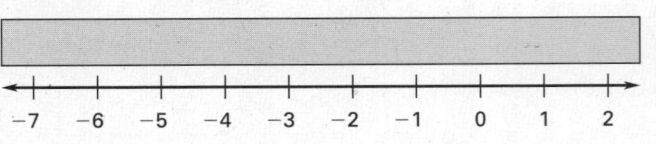

−1 is to the [ ] of −4.

Answer: −1 [ ] −4, or −4 [ ] −1.

b. Compare −3 and 0.

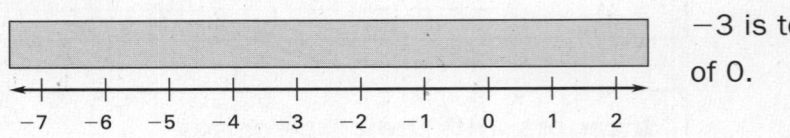

−3 is to the [ ] of 0.

Answer: −3 [ ] 0, or 0 [ ] −3.

Guided Practice Copy and complete the statement using < or >.

5. 3 _?_ −5	**6.** −7 _?_ 2	**7.** −6 _?_ −8	**8.** −2 _?_ −10

EXAMPLE **3** **Ordering Integers Using a Number Line**

Football The table shows the number of yards gained by the West High School football team during the first play in each quarter during their first game of the season. Which quarter had the first play with the least yards gained?

Quarter	1	2	3	4	OT
Yards Gained During First Play	15	−7	−12	9	19

Solution

You can graph each integer on a number line to order the yards gained.

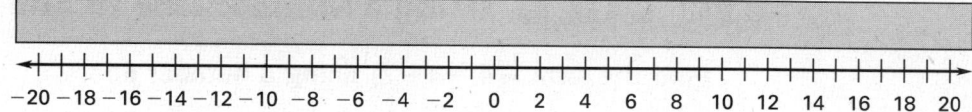

The yardages from least to greatest are: [   ].

Answer: At [   ] yards, the first play of the [   ] quarter had the least yards gained.

Adding Integers

Goal: Add integers.

Vocabulary

Absolute value:

EXAMPLE 1 **Using a Number Line to Add Integers**

Find the sum −4 + (−2) using a number line.

Start at 0. Move ☐ units to the ☐ .

Then move ☐ more units to the ☐ .

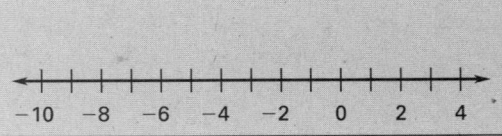

Answer: The final position is ☐ , so −4 + (−2) = ☐ .

EXAMPLE 2 **Standardized Test Practice**

The number line shows changes in altitude of a glider. Which expression represents the new altitude of the glider?

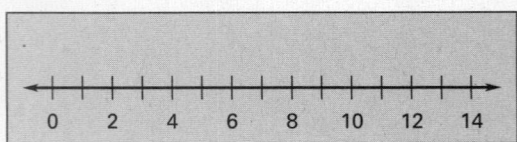

A −14 + 8   **B** 14 + 0   **C** 14 + (−8)   **D** 14 + (−6)

Solution

The model represents moving ☐ units to the right and then ☐ units to the left, or ☐ + ☐ = ☐ .

Answer: The correct answer is ☐ .   Ⓐ Ⓑ Ⓒ Ⓓ

1. $-7 + (-2)$	**2.** $-9 + 5$	**3.** $7 + (-12)$	**4.** $18 + (-5)$

EXAMPLE 3 **Finding Absolute Value**

Find the absolute value of the number.

a. 4   **b.** -5

Solution

Because distance cannot be negative, the absolute value of a number cannot be negative.

a. The distance between 4 and 0 is ☐. So, $|4| = $ ☐.

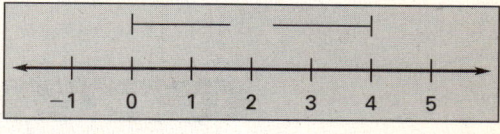

b. The distance between -5 and 0 is ☐. So, $|-5| = $ ☐.

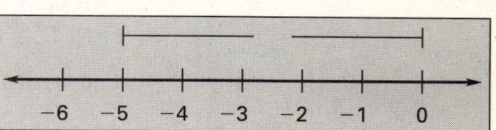

Guided Practice Find the absolute value of the number.

5. 75	**6.** -10	**7.** -60	**8.** 36

Adding Integers with Absolute Value

Words

Same Sign Add the [_____]

and use the [_____] sign.

Different Signs Subtract the

[_____] from the

[_____] and use the sign of

the integer with the [_____].

Opposites The sum of an integer and

its [_____] is [____].

Numbers

$10 + 14 =$ [____]

$-7 + (-5) =$ [____]

$13 + (-9) =$ [____]

$-11 + 6 =$ [____]

$-4 + 4 =$ [____]

EXAMPLE 4 **Adding Two Integers Using Absolute Value**

a. Find the sum $-2 + (-11)$.

These integers have [_____].

Add $\left|\;[\quad]\;\right|$ and $\left|\;[\quad]\;\right|$.

$-2 + (-11) =$ [_____]

Both integers are [_____], so the

sum is [_____].

b. Find the sum $-4 + 7$.

These integers have [_____].

Subtract $\left|\;[\quad]\;\right|$ from $\left|\;[\quad]\;\right|$.

$-4 + 7 =$ [____]

Because $\left|\;[\quad]\;\right|\;[\quad]\;\left|\;[\quad]\;\right|$, the

sum has the same sign as [____].

Use absolute values to find the sum.

9. $-3 + (-9)$	**10.** $-8 + 4$	**11.** $0 + (-13)$
12. $-10 + 12$	**13.** $18 + (-10)$	**14.** $-25 + 25$

EXAMPLE 5 **Adding Three or More Integers**

Stock Market The stock price of the Morello Corporation changed every day this week. Find the value of the stock at the end of the week.

Starting Price: $12	
Monday	$4
Tuesday	−$5
Wednesday	−$2
Thursday	$1
Friday	−$3

Solution

You can find the sum by adding the integers two at a time.

$12 + 4 + (-5) + (-2) + 1 + (-3)$

$= \boxed{} + (-5) + (-2) + 1 + (-3)$ Add 12 and 4.

$= \boxed{} + (-2) + 1 + (-3)$ Add $\boxed{}$ and −5.

$= \boxed{} + 1 + (-3)$ Add $\boxed{}$ and −2.

$= \boxed{} + (-3)$ Add $\boxed{}$ and 1.

$= \boxed{}$ Add $\boxed{}$ and −3.

Answer: The sum of the starting price and the changes in the stock price is $\boxed{}$. The stock was valued at $\boxed{}$ at the end of the week.

Refer to Example 5.

15. During the next week, the stock changed value again.

$3, $5, −$2, −$4, $6

Find the value of the stock at the end of the next week.

Subtracting Integers

LESSON 6.3

Goal: Subtract integers.

Subtracting Integers

Words To subtract an integer, add its [ ].

Numbers $5 - 7 = 5 +$ [ ]   **Algebra** $a - b = a +$ [ ]

> Need help with finding opposites? See page 269 of your textbook.

EXAMPLE 1 **Subtracting Integers**

a. $4 - 9 = 4 +$ [ ]   To subtract 9, add its opposite, [ ].

   $=$ [ ]   Use rule for adding integers.

b. $-3 - 7 = -3 +$ [ ]   To subtract 7, add its opposite, [ ].

   $=$ [ ]   Use rule for adding integers.

c. $15 - (-4) = 15 +$ [ ]   To subtract -4, add its opposite, [ ].

   $=$ [ ]   Use rule for adding integers.

d. $-12 - (-7) = -12 +$ [ ]   To subtract -7, add its opposite, [ ].

   $=$ [ ]   Use rule for adding integers.

Guided Practice Find the difference.

1. $7 - 2$	**2.** $-4 - (-7)$	**3.** $-2 - 1$	**4.** $12 - (-9)$

EXAMPLE **2** **Using Integer Subtraction**

Diving A snorkeler explores the Great Barrier Reef at 3 feet below sea level. A diver explores the reef at 27 feet below sea level. What is the difference between these elevations?

Solution

1. Use integers to represent the two elevations.

Snorkeler: ▢ feet   Diver: ▢ feet

2. Find the difference of ▢ and ▢ feet.

▢ − ▢ = ▢ + ▢   Rule for subtracting integers

= ▢   Add.

Answer: The difference between the elevations is ▢ feet.

EXAMPLE **3** **Finding a Change in Temperature**

Weather In Spearfish, South Dakota, weather observers recorded the fastest change in temperature. In two minutes' time, the temperature changed from −20°C to 7°C. What was the change in temperature?

Solution

Change in temperature = ▢ temperature − ▢ temperature

= ▢ − ▢   Substitute values.

= ▢ + ▢   Rule for subtracting integers.

= ▢   Add.

Answer: The change in temperature was ▢ °C, so the temperature rose ▢ °C.

Guided Practice **Solve the following problems.**

5. Find the difference between an elevation of 620 feet above sea level and an elevation of 15 feet below sea level.

6. The temperature at 7 A.M. was −4°F. At 7 P.M. the temperature was −18°F. What was the change in temperature?

Multiplying Integers

Goal: Multiply integers.

Multiplying Integers

Words

Same Sign The product of two integers with the same sign is [ ].

Different Signs The product of two integers with different signs is [ ].

Zero The product of an integer and 0 is [ ].

Numbers

$5 \cdot 3 = $ [ ]

$-5 \cdot (-3) = $ [ ]

$5 \cdot (-3) = $ [ ]

$-5 \cdot 3 = $ [ ]

$5 \cdot 0 = $ [ ]

$-5 \cdot 0 = $ [ ]

EXAMPLE 1 Multiplying Integers

a. $-4(-8) = $ [ ]

The product of two integers with the same sign is [ ].

b. $-9(3) = $ [ ]

The product of two integers with different signs is [ ].

c. $-1(0) = $ [ ]

The product of an integer and 0 is [ ].

EXAMPLE 2 **Evaluating Variable Expressions**

 a. Evaluate a^2 when $a = -5$.

 b. Evaluate xyz when $x = 3$, $y = -6$, and $z = 2$.

Solution

 a. $a^2 = \boxed{}$ Substitute $\boxed{}$ for a.

 $= \boxed{}$ Write $\boxed{}$ as a factor $\boxed{}$ times.

 $= \boxed{}$ Multiply $\boxed{}$ and $\boxed{}$.

 b. $xyz = \boxed{}$ Substitute $\boxed{}$ for x, $\boxed{}$ for y, and $\boxed{}$ for z.

 $= \boxed{}$ Multiply $\boxed{}$ and $\boxed{}$.

 $= \boxed{}$ Multiply $\boxed{}$ and $\boxed{}$.

Guided Practice **Find the product.**

1. $7(5)$	**2.** $-2(-6)$	**3.** $6(-6)$	**4.** $-8(8)$	**5.** $0(-20)$

EXAMPLE 3 **Using Integer Multiplication**

After-School Business Chris withdraws $5 from his savings account every day for 6 days to invest the money in his after-school business. Use multiplication to find the change in his balance after those 6 days.

Solution

You can find the total change in the account balance by multiplying the daily balance change by the number of days of withdrawals.

Change in balance $= \boxed{} \left(\boxed{} \right) = \boxed{}$

Answer: The account balance will decrease $\$\boxed{}$.

Dividing Integers

Goal: Divide integers.

Dividing Integers

Words   **Numbers**

Same Sign The quotient of two integers with the same sign is ☐ .

$14 \div 2 = \boxed{}$

$\dfrac{-16}{-4} = \boxed{}$

Different Signs The quotient of two integers with different signs is ☐ .

$25 \div (-5) = \boxed{}$

$\dfrac{-32}{8} = \boxed{}$

Zero The quotient of 0 and any nonzero integer is ☐ .

$0 \div 13 = \boxed{}$

$\dfrac{0}{-11} = \boxed{}$

WATCH OUT!
You cannot divide a number by 0. Any number divided by 0 is *undefined*. For example, $8 \div 0 = \underline{\ ?\ }$ can be rewritten as $\underline{\ ?\ } \cdot 0 = 8$. No number times 0 will result in a nonzero product.

EXAMPLE 1   **Dividing Integers**

a. $36 \div (-9) = \boxed{}$ The quotient of two integers with different signs is ☐ .

b. $\dfrac{-50}{-10} = \boxed{}$ The quotient of two integers with the same sign is ☐ .

c. $0 \div (-14) = \boxed{}$ The quotient of 0 and any nonzero integer is ☐ .

Guided Practice   Find the quotient.

1. $-18 \div 9$	**2.** $\dfrac{0}{-6}$	**3.** $\dfrac{-30}{-2}$	**4.** $22 \div (-1)$

EXAMPLE 2 **Standardized Test Practice**

Wall Street Stock brokers for a Wall Street firm tracked the changes in stock prices of the market over a 5-day period. Which expression can be used to find the mean change in stock prices?

A $60 + 17 + 23 + 45 + 19 \div 5$

B $60 + (-17) + 23 + (-45) + 19 \div 5$

C $(60 + 17 + 23 + 45 + 19) \div 5$

D $[60 + (-17) + 23 + (-45) + 19] \div 5$

Day	Change in Market Value
Monday	$60
Tuesday	-$17
Wednesday	$23
Thursday	-$45
Friday	$19

Solution

The mean is calculated by finding the sum of the stock price changes and then dividing by the number of days.

Mean = [   ] = [   ]

The mean change in stock prices is $[   ].

Answer: The correct answer is [   ]. **A** **B** **C** **D**

Guided Practice Solve the following problem.

5. The low temperature was recorded over several hours' time. Find the mean of the temperatures.

$-15°F, -8°F, 2°F, 0°F, -4°F, 19°F$

EXAMPLE 3 **Converting a Temperature**

Chemistry A chemical solution has a melting point of −70°C. Convert the temperature to degrees Fahrenheit.

Solution

$F = \dfrac{9}{5}C + 32$ Write formula for degrees Fahrenheit.

$= \dfrac{9}{5}\left(\boxed{} \right) + 32$ Substitute $\boxed{}$ for C.

$= \dfrac{\boxed{}}{\boxed{}} + 32$ Use rule for multiplying fractions.
Divide out common factor.

$= \boxed{} + \boxed{}$ Multiply.

$= \boxed{}$ Add.

Answer: The temperature −70°C is equal to $\boxed{}$ °F.

Guided Practice **Convert the temperature from degrees Fahrenheit to degrees Celsius or from degrees Celsius to degrees Fahrenheit.**

6. 40°C	**7.** 68°F	**8.** −58°F	**9.** −10°C

Rational Numbers

Goal: Perform operations on rational numbers.

Vocabulary

Rational number:

Additive inverse:

Multiplicative inverse:

Additive identity:

Multiplicative identity:

EXAMPLE 1 Identifying Rational Numbers

Show that the number is rational by writing it in $\frac{a}{b}$ form.

a. $12 =$

b. $-\frac{1}{2} =$

c. $0.6 =$

d. $-1\frac{1}{12} =$

The negative sign in a negative fraction usually appears in front of the fraction bar. However, it can also appear in the numerator or in the denominator.

EXAMPLE 2 **Ordering Rational Numbers**

Order -2, -2.4, $1\frac{4}{5}$, $-1\frac{1}{4}$, and $-2\frac{4}{5}$ from least to greatest.

Graph each number on a number line.

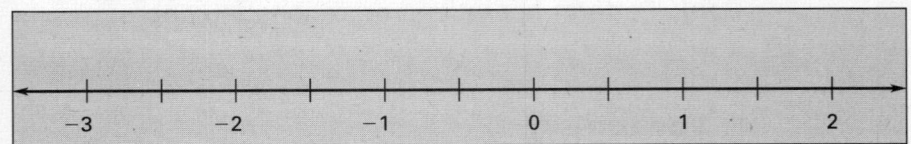

Answer: From least to greatest, the numbers are:

Guided Practice Show that each number is rational by writing it in $\frac{a}{b}$ form. Then order the numbers from least to greatest.

1. 1.6, -6, $-\frac{6}{7}$, -0.7	**2.** $5\frac{1}{4}$, -4.5, $-4\frac{4}{5}$, 0

Commutative and Associative Properties

> To remember the commutative property, remember that *commuters* are people who *move* or travel. To remember the associative property, remember that the people you *associate* with are the friends in your group.

Commutative Property of Addition

Words In a sum, you can add terms in any order.

Numbers $5 + (-6) = \boxed{} + \boxed{}$

Algebra $a + b = \boxed{} + \boxed{}$

Commutative Property of Multiplication

Words In a product, you can multiply factors in any order.

Numbers $4(-7) = \boxed{}\left(\boxed{}\right)$

Algebra $ab = \boxed{}$

Associative Property of Addition

Words Changing the grouping of terms will not change the sum.

Numbers

$(9 + 8) + 6 = \boxed{} + \left(\boxed{} + \boxed{}\right)$

Algebra

$(a + b) + c = \boxed{} + \left(\boxed{} + \boxed{}\right)$

Associative Property of Multiplication

Words Changing the grouping of factors will not change the product.

Numbers

$(2 \cdot 3) \cdot 4 = \boxed{} \cdot \left(\boxed{} \cdot \boxed{}\right)$

Algebra

$(ab)c = \boxed{}\left(\boxed{}\right)$

EXAMPLE 3 **Using Commutative, Associative Properties**

Evaluate the expression. Justify each step you take.

a. $-5.2 + 4 + (-6.8)$ **b.** $-20(12)(-5)$

Solution

Remember that recording the steps you take in a multi-step calculation can help you perform similar calculations.

a. $-5.2 + 4 + (-6.8)$

$= \boxed{} + \boxed{} + (-6.8)$ — Commutative property of addition

$= \boxed{} + \boxed{}$ — Associative property of addition

$= \boxed{} + \boxed{} = \boxed{}$ — Add $\boxed{}$ and $\boxed{}$, then $\boxed{}$ and $\boxed{}$.

b. $-20(12)(-5)$

$= \boxed{}(-5)$ — Commutative property of multiplication

$= \boxed{}$ — Associative property of multiplication

$= \boxed{} = \boxed{}$ — Multiply $\boxed{}$ and $\boxed{}$, then $\boxed{}$ and $\boxed{}$.

Guided Practice Evaluate the expression. Justify each step you take.

3. $2.6 + [(-5) + 3.4]$

4. $5(-12)(2)$

5. $-8(9)(-5)$

Inverse and Identity Properties

Inverse Property of Addition	**Inverse Property of Multiplication**
Words The sum of a number and its additive inverse, or opposite, is ☐ .	**Words** The product of a number and its multiplicative inverse, or reciprocal, is ☐ .
Numbers $7 + (-7) =$ ☐	**Numbers** $\dfrac{2}{3} \cdot \dfrac{3}{2} =$ ☐
Algebra $a + (-a) =$ ☐	**Algebra** For nonzero integers a and b, $\dfrac{a}{b} \cdot \dfrac{b}{a} =$ ☐ .
Identity Property of Addition	**Identity Property of Multiplication**
Words The sum of a number and the additive identity, 0, is ☐ .	**Words** The product of a number and the multiplicative identity, 1, is ☐ .
Numbers $-9 + 0 =$ ☐	**Numbers** $3 \cdot 1 =$ ☐
Algebra $a + 0 =$ ☐	**Algebra** $a \cdot 1 =$ ☐

EXAMPLE 4 **Using Inverse and Identity Properties**

Evaluate the expression. Justify each step you take.

$$\frac{1}{7} + \frac{2}{3} + \left(-\frac{1}{7}\right) = \frac{1}{7} + \boxed{} + \boxed{} \qquad \text{Commutative property of addition}$$

$$= \boxed{} + \boxed{} \qquad \text{Inverse property of addition}$$

$$= \boxed{} \qquad \text{Identity property of addition}$$

6. $66 + 102 + (-66)$

7. $4 \cdot 18 \cdot \frac{1}{4}$

8. $-\frac{2}{5} + \frac{7}{8} + \frac{2}{5}$

The Distributive Property

Goal: Evaluate expressions using the distributive property.

Vocabulary

Equivalent expressions:

Distributive property:

EXAMPLE 1 **Writing Equivalent Expressions**

Tea Party A tea party has two rectangular tables: one that is 6 feet by 5 feet, and one that is 6 feet by 4 feet. What two expressions could be used to find the total area of the tables?

Solution

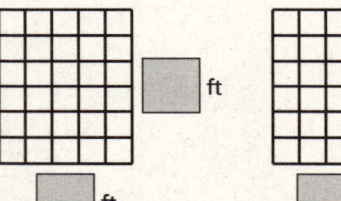 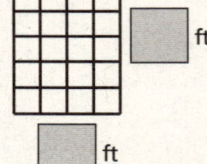

ft   ft   ft

ft   ft $\left(\boxed{} + \boxed{} \right)$ ft

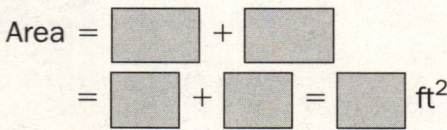 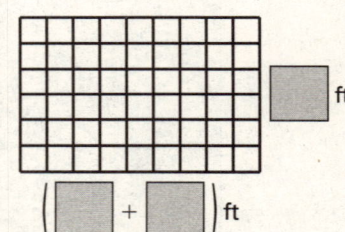

Area = $\boxed{}$ + $\boxed{}$ Area = $\boxed{}$

= $\boxed{}$ + $\boxed{}$ = $\boxed{}$ ft^2 = $\boxed{}$ = $\boxed{}$ ft^2

The Distributive Property

Algebra For all numbers a, b, and c, $a(b + c) = \boxed{} + \boxed{}$ and

$a(b - c) = \boxed{} - \boxed{}$.

Numbers $8(10 + 4) = \boxed{} + \boxed{}$ and $3(4 - 2) = \boxed{} - \boxed{}$

EXAMPLE 2 **Writing Equivalent Expressions**

Use the distributive property to write an equivalent expression.
Check your answer.

a. $-6(2 + 7)$ **b.** $3(75 - 25)$ **c.** $8(2) + 8(9)$

Solution

a. $-6(2 + 7) =$ ☐ $+$ ☐   Distributive property

     Check: $-6(9) \overset{?}{=}$ ☐ $+$ ☐   Simplify.

             $-54 =$ ☐ ✓   Answer checks.

b. $3(75 - 25) =$ ☐ $-$ ☐   Distributive property

     Check: $3(50) \overset{?}{=}$ ☐ $-$ ☐   Simplify.

             $150 =$ ☐ ✓   Answer checks.

c. $8(2) + 8(9) =$ ☐   Distributive property

     Check: $16 + 72 \overset{?}{=}$ ☐   Simplify.

             $88 =$ ☐ ✓   Answer checks.

Guided Practice Use the distributive property to write an equivalent
expression. Check your answer.

1. $5\left(\dfrac{1}{4}\right) + 5\left(\dfrac{3}{4}\right)$	**2.** $-4(7 + 5)$
3. $9(15 - 8)$	**4.** $10(6) - 10(2)$

EXAMPLE **3** **Using the Distributive Property**

Scrapbooks Leslie is making a scrapbook for her mother's birthday. She bought 6 packs of stickers for $6.95 each. Use the distributive property to find the total cost of the stickers.

Solution

$6(6.95) = $ ☐   Write 6.95 as a difference of a whole number and a decimal.

$= $ ☐ $-$ ☐   Distributive property

$= $ ☐ $-$ ☐ $= $ ☐   Multiply. Then subtract.

Answer: The total cost of the stickers is $ ☐ .

The Coordinate Plane

Goal: Identify and plot points in a coordinate plane.

Vocabulary

Coordinate plane:

x-axis:

y-axis:

Origin:

Quadrant:

Ordered pair:

x-coordinate:

y-coordinate:

Scatter plot:

EXAMPLE 1   Naming Ordered Pairs

Name the ordered pair that represents the point.

  a. *A*   **b.** *B*

Solution

  a. Point *A* is ☐ units to the ☐ of

      the origin and ☐ units ☐. So, the

      x-coordinate is ☐ and the

      y-coordinate is ☐. Point *A* is

      represented by the ordered pair (☐ , ☐).

  b. Point *B* is ☐ units to the ☐ of the origin and ☐ unit ☐.

      So, the *x*-coordinate is ☐ and the *y*-coordinate is ☐. Point *B* is

      represented by the ordered pair (☐ , ☐).

EXAMPLE 2   Standardized Test Practice

Which of the following points is located in Quadrant IV?

  (A) $P(2, -3)$ **(B)** $Q(-4, 3)$ **(C)** $R(1, 0)$ **(D)** $S(-4, -2)$

> The notation
> $P(2, -3)$ means that
> point *P* is represented
> by the ordered
> pair (2, −3).

Solution

Plot points *P*, *Q*, *R*, and *S* in a coordinate plane.

Point ☐ lies on the *x*-axis. Point ☐ is located

in Quadrant II. Point ☐ is located in Quadrant III.

Point ☐ is located in Quadrant IV.

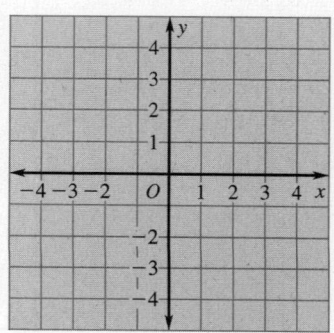

Answer: Point ☐ . The correct answer

is ☐ . **(A)** **(B)** **(C)** **(D)**

Plot the point and describe its location.

1. $W(6, 1)$ **2.** $X(0, 4)$ **3.** $Y(-1, 3)$ **4.** $Z(-2, -4)$

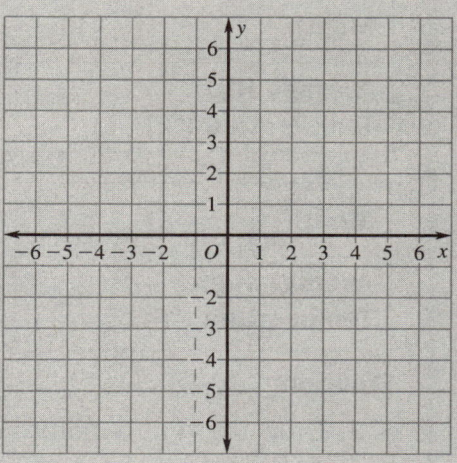

EXAMPLE 3   **Finding Segment Lengths and Area**

Find the length, width, and area of rectangle *ABCD* shown.

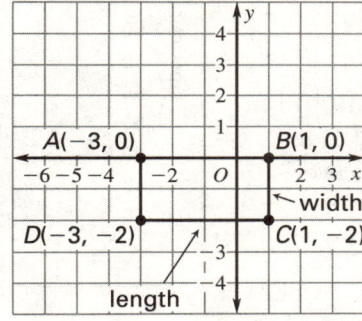

The length of the rectangle is the *horizontal* distance between *A* and *B*.
To find this distance, find the absolute value of the difference between the
x-coordinates of *A* and *B*.

Length $= |x\text{-coordinate of } A - x\text{-coordinate of } B|$

$= \boxed{} = \boxed{} = \boxed{}$ units

The width of the rectangle is the *vertical* distance between *A* and *D*.
To find this distance, find the absolute value of the difference between
the *y*-coordinates of *A* and *D*.

Width $= |y\text{-coordinate of } A - y\text{-coordinate of } D|$

$= \boxed{} = \boxed{} = \boxed{}$ units

The area of the rectangle is found by multiplying the length and width.

Area $= \ell w = \boxed{} = \boxed{}$ square units

EXAMPLE 4 **Making a Scatter Plot**

Average High Temperature The monthly average high temperatures in Myrtle Beach are listed in the table below. Make a scatter plot of the data. Then make a conclusion about the data.

Month	1	2	3	4	5	6
Average High Temperature (°F)	56	60	68	76	83	88

Month	7	8	9	10	11	12
Average High Temperature (°F)	91	89	85	77	69	60

Solution

1. Draw the first quadrant of a coordinate plane, and show the month on the *x*-axis and the temperature on the *y*-axis.

2. Plot the ordered pairs in the table.

3. Look for a pattern. The points tend to rise from left to right from Month 1 to Month 7 and then lower from left to right from Month 7 to Month 12.

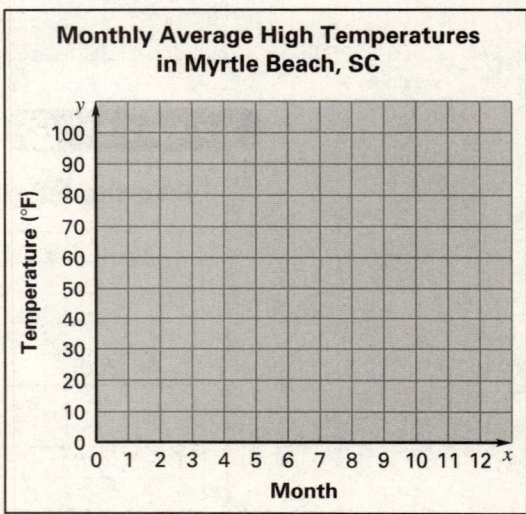

Monthly Average High Temperatures in Myrtle Beach, SC

Answer: From January to July, the monthly average high temperature
[ ] and from July to December, the monthly average high temperature [ ].

CHAPTER 6

Words to Review

Give an example of the vocabulary word.

Integer

Negative integer

Positive integer

Opposite

Absolute value

Rational number

Additive inverse

Multiplicative inverse

Additive identity

Multiplicative identity

Equivalent expressions

Distributive property

Coordinate plane

x-axis

y-axis

Origin

Quadrant

Ordered pair

x-coordinate

y-coordinate

Scatter plot

Review your notes and Chapter 6 by using the Chapter Review on pages 322–326 of your textbook.

Writing Expressions and Equations

Goal: Write variable expressions and equations.

Vocabulary

Verbal model:

EXAMPLE 1 **Translating Verbal Phrases**

Verbal phrase   **Expression**

a. A number increased by 3

b. 9 less than a number

c. 1 more than three times a number

d. 5 decreased by the quotient of a number and 2

When translating verbal sentences into equations, look for the key words "is" and "equals," which can be represented by the symbol =.

EXAMPLE 2 **Translating Verbal Sentences**

Verbal sentence   **Equation**

a. 12 increased by a number is 18.

b. The difference of a number and 6 equals −2.

c. The product of $\frac{2}{3}$ and a number is 15.

d. −2 is equal to five times the sum of a number and 3.

Guided Practice Write the verbal phrase or sentence as a variable expression or equation. Let *n* represent the number.

1. 9 added to a number	**2.** $\frac{1}{4}$ of a number increased by 18
3. 24 divided by a number equals 6.	**4.** 26 minus 4 times a number is 10.

EXAMPLE 3 **Writing and Solving an Equation**

Dinner The cost of a fish dinner is 3 times the cost of a chef salad. The fish dinner costs $21. Find the cost of the chef salad.

Solution

Write a verbal model.

Let *s* represent the cost of the salad.

3 times the cost of a ⬜ = Cost of a ⬜

⬜ = ⬜

Use mental math: Because 3 times ⬜ is 21, $s =$ ⬜.

Answer: The cost of a chef salad is $⬜.

> Assign a meaningful variable to represent what you need to find. In Example 3, *s* is chosen to represent the price of a salad.

Guided Practice Use mental math to solve the following problem.

5. This year, the enrollment at the local junior college dropped by 500 to 4250. Write and solve an equation to find the enrollment last year.

Simplifying Expressions

LESSON 7.2

Goal: Simplify variable expressions.

Vocabulary

Term:

Like terms:

Equivalent variable expressions:

Coefficient:

Constant term:

EXAMPLE 1 Combining Like Terms

Simplify the expression 8x − 2 + 4x.

After Example 1, the step of using the distributive property in order to combine like terms will not be shown.

$8x - 2 + 4x =$ ⬚   Write expression as a sum.

$= 8x +$ ⬚   Commutative property of addition

$=$ ⬚   Distributive property

$=$ ⬚   Simplify.

$=$ ⬚   Rewrite without parentheses.

EXAMPLE 2 Coefficients, Constant Terms, Like Terms

Identify the coefficients, constant terms, and like terms of the expression $x - 7 + 3x - 1$.

First, write the expression as a sum: $x + \left(\boxed{} \right) + 3x + \left(\boxed{} \right)$.

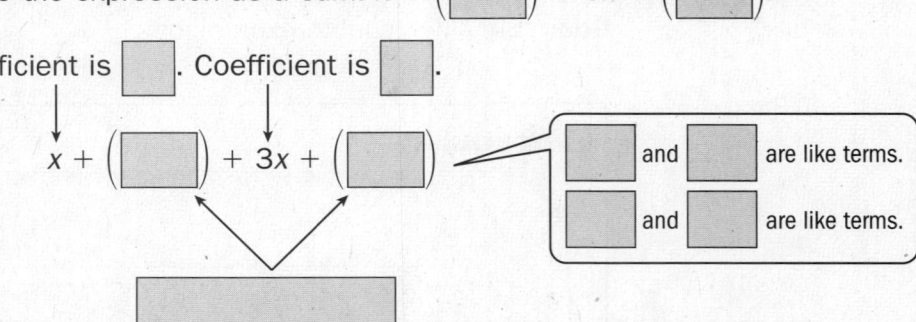

Coefficient is $\boxed{}$. Coefficient is $\boxed{}$.

$x + \left(\boxed{} \right) + 3x + \left(\boxed{} \right)$

$\boxed{}$ and $\boxed{}$ are like terms.

$\boxed{}$ and $\boxed{}$ are like terms.

$\boxed{}$

EXAMPLE 3 Simplifying an Expression

Simplify the expression $2(m - 1) + 6$.

$2(m - 1) + 6 = \boxed{}$ Distributive property

$= \boxed{}$ Write as a sum.

$= \boxed{}$ Combine like terms.

Guided Practice Identify the coefficients, constant term(s), and like terms of the expression. Then simplify the expression.

1. $-2n + 4 - 3n$	2. $10 - 6p + 5p - 4$	3. $3\ell + 9 - \ell - 6$

EXAMPLE 4 **Writing and Simplifying an Expression**

Construction A rectangular skylight in an office building is 3 times as long as it is wide. Write and simplify an expression for the perimeter of the skylight in terms of the width *w*.

Solution

Because the skylight is 3 times as long as it is wide, its length is ▢ .

$$\text{Perimeter} = 2\ell + 2w \qquad \text{Formula for perimeter of a rectangle}$$

$$= 2\left(\boxed{}\right) + 2w \qquad \text{Substitute } \boxed{} \text{ for } \ell.$$

$$= \boxed{} + 2w \qquad \text{Multiply.}$$

$$= \boxed{} \qquad \text{Combine like terms.}$$

Answer: An expression for the perimeter of the skylight is ▢ .

Guided Practice **Complete the following exercise.**

4. A rectangle is 4 inches longer than it is wide. Write and simplify an expression for the perimeter of the rectangle in terms of the width *w*.

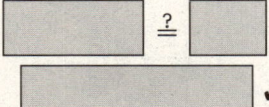

Solving Addition and Subtraction Equations

Goal: Solve addition and subtraction equations.

Vocabulary

Inverse operations:

Equivalent equations:

Subtraction Property of Equality

Words Subtracting the same number from each side of an equation

produces an ⬜ equation.

Algebra $x + a = b \longrightarrow x + a - a = b$ ⬜ ⬜

EXAMPLE 1 **Solving an Addition Equation**

Solve $x + 3 = -1$.

$$x + 3 = -1$$ Write original equation.

⬜ ⬜   ⬜ from each side.

⬜ = ⬜   Simplify.

✓ **Check** $x + 3 = -1$ Write original equation.

⬜ $\overset{?}{=}$ ⬜   Substitute ⬜ for x.

⬜ ✓   Solution checks.

Addition Property of Equality

Words Adding the same number to each side of an equation produces an [ ] equation.

Algebra $x - a = b$ ⟶ $x - a + a = b$ [ ] [ ]

EXAMPLE 2 **Solving a Subtraction Equation**

WATCH OUT!
You can add or subtract vertically or horizontally to solve equations, but remember to perform the same operation on each side of the equation.

Solve $-4 = y - 9$.

$-4 = y - 9$ Write original equation.

[ ] = [ ]   [ ] to each side.

[ ] = [ ]   Simplify.

✓ **Check** $-4 = y - 9$ Write original equation.

[ ] $\overset{?}{=}$ [ ]   Substitute [ ] for y.

[ ] ✓   Solution checks.

EXAMPLE 3 **Combining Like Terms**

Solve $7 = 4.1 + b + 1$.

$7 = 4.1 + b + 1$ Write original equation.

[ ] $= 4.1 +$ [ ]   Commutative property of addition

[ ] = [ ]   Combine like terms.

[ ] = [ ]   [ ] from each side.

[ ] = [ ]   Simplify.

✓ **Check** $7 = 4.1 + b + 1$ Write original equation.

[ ] $\overset{?}{=}$ [ ]   Substitute [ ] for b.

[ ] ✓   Solution checks.

Guided Practice Solve the equation. Check your solution.

1. $t + 7 = 12$	**2.** $n + 8 = 0$	**3.** $6 = y - 4$
4. $r - 12 = 15$	**5.** $p - (-3.6) = 4.9$	**6.** $2.7 + s - 1.9 = 5.2$

EXAMPLE 4 Writing and Solving an Equation

Business Travel Carol is out of the office for 8 hours meeting with a client. She spends 0.75 hour driving to the client's office, and 1.25 hours driving back from the client's office. How long was Carol at the client's office?

Solution

Write a verbal model. Let h represent the number of hours Carol spent at the client's office.

Time away from office = [ ] + [ ] + [ ]

[ ] = [ ]　　Write equation.

[ ] = [ ]　　Combine like terms.

[ ] = [ ]　　[ ] from each side.

[ ] = [ ]　　Simplify.

Answer: Carol spent [ ] hours at the client's office.

LESSON 7.4

Solving Multiplication and Division Equations

Goal: Solve multiplication and division equations.

Division Property of Equality

Words Dividing each side of an equation by the same nonzero number

produces an [   ] equation.

Algebra $ax = b \ (a \neq 0) \longrightarrow \dfrac{ax}{a} = $ [   ]

EXAMPLE 1 Solving a Multiplication Equation

Solve $-30 = 6x$.

$-30 = 6x$	Write original equation.
$\dfrac{-30}{\boxed{}} = \dfrac{6x}{\boxed{}}$	[ ] each side by [ ].
$\boxed{} = \boxed{}$	Simplify.

✓ Check $-30 = 6x$ Write original equation.

$\boxed{} \overset{?}{=} \boxed{}$ Substitute [   ] for x.

$\boxed{}$ ✓ Solution checks.

Multiplication Property of Equality

Words Multiplying each side of an equation by the same nonzero number

produces an [   ] equation.

Algebra $\dfrac{x}{a} = b \ (a \neq 0) \longrightarrow a \cdot \dfrac{x}{a} = $ [   ]

In your notebook, you may want to compare and contrast solving mulitiplication and division equations. This will help you remember how to solve these types of equations.

EXAMPLE 2 Solving a Division Equation

Solve $\dfrac{x}{4} = 0.3$.

$\dfrac{x}{4} = 0.3$ Write original equation.

☐ = ☐    each side by ☐.

☐ = ☐   Simplify.

EXAMPLE 3 Solving an Equation Using a Reciprocal

Need help with multiplying by a reciprocal? See page 237 of your textbook.

Solve $\dfrac{3}{4}x = -6$.

$\dfrac{3}{4}x = -6$ Write original equation.

☐ = ☐    each side by ☐.

☐ = ☐   Simplify.

Guided Practice   Solve the equation. Check your solution.

1. $9v = 36$	**2.** $-8b = 96$
3. $-1.7 = \dfrac{k}{3}$	**4.** $\dfrac{d}{4} = 15$

5. $6q - 4q = 16$

6. $\dfrac{5}{8}m = 10$

EXAMPLE 4 **Standardized Test Practice**

Rollerblading A woman is rollerblading through the park. You measure a 75-foot stretch of sidewalk, and count that she skates that portion of the sidewalk in 12 seconds. What is the speed of the woman?

Ⓐ −625 feet per second

Ⓑ 3 feet per second

Ⓒ 6.25 feet per second

Ⓓ 50 feet per second

Solution

Use the formula $d = rt$.

$$d = rt$$

$$\boxed{} = \boxed{}$$

Write formula for distance.

Substitute $\boxed{}$ for d and $\boxed{}$ for t.

$$\boxed{} = \boxed{}$$

$$\boxed{} = \boxed{}$$

$\boxed{}$ each side by $\boxed{}$.

Simplify.

Answer: The speed of the woman is $\boxed{}$ feet per second. The correct answer is $\boxed{}$. Ⓐ Ⓑ Ⓒ Ⓓ

Guided Practice Solve the following problem.

7. A filmmaker makes an edited version of his movie that is 120 minutes long. The unedited footage is 7 times as long as the edited version. Write and solve an equation to find the length of the unedited film.

Solving Two-Step Equations

Goal: Solve two-step equations.

EXAMPLE 1 Solving a Two-Step Equation

Solve $2m - 7 = -19$.

$$2m - 7 = -19$$ Write original equation.

[ ] = [ ] [ ] to each side.

[ ] = [ ] Simplify.

[ ] = [ ] [ ] each side by [ ].

[ ] = [ ] Simplify.

> Don't forget to check your solution by substituting back into the original equation.

EXAMPLE 2 Solving a Two-Step Equation

Solve $\frac{p}{5} + 7 = -2$.

$$\frac{p}{5} + 7 = -2$$ Write original equation.

[ ] = [ ] [ ] from each side.

[ ] = [ ] Simplify.

[ ] = [ ] [ ] each side by [ ].

[ ] = [ ] Simplify.

Solve the equation. Check your solution.

1. $7q - 4 = 10$	**2.** $\frac{j}{6} + 2 = 0$	**3.** $\frac{y}{5} - 6 = -6$

EXAMPLE 3 Writing and Solving a Two-Step Equation

Long Distance Calls A long distance phone company charges customers a $5 monthly fee plus $3 per hour for long distance phone calls. One customer's bill was $23. How many hours of long distance calls did the customer make?

Solution

Write a verbal model. Let *h* represent the number of hours of long distance the customer used.

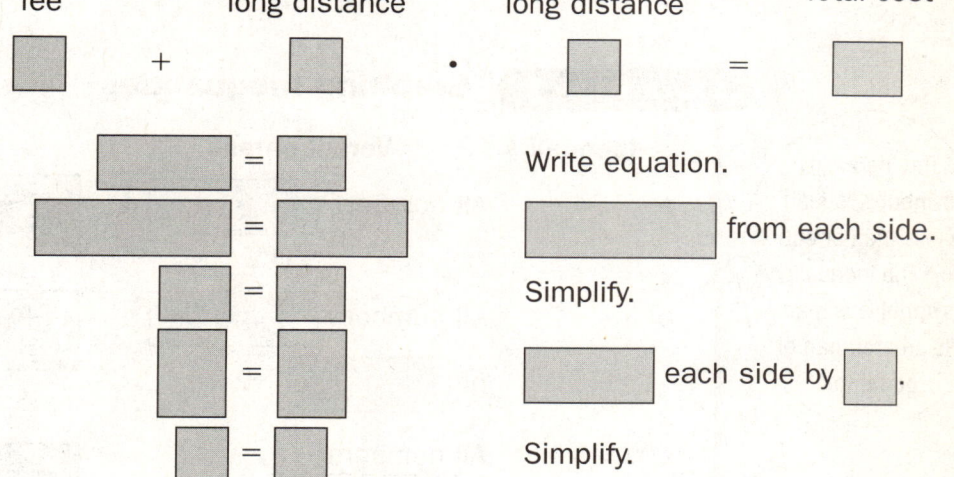

Answer: The customer made ⬜ hours of long distance phone calls.

Solving Inequalities

Goal: Write and solve inequalities.

Vocabulary

Inequality:

Solution of an inequality:

Graph of an inequality:

Equivalent inequalities:

EXAMPLE 1 **Graphing Inequalities**

> The inequality symbol ≤ is read "is less than or equal to." The inequality symbol ≥ is read "is greater than or equal to."

Inequality	Verbal phrase	Graph
a. $x < 4$	All numbers [　　] 4	−5 −4 −3 −2 −1 0 1 2 3 4 5
b. $x \le -2$	All numbers [　　] or [　　] −2	−5 −4 −3 −2 −1 0 1 2 3 4 5
c. $x > 3$	All numbers [　　] 3	−5 −4 −3 −2 −1 0 1 2 3 4 5
d. $x \ge -1$	All numbers [　　] or [　　] −1	−5 −4 −3 −2 −1 0 1 2 3 4 5

EXAMPLE 2 **Solving an Inequality**

Solve $f - 3 \leq -1$. Then graph the solution.

$f - 3 \leq -1$ Write original inequality.

[_____]   [_____] to each side.

[_____]   Simplify.

To graph [_____], use a(n) [_____] dot and draw the arrow pointing

to the [_____].

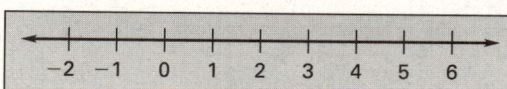

$$\begin{array}{ccccccccc} & & & & & & & & \\ \hline -2 & -1 & 0 & 1 & 2 & 3 & 4 & 5 & 6 \end{array}$$

✓ **Check** To check the solution [_____], choose any number

[_____] to substitute for f. Use $f = 1$ in the check below.

$f - 3 \leq -1$ Write original inequality.

[_____] $- 3 \overset{?}{\leq} -1$ Substitute [_____] for f.

[_____] ≤ -1 Solution checks.

Guided Practice Solve the inequality. Then graph the solution.

1. $s - 1 \geq 4$	**2.** $4 < b - 3$	**3.** $w + 1 > -1$
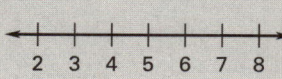	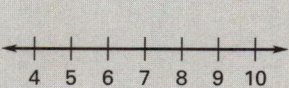	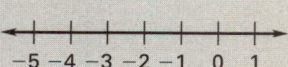

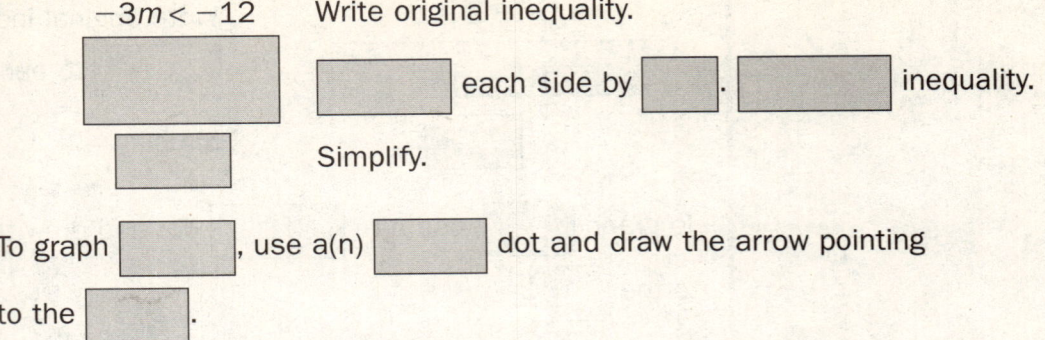

EXAMPLE 3 Solving an Inequality

Solve $-3m < -12$**. Then graph the solution.**

$-3m < -12$ Write original inequality.

[ ]   [ ] each side by [ ]. [ ] inequality.

[ ]   Simplify.

To graph [ ], use a(n) [ ] dot and draw the arrow pointing

to the [ ].

WATCH OUT!

Don't forget to reverse the inequality when you multiply or divide each side of an inequality by a negative number.

```
←+—+—+—+—+—+—+—+—+→
  0  1  2  3  4  5  6  7  8
```

Guided Practice **Solve the inequality. Then graph the solution.**

4. $\dfrac{x}{4} \geq 1$

```
←+—+—+—+—+—+—+→
  1  2  3  4  5  6  7
```

5. $5s < -30$

```
←+—+—+—+—+—+—+→
 -9 -8 -7 -6 -5 -4 -3
```

6. $-n \geq -10$

```
←+—+—+—+—+—+—+→
  7  8  9 10 11 12 13
```

Functions and Equations

Goal: Write and evaluate function rules.

Vocabulary

Function:

Input:

Output:

Domain:

Range:

EXAMPLE 1 Evaluating a Function

Evaluate the function $y = 3x$ when $x = 8$.

$y = 3x$ Write rule for function.

$ = \boxed{}$ Substitute $\boxed{}$ for x.

$ = \boxed{}$ Multiply.

EXAMPLE **2** **Making an Input-Output Table**

Make an input-output table for the function $y = x - 4.2$ using the domain 0, 1, 2, and 3. Then state the range of the function.

Solution

Input x	0	1	2	3
Substitution	$y = \boxed{} - 4.2$	$y = \boxed{} - 4.2$	$y = \boxed{} - 4.2$	$y = \boxed{} - 4.2$
Output y				

The range of the function is the set of outputs: $\boxed{}$, $\boxed{}$, $\boxed{}$, and $\boxed{}$.

Guided Practice **Complete the following exercise.**

1. Make an input-output table for the function $y = 4 - x$ using the domain $-2, -1, 0, 1,$ and 2. Then state the range of the function.

EXAMPLE **3** **Writing a Function Rule**

Write a function rule for the input-output table.

Input x	-2	-1	0	1	2	3	4
Output y	-3.5	-2.5	-1.5	-0.5	0.5	1.5	2.5

Solution

You can see that you obtain each output by $\boxed{}$ the input.

Answer: The function rule given by the table is $\boxed{}$.

EXAMPLE 4 **Writing a Function Rule From a Pattern**

Squares In the diagram of the squares, the input *s* is the length of each side of a square. The output *P* is the perimeter of the square. Write a rule for the function. Then use the rule to find the perimeter of a square with sides 9 units.

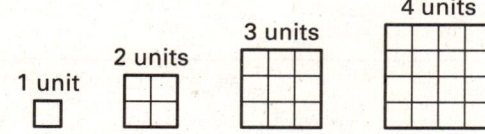

1 unit 2 units 3 units 4 units

Solution

1. Begin by making an input-output table.

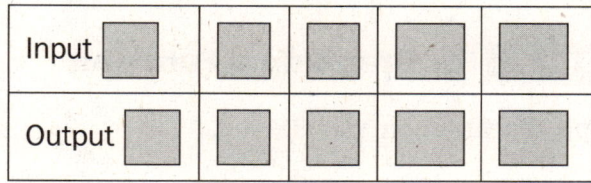

Input					
Output					

2. Notice that each output value is [ ] the input value. So, a rule for the function is [ ].

3. To find the perimeter of a square with sides 9 units, evaluate the function when *s* = 9. Because *P* = [ ] = [ ], the perimeter of the square is [ ].

Guided Practice Write a function rule for the input-output table.

2.

Input *x*	−1	0	1	2
Output *y*	−2	0	2	4

3.

Input *x*	2	4	6	8
Output *y*	$\frac{1}{2}$	1	$1\frac{1}{2}$	2

Graphing Functions

Goal: Graph functions in a coordinate plane.

Vocabulary

Linear function:

EXAMPLE 1 **Graphing a Function**

Graph the function $y = 3x - 1$.

> When the domain of a function is not given, assume that it includes every *x*-value for which the function can produce a corresponding *y*-value.

1. Make an input-output table by choosing several input values and evaluating the function for the output values.

2. Use the table to write a list of ordered pairs:

x	Substitution	y
−2		
−1		
0		
1		
2		

3. Plot the ordered pairs in a coordinate plane.

4. Notice that all of the points lie on a line. Any other ordered pairs satisfying $y = 3x - 1$ would also lie on the line when graphed. The line represents the complete graph of the function $y = 3x - 1$.

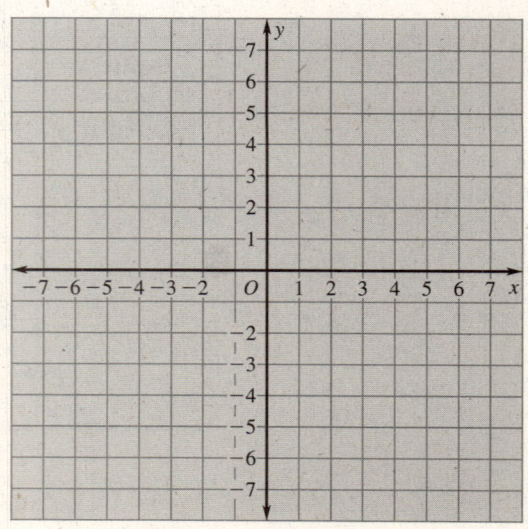

Graph the function.

1. $y = x - 2$

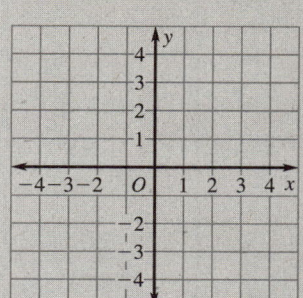

2. $y = \dfrac{x}{2}$

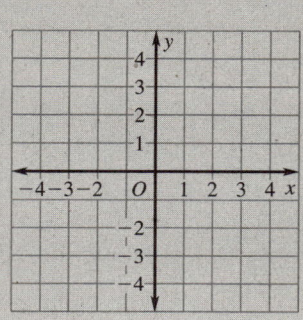

3. $y = 4x + 1$

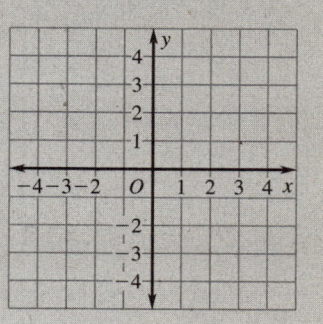

EXAMPLE 2 **Writing and Graphing a Function**

The cost of gasoline is $1.50 per gallon. Write and graph a function that represents the cost *y* of *x* gallons of gasoline.

The situation can be represented by the function  , where *y* is the total cost of *x* gallons of gasoline.

1. Make an input-output table.

Input *x*	Output *y*
0	
1	
2	
3	
4	

2. Plot the ordered pairs and connect them.

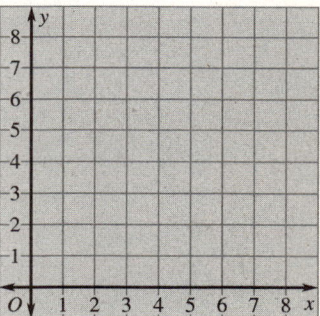

WATCH OUT!

In Example 2, note that you cannot have less than 0 gallons of gasoline, so you cannot use any numbers less than 0 in the domain.

EXAMPLE 3 **Identifying Linear Functions**

Tell whether each graph represents a function of *x*. If it does, tell whether the function is linear.

> Recall that a function pairs each input value with *exactly* one output value.

a.

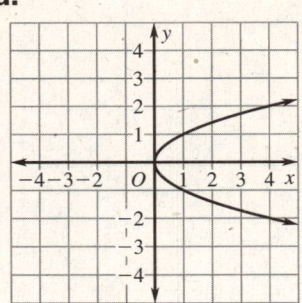

b.

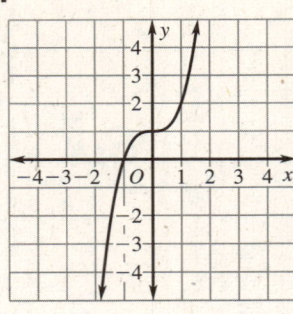

c.

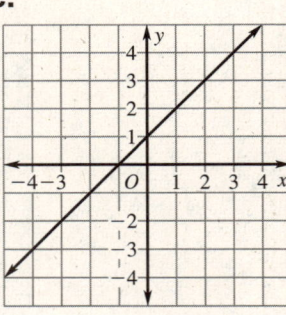

Solution

a.

b.

c.

Words to Review

Give an example of the vocabulary word.

Verbal model

Term

Like terms

Equivalent variable expressions

Coefficient

Constant term

Inverse operations

Equivalent equations

Inequality

Solution of an inequality

Graph of an inequality

Equivalent inequalities

Function

Input

Output

Domain

Range

Linear function

Review your notes and Chapter 7 by using the Chapter Review on pages 386–390 of your textbook.

Ratios

Goal: Write and compare ratios.

Vocabulary

Ratio:

Equivalent ratios:

Writing a Ratio

Words	**Numbers**	**Algebra**
wins to losses	16 to 10	a to b, where b is nonzero.
$\dfrac{wins}{losses}$		, where b is nonzero.
wins : losses		, where b is nonzero.

EXAMPLE 1 **Writing a Ratio**

You can make comparisons about 6th grade students in first period classes.

Silverlake Middle School's 6th Grade		
Teacher	**Students in 1st Period**	**Students in 2nd Period**
Ms. Black	29	23
Mr. Henderson	24	27
Ms. Solomon	25	26
Mr. O'Grady	24	25

a. Ms. Black's first period students to Mr. O'Grady's first period students

Ms. Black = 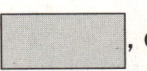 , Mr. O'Grady =

Answer: , or

b. Ms. Solomon's first period students to all first period students

Ms. Solomon = [____] ; all = [_____] = [____]

Answer: [____] , or [____]

Guided Practice Use the table on the previous page to write the ratios.

1. Ms. Black's 1st period students to Ms. Black's 2nd period students

2. All 1st period students to all 2nd period students

3. Mr. O'Grady's 2nd period students to all other 2nd period students

EXAMPLE 2 **Writing Ratios in Simplest Form**

Holiday Dinner Mrs. Carr spends $4\frac{1}{2}$ hours cooking a holiday meal that her family eats in 30 minutes. Follow the steps below to find the ratio of time spent cooking to time spent eating.

1. Write hours as minutes so that the units are the same.

$4\text{ h} + \frac{1}{2}\text{ h} = $ [____] min + [____] min   Write hours as minutes.

= [____] min   Add.

2. Write the ratio of time spent cooking to time spent eating.

$\dfrac{\text{Time cooking}}{\text{Time eating}} = $ [____]   Write ratio.

= [____]   Simplify fraction.

Answer: The ratio of time spent cooking to time spent eating is [____] : [____] .

EXAMPLE 3 **Comparing Ratios**

Books Kylie and Sophia compared their book collections. To determine who has the greater ratio of mysteries to biographies, write the ratios.

	Mystery	Fiction	Biography
Kylie	12	6	15
Sophia	7	15	10

Kylie: $\dfrac{\text{mysteries}}{\text{biographies}}$ = [ ] **Sophia:** $\dfrac{\text{mysteries}}{\text{biographies}}$ = [ ] Write ratios as fractions.

= [ ] = [ ] Write fractions as decimals.

Answer: Because [ ] > [ ], [ ] has the greater ratio of mysteries to biographies.

Need help with writing fractions as decimals? See page 199 of your textbook.

Guided Practice **Refer to Example 3.**

4. Does Kylie or Sophia have a greater ratio of fiction to mystery books?

5. Does Kylie or Sophia have a greater ratio of biography to fiction?

Rates

Goal: Use rates to compare two quantities with different units.

Vocabulary

Rate:

Unit rate:

EXAMPLE 1 **Finding a Unit Rate**

Microwave Cooking A microwave oven increases the temperature of a cup of water by 42°F in 14 seconds. What is the heating rate in degrees Fahrenheit per second?

Solution

First, write a rate comparing the temperature increase to the seconds it took to heat. Then rewrite the fraction so that the denominator is 1.

$$\frac{42°F}{14 \text{ sec}} = \frac{42°F \div \boxed{}}{14 \text{ sec} \div \boxed{}}$$ Divide numerator and denominator by $\boxed{}$.

$$= \boxed{}$$ Simplify.

Answer: The heating rate is about $\boxed{}$ °F per second.

Guided Practice Find the unit rate.

1. $72 in 8 hours	**2.** 90 miles in 6 days	**3.** 4 cups in 10 servings

EXAMPLE 2 **Finding an Average Speed**

Family Vacation A family drove their car 429 miles in 8 hours and 15 minutes. What was the average speed of the car?

Solution

1. Rewrite the time so that the units are the same.

$$8 \text{ h} + 15 \text{ min} = 8 \text{ h} + \boxed{} \text{ h} = \boxed{} \text{ h}$$

2. Find the average speed.

$$\frac{429 \text{ miles}}{8.25 \text{ hours}} = \frac{429 \text{ miles} \div \boxed{}}{8.25 \text{ hours} \div \boxed{}} \quad \text{Divide numerator and denominator by } \boxed{}.$$

$$= \boxed{} \quad \text{Simplify.}$$

Answer: The car's average speed was $\boxed{}$ miles per hour.

EXAMPLE 3 **Comparing Unit Rates**

A unit price is a type of unit rate.

Cereal A store sells the same cereal the following two ways: a small 48-ounce package for $1.92 and a large 64-ounce package for $3.20. To determine which is the better buy, find the unit price for both types.

Small package: $\dfrac{\$1.92}{48 \text{ oz}} = \boxed{}$ Write as unit rate.

Large package: $\dfrac{\$3.20}{64 \text{ oz}} = \boxed{}$ Write as unit rate.

Answer: The $\boxed{}$ package of cereal is a better buy because it costs less per ounce.

Guided Practice Solve the following problems.

4. It takes you 11 minutes and 40 seconds to ride your bike 2800 yards. What is your average speed in yards per second?

5. Which of the following is the better buy: 2 notebooks for $2.40 or 6 notebooks for $4.80?

Slope

Goal: Find the slope of a line.

Vocabulary

Slope:

EXAMPLE 1 **Finding the Slope of a Line**

To find the slope of a line, find the ratio of the rise to the run between two points on the line.

> Rise is positive when moving up and negative when moving down.

a.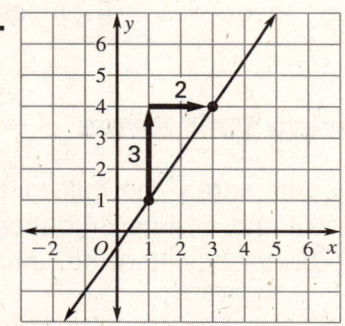

b.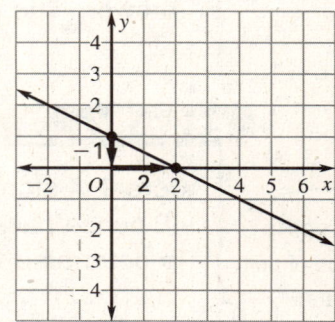

slope $= \dfrac{\text{rise}}{\text{run}} =$ ◻

slope $= \dfrac{\text{rise}}{\text{run}} =$ ◻ $=$ ◻

EXAMPLE 2 **Interpreting Slope as a Rate**

Lemonade Stand The graph represents the cups of lemonade sold over time. To find the rate of sales, find the slope of the line.

slope $= \dfrac{\text{rise}}{\text{run}} =$ ◻   Write rise over run.

$=$ ◻   Find unit rate.

Answer: The lemonade sold at a rate of ◻ cups per hour.

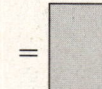

Lemonade Sales

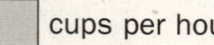

Guided Practice Complete the following exercises.

---

1. Plot the points (1, 5) and (0, 8). Then find the slope of the line that passes through the points.

---

2. In Example 2, suppose the line starts at the origin and passes through the point (2, 7). Find the rate of lemonade sales.

EXAMPLE 3 **Using Slope to Draw a Line**

Draw the line that has a slope of 4 and passes through (2, 1).

1. Plot (2, 1).

2. Write the slope as a fraction.

slope = ☐ = ☐

3. Move ☐ unit to the ☐ and

☐ units ☐ to plot the second point.

4. Draw a line through the two points.

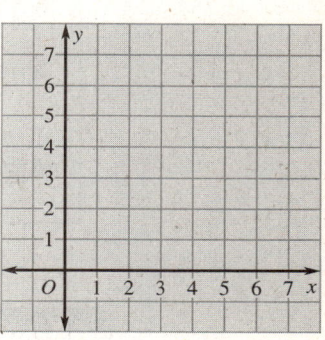

Guided Practice Refer to Example 3.

---

3. Draw the line that has a slope of $-\frac{2}{3}$ and passes through (5, 4).

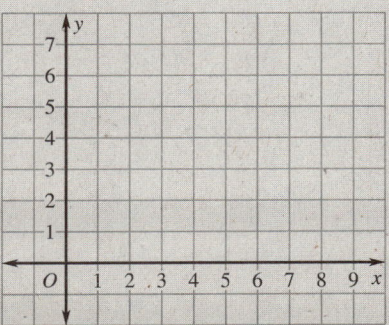

Writing and Solving Proportions

Goal: Solve proportions using equivalent ratios and algebra.

Vocabulary

Proportion:

Proportions

Words A **proportion** is an equation that states that two ⬚ are ⬚ .

Numbers ⬚/⬚ = ⬚/⬚ The proportion is read "4 is to 5 as 8 is to 10."

Algebra $\frac{a}{b} = \frac{c}{d}$, where b and d are nonzero numbers.

EXAMPLE 1 **Using Equivalent Ratios**

Skating Lessons A skating rink offers private skating lessons at a cost of $15 for 30 minutes. How much will it cost for 90 minutes of private lessons?

Solution

To find the price paid P for 90 minutes of lessons, solve the proportion $\frac{15}{30} = \frac{P}{90}$.

1. Ask yourself: What number can you multiply 30 by to get 90?

$$\frac{15}{30} = \frac{P}{90}$$

$\times\ ?$

2. Because $30 \times \boxed{} = 90$, multiply the numerator by $\boxed{}$ to find P.

$$\times \boxed{}$$

$$\frac{15}{30} = \frac{P}{90}$$

$$\times \boxed{}$$

Answer: Because $15 \times \boxed{} = \boxed{}$, $P = \boxed{}$. So, the price of 90 minutes of private lessons is \$$\boxed{}$.

EXAMPLE 2 **Solving Proportions Using Algebra**

Solve the proportion $\dfrac{4}{14} = \dfrac{x}{21}$.

$$\frac{4}{14} = \frac{x}{21} \qquad \text{Write original proportion.}$$

$$\boxed{} \cdot \frac{4}{14} = \boxed{} \cdot \frac{x}{21} \qquad \text{Multiply each side by } \boxed{}.$$

$$\frac{\boxed{}}{\boxed{}} = x \qquad \text{Simplify.}$$

$$\boxed{} = x \qquad \text{Simplify fraction.}$$

Answer: The solution is $\boxed{}$.

> As you learn different methods for solving a proportion, remember to write an example of each method in your notebook.

Guided Practice Use equivalent ratios to solve the proportion.

1. $\dfrac{2}{3} = \dfrac{z}{12}$	**2.** $\dfrac{4}{3} = \dfrac{x}{18}$	**3.** $\dfrac{30}{c} = \dfrac{5}{8}$	**4.** $\dfrac{4}{n} = \dfrac{48}{12}$

Use algebra to solve the proportion.

5. $\dfrac{4}{6} = \dfrac{m}{15}$	**6.** $\dfrac{10}{15} = \dfrac{n}{9}$	**7.** $\dfrac{h}{20} = \dfrac{6}{8}$	**8.** $\dfrac{b}{12} = \dfrac{3}{18}$

EXAMPLE **3** **Writing and Solving a Proportion**

Basketball Tyler scores an average of 10 points in 8 minutes of playing time. Follow the steps below to find the number of points that Tyler averages in 4 minutes of play.

1. Write a proportion. Let *x* represent the average number of points scored in 4 minutes.

WATCH OUT!
You cannot write a proportion that compares points to minutes and minutes to points.

$\dfrac{\text{points}}{\text{minutes}} \neq \dfrac{\text{minutes}}{\text{points}}$

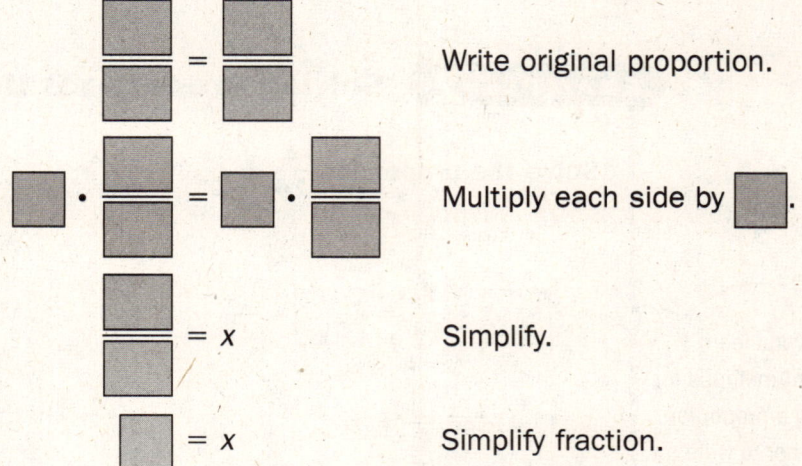 ← points
← minutes

2. Solve the proportion.

Write original proportion.

Multiply each side by ⬜.

⬜ = *x*   Simplify.

⬜ = *x*   Simplify fraction.

Answer: Tyler averages ⬜ points in 4 minutes of playing time.

Solving Proportions Using Cross Products

LESSON 8.5

Goal: Solve proportions using cross products.

Vocabulary

Cross products:

Cross Products Property

Words The cross products of a proportion are [ ].

Numbers $\frac{5}{7} = \frac{15}{21}$

[ ] = [ ]

[ ] = [ ]

Algebra If $\frac{a}{b} = \frac{c}{d}$ where b and d are nonzero numbers, then [ ] = [ ].

EXAMPLE 1 Solving a Proportion Using Cross Products

Use the cross products property to solve $\frac{2}{5} = \frac{x}{7}$.

> The phrase *cross products* comes from the "X" shape formed by the diagonal numbers in a proportion.

$$\frac{2}{5} = \frac{x}{7}$$ Write original proportion.

[ ] = [ ]   Cross products property

$\frac{[\ ]}{[\ ]} = \frac{[\ ]}{[\ ]}$ Divide each side by [ ].

[ ] = [ ]   Simplify.

EXAMPLE 2 **Writing and Solving a Proportion**

Currency Exchange When Jake visited Canada, he exchanged 10 U.S. dollars and he received 14 Canadian dollars. Find how many U.S. dollars he exchanged when he received 35 Canadian dollars.

$$\frac{\boxed{}}{\boxed{}} = \frac{u}{\boxed{}} \quad \longleftarrow \text{U.S. dollars}$$
$$\longleftarrow \text{Canadian dollars}$$

$$\boxed{} = \boxed{} \quad \text{Cross products property}$$

$$\frac{\boxed{}}{\boxed{}} = \frac{\boxed{}}{\boxed{}} \quad \text{Divide each side by } \boxed{}.$$

$$\boxed{} = \boxed{} \quad \text{Simplify.}$$

Answer: Jake exchanged $\boxed{}$ U.S. dollars when he received 35 Canadian dollars.

EXAMPLE 3 **Writing and Solving a Proportion**

Baseball The ratio of left-handed pitchers to right-handed pitchers on a baseball team is 2 to 5. If the team has 14 pitchers, how many are left-handed?

Solution

First, determine the ratio of left-handed pitchers to total pitchers.

$$\frac{\boxed{}}{\boxed{} + \boxed{}} = \frac{\boxed{}}{\boxed{}} \quad \text{For every } \boxed{} \text{ pitchers, } \boxed{} \text{ are left-handed.}$$

To find the number ℓ of left-handed pitchers, set up a proportion and solve it.

$$\frac{\boxed{}}{\boxed{}} = \frac{\boxed{}}{\boxed{}} \quad \longleftarrow \text{left-handed pitchers}$$
$$\longleftarrow \text{total pitchers}$$

$$\boxed{} = \boxed{} \quad \text{Cross products property}$$

$$\frac{\boxed{}}{\boxed{}} = \frac{\boxed{}}{\boxed{}} \quad \text{Divide each side by } \boxed{}.$$

$$\boxed{} = \boxed{} \quad \text{Simplify.}$$

Answer: There are $\boxed{}$ left-handed pitchers on the team.

1. In Example 2, if Jake exchanged 45 U.S. dollars, how many Canadian dollars would he receive?

2. A baseball team has a ratio of wins to losses of 5 to 3. If they played 24 games, how many games did they lose?

Scale Drawings and Models

LESSON 8.6

Goal: Use proportions with scale drawings.

Vocabulary

Scale drawing:

Scale:

Scale model:

EXAMPLE 1 **Using the Scale of a Map**

Maps Use the map of Nebraska to estimate the distance between the towns of Ogallala and Central City.

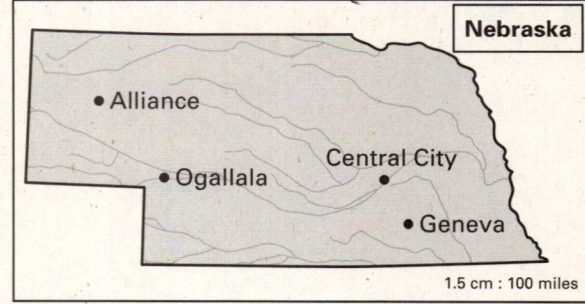

Solution

From the map's scale, 1.5 centimeters represent 100 miles. On the map, the distance between Ogallala and Central City is 3 centimeters.

Need help with writing a proportion? See page 419 in your textbook.

Write and solve a proportion to find the distance d between the towns.

$$\frac{\boxed{}}{\boxed{}} = \frac{\boxed{}}{\boxed{}}$$ ← centimeters
  ← miles

$\boxed{} = \boxed{}$ Cross products property

$\dfrac{\boxed{}}{\boxed{}} = \dfrac{\boxed{}}{\boxed{}}$ Divide each side by $\boxed{}$.

$\boxed{} = \boxed{}$ Simplify.

Answer: The actual distance between Ogallala and Central City is about $\boxed{}$ miles.

Guided Practice **Use a metric ruler and the map in Example 1.**

1. Estimate the distance, in miles, between the towns of Alliance and Geneva.

EXAMPLE 2 Finding a Dimension on a Scale Model

When a scale is written as a ratio, it usually takes the form shown below.

scale model: actual object

Model Cars A scale model of an Austin Healy automobile is for sale at the local Hobby Shop. The scale used is 1 : 15. The height of the actual car is 45 inches. Find the height of the model.

Solution

Write and solve a proportion to find the height h of the model of the Austin Healy.

$\frac{\square}{\square} = \frac{\square}{\square}$ ← scale model / ← car

$\square = \square$ Cross products property

$\frac{\square}{\square} = \frac{\square}{\square}$ Divide each side by $\square$.

$\square = \square$ Simplify.

Answer: The height of the model is $\square$ inches.

EXAMPLE 3 Finding the Scale

Architecture An architect is planning a theater complex. The model is 36 inches tall. The resulting theater complex will be 150 feet tall. What is the model's scale?

Solution

Write a ratio. Make sure that both measures are in feet. Then simplify the fraction.

$\square = \square = \square$ ← scale model / ← full size

Answer: The model's scale is $\square$: $\square$.

2. The parking garage for the theater complex is 175 feet long. Find the length of the model.

Words to Review

Give an example of the vocabulary word.

Ratio

Equivalent ratios

Rate

Unit rate

Slope

Proportion

Cross products

Scale drawing

Scale

Scale model

Review your notes and Chapter 8 by using the Chapter Review on pages 437–440 of your textbook.

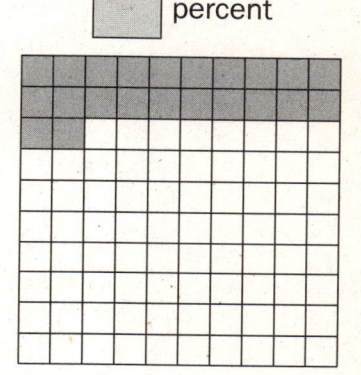

Percents and Fractions

LESSON 9.1

Goal: Use a fraction to find the percent of a number.

Vocabulary

Percent: ▭

Understanding Percent

The model at the right has 22 out of 100 squares shaded. You can say that ▭ percent of the squares are shaded.

Numbers You can write 22 percent as

▭ or as ▭%.

Algebra You can write *p* percent as

▭ or as ▭%.

▭ percent

EXAMPLE 1 Writing Percents as Fractions

Write the percent as a fraction.

a. 49%   **b.** 60%

Solution

a. 49% = ▭   **b.** 60% = ▭ = ▭

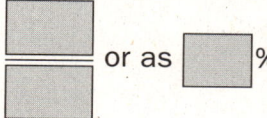

Write the percent as a fraction in simplest form.

1. 18%	**2.** 45%	**3.** 41%	**4.** 70%

EXAMPLE 2 **Writing Fractions as Percents**

To write a fraction as a percent, rewrite the fraction with a denominator of 100.

a. $\dfrac{3}{10} = \dfrac{3 \times \boxed{}}{10 \times \boxed{}} = \dfrac{\boxed{}}{\boxed{}} = \boxed{}\%$

b. $\dfrac{4}{5} = \dfrac{4 \times \boxed{}}{5 \times \boxed{}} = \dfrac{\boxed{}}{\boxed{}} = \boxed{}\%$

EXAMPLE 3 **Finding a Percent of a Number**

To find 20% of 55, use the fact that $20\% = \frac{1}{5}$ and multiply.

20% of 55 = 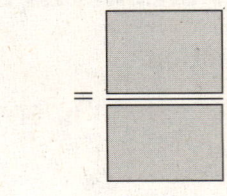 Write percent as a fraction.

= $\dfrac{\boxed{}}{\boxed{}}$ Use rule for multiplying fractions. Divide out common factor.

= 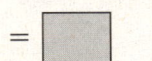 Simplify.

Guided Practice In Exercises 5–8, write the fraction as a percent.

5. $\frac{7}{25}$	6. $\frac{11}{20}$	7. $\frac{9}{10}$	8. $\frac{13}{50}$
9. Find 30% of 400.		10. Find 75% of 280.	

EXAMPLE 4 **Using Percents**

Soccer According to the Smithville Athletic Club, 47 of the 100 children playing Pee Wee Soccer this year are boys. What percent of the players are girls?

Solution

You know that $\frac{47}{100} = \boxed{}$ % of the soccer players are boys. To find the percent of soccer players who are girls, use the fact that the entire group of players represent 100%.

$$\boxed{}\% - \boxed{}\% = \boxed{}\%$$

Answer: $\boxed{}$ % of the Pee Wee soccer players are girls.

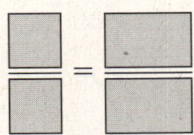

Percents and Proportions

Goal: Use proportions to solve percent problems.

Solving Percent Problems

You can represent "*a* is *p* percent of *b*" with the proportion

$$\frac{\boxed{}}{\boxed{}} = \frac{\boxed{}}{\boxed{}}$$

where *a* is part of the base *b* and *p*%, or $\frac{p}{100}$, is the percent.

EXAMPLE 1 **Finding a Percent**

What percent of 4 is 3?

In a percent problem, the word that follows "of" is usually the base b.

$$\frac{a}{b} = \frac{p}{100}$$ Write proportion.

 $$= \frac{p}{100}$$ Substitute $\boxed{}$ for *a* and $\boxed{}$ for *b*.

$$\boxed{} \cdot \frac{\boxed{}}{\boxed{}} = \boxed{} = \frac{p}{100}$$ Multiply each side by $\boxed{}$.

$$\boxed{} = \boxed{}$$ Simplify.

Answer: 3 is $\boxed{}$% of 4.

1. What percent of 25 is 10?	**2.** What percent of 300 is 9?

3. In a grocery store, 6 of the 30 breakfast cereals are generic brand. What percent of the breakfast cereals are generic brand?

EXAMPLE 2 **Finding a Part of a Base**

Tennis 328 fans attended a tennis tournament. In a survey, 25% of the fans wanted players to wear traditional white tennis clothes. How many fans wanted players to wear traditional white clothing?

$$\frac{a}{b} = \frac{p}{100}$$ Write proportion.

$$\frac{\boxed{}}{\boxed{}} = \frac{\boxed{}}{100}$$ Substitute $\boxed{}$ for b and $\boxed{}$ for p.

$$\boxed{} \cdot \frac{\boxed{}}{\boxed{}} = \boxed{} \cdot \frac{\boxed{}}{100}$$ Multiply each side by $\boxed{}$.

$$\boxed{} = 328 \cdot \frac{\overset{1}{\boxed{}}}{\underset{\underset{1}{4}}{100}}$$ Use rule for multiplying fractions. Divide out common factors.

$$\boxed{} = \boxed{}$$ Simplify.

Answer: In the survey, $\boxed{}$ of the fans wanted players in traditional white clothing.

✓ **Check:** 25% of 328 is about $\frac{1}{4}$ of 300, or about 75. So, 82 is reasonable.

4. What number is 85% of 120?	**5.** What number is 7% of 200?
6. What number is 21% of 80?	**7.** What number is 62% of 900?

EXAMPLE 3 **Finding a Base**

48 is 40% of what number?

$$\frac{a}{b} = \frac{p}{100}$$ Write proportion.

$$\frac{\boxed{}}{\boxed{}} = \frac{\boxed{}}{100}$$ Substitute.

$$\boxed{} = \boxed{}$$ Cross products property

$$\frac{\boxed{}}{\boxed{}} = \frac{\boxed{}}{\boxed{}}$$ Divide each side by $\boxed{}$.

$$\boxed{} = \boxed{}$$ Simplify.

To help you remember the process of solving a percent problem, you may want to highlight the key step in the process.

Answer: 48 is 40% of $\boxed{}$.

Percents and Decimals

LESSON 9.3

Goal: Write percents as decimals and decimals as percents.

EXAMPLE 1 **Writing Percents as Decimals**

a. 52% = 52%

= [ ]

b. 4% = 04%

= [ ]

c. 18.4% = 18.4%

= [ ]

EXAMPLE 2 **Writing Decimals as Percents**

a. 0.27 = .27

= [ ]

b. 0.03 = .03

= [ ]

c. 0.091 = .091

= [ ]

Guided Practice Write the percent as a decimal or the decimal as a percent.

1. 30%	**2.** 7%	**3.** 17.4%
4. 0.043	**5.** 0.01	**6.** 0.169

EXAMPLE 3 **Standardized Test Practice**

Mary saves $\frac{5}{9}$ of her paycheck. What percent of her paycheck does Mary save?

(A) 23%   **(B)** 50%   **(C)** 55.6%   **(D)** 80%

Solution

> The symbol ≈ is read "approximately equal to." It indicates that a result has been rounded and is not exact.

$\frac{5}{9} \approx$ Divide 5 by 9. Round to the nearest thousandth.

$=$ [   ]   Write as a percent.

Answer: Mary saves about [   ] % of her paycheck. The correct answer

is [   ] .   **(A)**   **(B)**   **(C)**   **(D)**

EXAMPLE 4 **Rewriting Small and Large Percents**

Video Store A video store carries 0.8% of their videos in foreign languages. The store increased their inventory of DVDs by 500%. Write these percents as decimals.

Foreign language: 0.8% = **0**0.8%   DVDs: 500% = 500%

$=$ [   ] $=$ [   ]

Guided Practice Write the fraction as a percent. Round to the nearest tenth of a percent.

7. $\frac{1}{6}$	**8.** $\frac{7}{9}$	**9.** $\frac{6}{7}$	**10.** $\frac{9}{13}$

Write the percent as a decimal.

11. 0.36%	**12.** 740%	**13.** 0.0026%	**14.** 0.08%

EXAMPLE 5 **Using a Percent Less Than 1%**

Chemistry A chemical solution in a container has a volume of 85,000 milliliters. The solution contains 0.04% saline. How much of the solution is saline?

Solution

0.04% of 85,000 = [   ]   Write percent as a decimal.

= [   ]   Multiply.

Answer: The solution contains [   ] milliliters of saline.

Guided Practice **Solve the following problem.**

15. The enrollment at Little Angel's Preschool last year was 50 students. This year's enrollment is 220% of last year's. How many students enrolled this year?

The Percent Equation

Goal: Use equations to solve percent problems.

The Percent Equation

You can represent "*a* is *p* percent of *b*" with the equation

[ ]

where *a* is part of the base *b* and *p*% is the percent.

EXAMPLE 1 **Finding a Part of a Base**

Pharmacy The pharmacy has 75% of the 300 tablets that Dr. Cole prescribed for her patient. How many tablets does the pharmacy have?

$a = p\% \cdot b$ Write percent equation.

$\quad = \boxed{}\% \cdot \boxed{}$ Substitute $\boxed{}$ for *p* and $\boxed{}$ for *b*.

$\quad = \boxed{} \cdot \boxed{}$ Write percent as a decimal.

$\quad = \boxed{}$ Multiply.

Answer: The pharmacy has $\boxed{}$ of the tablets.

Guided Practice Use the percent equation to answer the question.

1. What is 30% of 250?	**2.** What is 32% of 65?

EXAMPLE 2 **Finding a Percent**

What percent of 240 is 72?

In Example 2, you can use common percents to check the reasonableness of the answer. You know that 50%, or $\frac{1}{2}$, of 240 is 120. Because 72 is less than 50% of 240, 30% seems reasonable.

$a = p\% \cdot b$ Write percent equation.

$\boxed{} = p\% \cdot \boxed{}$ Substitute $\boxed{}$ for a and $\boxed{}$ for b.

$\dfrac{\boxed{}}{\boxed{}} = \dfrac{p\% \cdot \boxed{}}{\boxed{}}$ Divide each side by $\boxed{}$.

$\boxed{} = p\% = \boxed{}\%$ Simplify fraction. Then write as a percent.

Answer: The number 72 is $\boxed{}$% of 240.

EXAMPLE 3   **Finding a Base**

The number 80 is 32% of what number?

$a = p\% \cdot b$ Write percent equation.

$\boxed{} = \boxed{}\% \cdot b$ Substitute $\boxed{}$ for a and $\boxed{}$ for p.

$\dfrac{\boxed{}}{\boxed{}} = \dfrac{\boxed{} \cdot b}{\boxed{}}$ Write percent as a decimal. Then divide each side by $\boxed{}$.

$\boxed{} = \boxed{}$ Simplify.

Answer: The number 80 is 32% of $\boxed{}$.

Guided Practice   **Use the percent equation to answer the question.**

3. 99 is what percent of 396?	**4.** 30 is 250% of what number?

EXAMPLE 4 **Finding a Commission**

Jewelry A jewelry salesperson sells a bracelet for $350. The salesperson earns an 8% commission on the sale. How much is the commission?

Solution

$a = p\% \cdot b$ Write percent equation.

$= \boxed{}\% \cdot \boxed{}$ Substitute $\boxed{}$ for p and $\boxed{}$ for b.

$= \boxed{} \cdot \boxed{}$ Write percent as a decimal.

$= \boxed{}$ Multiply.

Answer: The commission is $\$\boxed{}$.

EXAMPLE 5 **Standardized Test Practice**

Baseball A baseball team has 14 pitchers. Nine of the pitchers are right-handed. Which best represents the percent of pitchers on the team that are *not* right-handed?

Ⓐ 36%   **Ⓑ** 44%   **Ⓒ** 64%   **Ⓓ** 136%

Solution

You know that $\boxed{}$ $\boxed{}$ = $\boxed{}$

$a = p\% \cdot b$ Write percent equation.

$\boxed{} = \%\cdot\boxed{}$ Substitute $\boxed{}$ for a and $\boxed{}$ for b.

$\dfrac{\boxed{}}{\boxed{}} = \dfrac{p\% \cdot \boxed{}}{\boxed{}}$ Divide each side by $\boxed{}$.

$\boxed{} = \%$ Simplify.

$\approx \boxed{}\%$ Write as a percent. Round to the nearest hundredth.

Answer: Approximately $\boxed{}$% of the pitchers are not right-handed.

The correct answer is . Ⓐ Ⓑ Ⓒ Ⓓ

Circle Graphs

Goal: Use percents to interpret and make circle graphs.

Vocabulary

Circle graph:

Ray:

Angle:

Vertex:

Degrees:

EXAMPLE 1 **Interpreting a Circle Graph**

Class Survey The results of a survey are displayed in the circle graph. What conclusions can you make about the data?

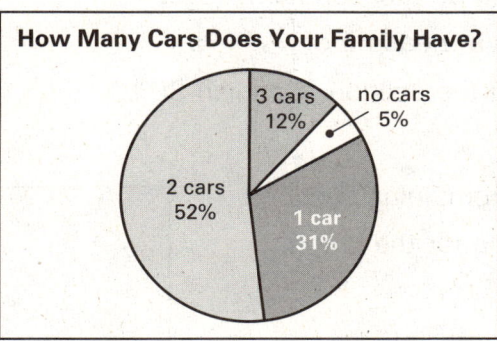

How Many Cars Does Your Family Have?

3 cars 12% no cars 5%

2 cars 52%

1 car 31%

Solution

You can make conclusions about the data in the circle graph above.

- The largest section in the circle graph is labeled "[   ]." So, this is how many cars most families have.

- More families have "3 cars" than have "[   ] cars".

EXAMPLE 2 **Making a Circle Graph Given Percents**

Second Language The table shows the results of a survey that asked students what second language they speak. Display the data in a circle graph.

Language	Percent
Spanish	30%
Vietnamese	25%
Portuguese	5%
None	40%

Solution

1. Find the angle measure of each section.

Spanish

30% of 360° = [   ]

= [   ]

Vietnamese

25% of 360° = [   ]

= [   ]

Portuguese

5% of 360° = [   ]

= [   ]

None

40% of 360° = [   ]

= [   ]

2. Draw a circle using a compass.

3. Use a protractor to draw the angle for Spanish as a second language, which has a measure of [   ].
Then label the section "Spanish 30%."

4. Draw the remaining sections.

5. Write a title for the graph.

Need help using a compass? See page 754 of your textbook.

1. Can you determine from the circle graph the number of families that have three cars? Explain your reasoning.

2. The table shows the results of a survey that asked students to name their favorite pet. Display the data in a circle graph.

Pet	Percent
Dog	45%
Cat	30%
Rodent	15%
Amphibian	10%

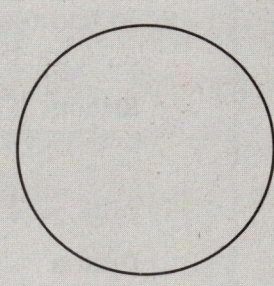

EXAMPLE 3 **Making a Circle Graph Given Data**

The table shows the results of a survey that asked people their favorite type of television show. Display the data in a circle graph.

Show	Sitcom	Drama	Cartoon	News
People	30	9	6	15

Solution

1. Find the total number of people surveyed.

   $30 + 9 + 6 + 15 = $ ☐

2. To find the angle measure of each section, write each group of people as a fraction of all the people and multiply by 360°.

   Sitcom

   Drama

   ☐ = ☐ = ☐

   Cartoon

   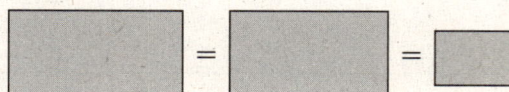

   News

   ☐ = ☐ = ☐

3. Draw and label the circle graph.

Percent of Increase and Decrease

LESSON 9.6

Goal: Find a percent of change in a quantity.

Vocabulary

Percent of change:

Percent of increase:

Percent of decrease:

EXAMPLE 1 **Finding a Percent of Increase**

What is the percent of increase from 5 to 7?

$$p\% = \frac{\text{Amount of increase}}{\text{Original amount}}$$ Write percent of increase formula.

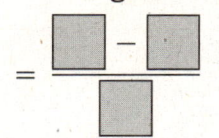   Substitute amount of increase and original amount.

 = ☐ %   Subtract. Then express fraction as a percent.

Answer: The percent of increase is ☐ %.

> Need help with common percents? See pages 450 and 455 of your textbook.

EXAMPLE **2** **Finding a Percent of Decrease**

What is the percent of decrease from 30 to 25?

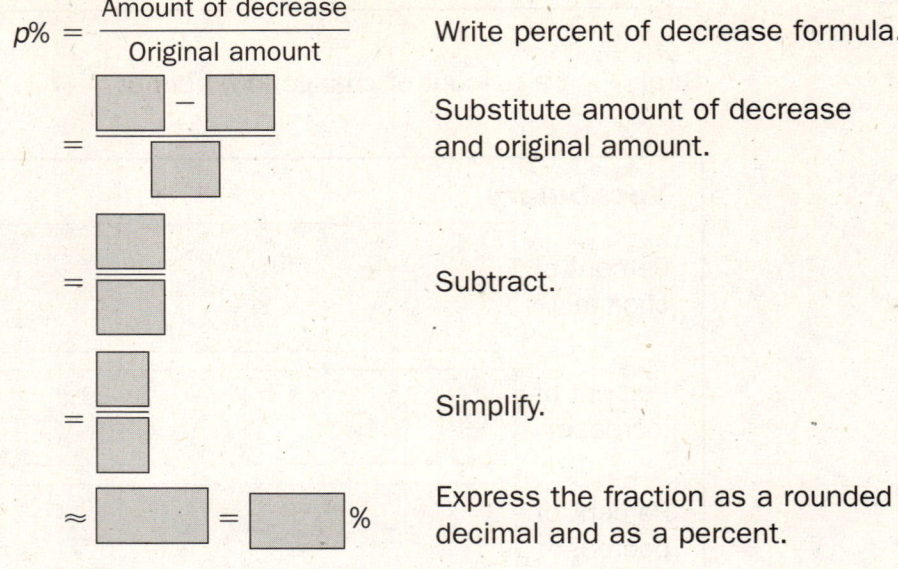

In Example 2, note that decreasing from 30 to 25 is about the same as decreasing from 30 to 24. Because $\frac{30-24}{30} = \frac{1}{5} = 20\%$, the answer is reasonable.

$$p\% = \frac{\text{Amount of decrease}}{\text{Original amount}}$$

Write percent of decrease formula.

$$= \frac{\boxed{} - \boxed{}}{\boxed{}}$$

Substitute amount of decrease and original amount.

$$= \frac{\boxed{}}{\boxed{}}$$

Subtract.

$$= \frac{\boxed{}}{\boxed{}}$$

Simplify.

$$\approx \boxed{} = \boxed{}\%$$

Express the fraction as a rounded decimal and as a percent.

Answer: The percent of decrease is about $\boxed{}$ %.

Guided Practice Identify the percent of change as an *increase* or a *decrease*. Then find the percent of change. Use estimation to check your answer.

1. Original: 10 New: 12	**2.** Original: 125 New: 25	**3.** Original: 250 New: 150

EXAMPLE 3 Using a Percent of Change

Salary An employee's salary recently increased 15% from $28,000 per year. How much does the employee earn now?

Solution

Find the amount of increase, 15% of $28,000.

Increase = 15% × 28,000

$\qquad$ = [ ] Write percent as a decimal.

$\qquad$ = [ ] Multiply.

Add the increase to the original amount.

New amount = Original amount + Increase

$\qquad$ = [ ] + [ ] = [ ]

Answer: The new salary is $[ ].

Discounts, Markups, Sales Tax, and Tips

Goal: Find discounts, markups, sales tax, and tips.

EXAMPLE 1 **Finding a Sale Price**

Music You buy a CD that is 40% off the original price of $12. What is the sale price?

Solution

1. Find the amount of the discount.

Discount = 40% of $12

= [　　　]   Write 40% as a decimal.

= [　　]   Multiply.

2. Subtract the discount from the original price.

Sale Price = Original price − Discount

= [　　] − [　　] = [　　]

Answer: The sale price is $[　　].

EXAMPLE 2 **Finding a Retail Price**

Furniture A furniture store that sells sofas buys them from a manufacturer at a wholesale price of $350. The store's markup is 200%. What is the retail price of the sofa?

1. Find the amount of the markup.

Markup = 200% of $350

= [　　　]   Write 200% as a decimal.

= [　　]   Multiply.

2. Add the markup to the wholesale price.

Retail Price = Wholesale price + Markup

= [　　] + [　　] = [　　]

Answer: The retail price is $[　　].

1. A store is selling all shoes at 20% off the original price. What is the sale price of a pair of shoes originally priced at $65?

2. A store buys software from a manufacturer at a wholesale price of $72. The store's markup is 75%. What is the retail price?

EXAMPLE 3 **Finding Sales Tax and Tip**

Diner At a diner, Maddie orders a meal that costs $8. She leaves a 15% tip. The sales tax is 6%. What is the total cost of the meal?

Solution

1. Find the tip. 15% of $8 = [   ] = [   ]

2. Find the sales tax. 6% of $8 = [   ] = [   ]

3. Add the food bill, tip, and sales tax. [   ] = [   ]

Answer: The total cost of the meal is $[   ].

Simple Interest

Goal: Calculate simple interest.

Vocabulary

Interest:

Principal:

Simple interest:

Annual interest rate:

Balance:

Simple Interest

Words Simple interest *I* is the product of the [____] *P*, the

[_____] *r* written as a decimal, and the [____] *t* in years.

Algebra [____]

Numbers A $1000 deposit earns 5% simple annual interest for 3 years.

$$I = (\quad)(\quad)(\quad) = \$ \quad$$

EXAMPLE 1 **Finding a Balance**

Carol deposits $30 in a bank account that pays 5% simple annual interest. What will be the total amount that she has in the account after 2 years?

$I = Prt$ Write simple interest formula.

$= (\boxed{})(\boxed{})(\boxed{})$ Substitute $\boxed{}$ for P, $\boxed{}$ for r, and $\boxed{}$ for t.

$= \boxed{}$ Multiply.

To find the balance, add the interest to the principal.

Answer: Carol will have $30 + $$\boxed{}$, or $$\boxed{}$ in her account.

EXAMPLE 2 **Finding an Interest Rate**

You deposit $750 into an 8 month certificate of deposit. After 8 months the balance is $770. Find the simple annual interest rate.

To find the interest, subtract the principal from the balance.

$\boxed{} - \boxed{} = \boxed{}$

Then use the simple interest formula and solve for r.

$I = Prt$ Write simple interest formula.

$\boxed{} = (\boxed{})(\boxed{})\left(\boxed{} \right)$ Substitute $\boxed{}$ for I, $\boxed{}$ for P, and $\frac{8}{12}$ for t.

$\boxed{} = \boxed{}$ Multiply.

$\dfrac{\boxed{}}{\boxed{}} = \dfrac{\boxed{}}{\boxed{}}$ Divide each side by $\boxed{}$.

$\boxed{} = \boxed{}$ Simplify.

$\boxed{}\% = \boxed{}$ Write decimal as a percent.

Answer: The simple annual interest rate is $\boxed{}$%.

WATCH OUT!

When using the simple interest formula, make sure you write the number of months as a fraction of a year. For example, 7 months should be written as $\frac{7}{12}$.

Guided Practice Solve the following problems.

1. If you deposit $1500 into an account that earns 5% simple annual interest, what will the account's balance be after 4 months?

2. You deposit $800 into a 9 month certificate of deposit. After 9 months the balance is $848. Find the simple annual interest rate.

EXAMPLE 3 **Finding an Amount of Time**

Mario borrows $500 from a bank to pay for car repairs. His simple annual interest rate is 10%. Mario pays a total of $100 in interest on the loan. How long did Mario have the loan?

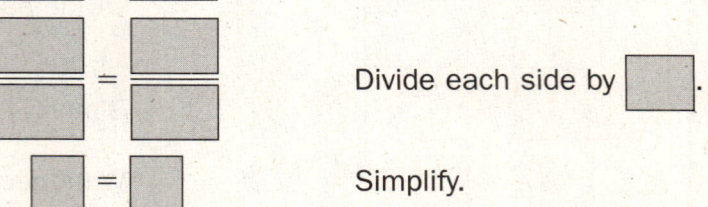

$I = Prt$ Write simple interest formula.

☐ = (☐)(☐)☐   Substitute ☐ for I, ☐ for P, and ☐ for r.

☐ = ☐   Multiply.

$\dfrac{☐}{☐} = \dfrac{☐}{☐}$ Divide each side by ☐.

☐ = ☐   Simplify.

Answer: Mario had the loan for ☐.

Words to Review

Give an example of the vocabulary word.

Percent

Circle graph

Ray

Angle

Vertex

Degrees

Percent of change

Percent of increase

Percent of decrease

Interest

Principal

Simple interest

Annual interest rate

Balance

Review your notes and Chapter 9 by using the Chapter Review on pages 496–500 of your textbook.

Angles

Goal: Classify angles by their measures.

Vocabulary

Acute angle:

Right angle:

Obtuse angle:

Straight angle:

Complementary:

Supplementary:

EXAMPLE 1   **Classifying an Angle**

A quick way to check the size of an angle is to use the corner of a piece of paper. Because the corner forms a right angle, it is easy to determine whether the angle's measure is less than 90°, exactly 90°, or greater than 90°.

Estimate to classify the angle as *acute*, *right*, *obtuse*, or *straight*.

a.

G

b.

D

Solution

a. Because $m\angle G$ is [   ], $\angle G$ is [   ].

b. Because $m\angle D$ is [   ], $\angle D$ is [   ].

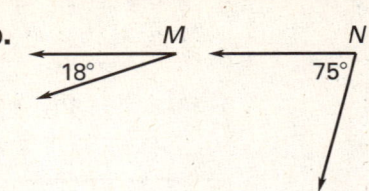

EXAMPLE 2 Complementary and Supplementary Angles

Tell whether the angles are *complementary*, *supplementary*, or *neither*.

a.

49°   131°
X Y

b.

M   N
18°   75°

The angle above can be named in several ways: ∠ABC, ∠CBA, ∠B, and ∠1. Notice that the vertex must be in the middle or the only letter used in the name of the angle.

Solution

a. $m\angle X + m\angle Y =$ ☐ $+$ ☐ $=$ ☐ . So, ∠X and ∠Y are

☐ .

b. $m\angle M + m\angle N =$ ☐ $+$ ☐ $=$ ☐ . So, ∠M and ∠N are

☐ .

Guided Practice Classify the angle as *acute*, *obtuse*, *right*, or *straight*.

1. $m\angle D = 18°$	**2.** $m\angle V = 90°$	**3.** $m\angle S = 180°$	**4.** $m\angle J = 150°$

5. Give the measures of two angles that are complementary.

EXAMPLE 3 Standardized Test Practice

For the two skateboard ramps at the right, ∠1 and ∠2 are complementary. If *m*∠1 = 38°, find *m*∠2.

 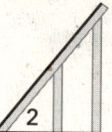

Ⓐ 12°   Ⓑ 52°

Ⓒ 142°   Ⓓ 322°

Solution

m∠1 + *m*∠2 = ☐	Definition of ☐ angles
☐ + *m*∠2 = ☐	Substitute ☐ for *m*∠1.
m∠2 = ☐	Subtract ☐ from each side.

Answer: The measure of ∠2 is ☐ . The correct answer is ☐ .

Ⓐ   Ⓑ   Ⓒ   Ⓓ

Guided Practice Use the definitions of complementary and supplementary angles to find the measure of the angle.

6. ∠P and ∠Q are supplementary. If *m*∠P = 98°, find *m*∠Q.

7. ∠T and ∠U are complementary. If *m*∠T = 16°, find *m*∠U.

Special Pairs of Angles

Goal: Identify special pairs of angles and types of lines.

Vocabulary

Adjacent angles:

Vertical angles:

Congruent angles:

Parallel lines:

Intersecting lines:

Perpendicular lines:

Corresponding angles:

EXAMPLE 1 **Identifying Adjacent Angles**

Name all pairs of adjacent, supplementary angles.

Adjacent, supplementary angles:

EXAMPLE 2 **Using Vertical Angles**

Given that $m\angle 1 = 68°$, find $m\angle 3$.

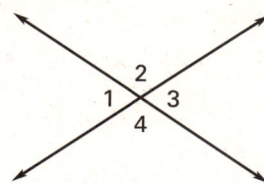

Because ⬜ and $\angle 3$ are ⬜ angles, they are ⬜.

So, $m\angle 3 = $ ⬜ $= $ ⬜.

Guided Practice **Refer to the diagram in Example 2.**

1. Name all pairs of adjacent, supplementary angles.

2. Given that $m\angle 1 = 68°$, find $m\angle 2$.

3. Use your answer from Exercise 2 to find $m\angle 4$.

EXAMPLE 3 **Using Corresponding Angles**

Maps The map shows a section of Houston. Streets shown on maps often appear to form parallel or intersecting lines.

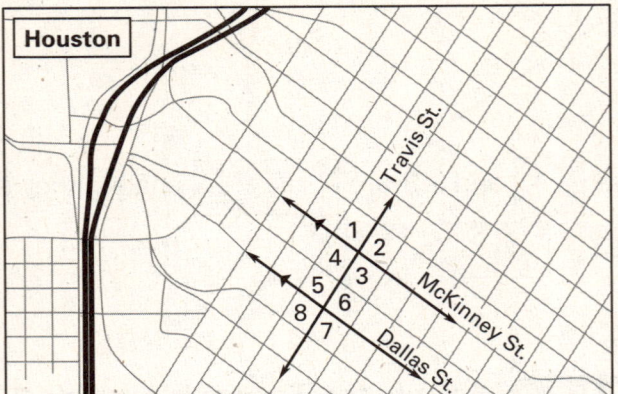

> Arrowheads are used to indicate that lines are parallel.

a. Name two streets that are parallel and two streets that intersect.

b. If $m\angle 1 = 85°$, find $m\angle 7$.

Solution

a. [   ] is parallel to [   ]. [   ]
intersects both [   ] and [   ].

b. Because $\angle$[ ] and $\angle$[ ] are [   ] angles,
[   ] = [   ] = [   ]. Because McKinney Street and Dallas Street
are [   ] lines, $\angle$[ ] and $\angle$[ ] are [   ]
angles. So, [   ] = [   ] = [   ].

Guided Practice Refer to the map in Example 3.

4. Find $m\angle 2$ and $m\angle 6$. Explain your reasoning.

Triangles

Goal: Classify triangles.

Vocabulary

Acute triangle:

Right triangle:

Obtuse triangle:

Congruent sides:

Equilateral triangle:

Isosceles triangle:

Scalene triangle:

EXAMPLE 1 **Finding an Angle Measure in a Triangle**

Find the value of _x_ in the triangle shown.

$x° +$ ☐ $° +$ ☐ $° =$ ☐ $°$ Sum of angle measures in a triangle is ☐.

$x +$ ☐ $=$ ☐   Add ☐ and ☐.

$x =$ ☐   Subtract ☐ from each side.

Answer: The value of _x_ is ☐.

Triangles are named by their *vertices*. The vertices of the triangle in Example 1 are *L*, *M*, and *N*, so the triangle can be named with the notation △*LMN*. This notation is read "triangle *LMN*."

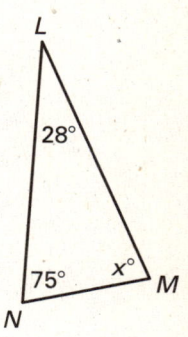

EXAMPLE 2 **Finding the Measure of an Exterior Angle**

Find the value of _y_ in the figure.

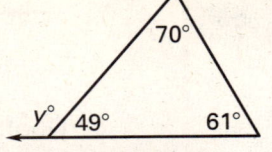

To find the value of _y_, use the fact that adjacent interior and exterior angles of a triangle are supplementary.

$y° + \boxed{}° = \boxed{}°$ Definition of $\boxed{}$ angles

$y = \boxed{}$ Subtract $\boxed{}$ from each side.

Answer: The value of _y_ is $\boxed{}$.

Guided Practice   **Find the value of _y_.**

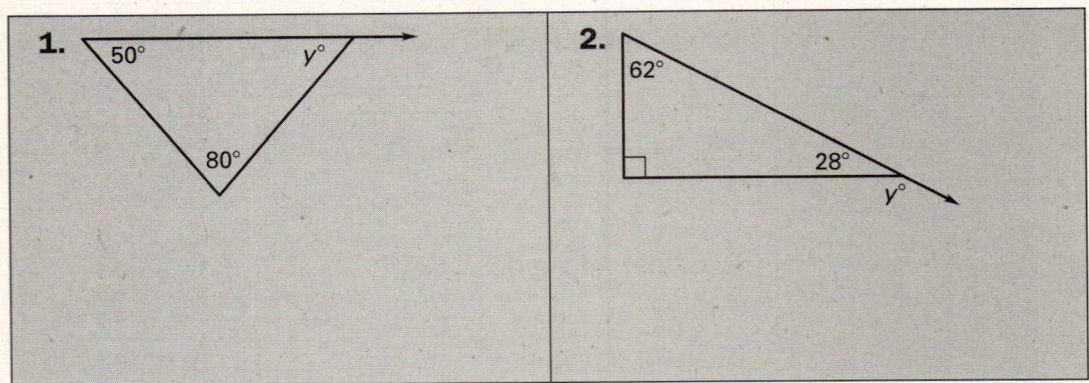

1.

2.

EXAMPLE 3   **Classifying a Triangle by Angle Measures**

Classify the triangle by its angle measures.

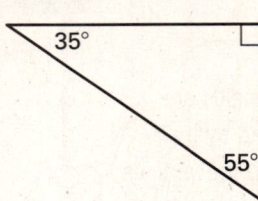

The triangle has $\boxed{}$ angle, so it is a(n) $\boxed{}$ triangle.

EXAMPLE 4 **Standardized Test Practice**

Which statement about the triangle is true?

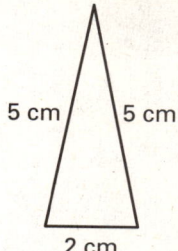

5 cm   5 cm

2 cm

Ⓐ It is scalene.

Ⓑ It is equilateral.

Ⓒ It is isosceles.

Ⓓ Its 3 angles are congruent.

Solution

The triangle is not ▭ because two sides are congruent. The triangle is not ▭ because only two sides are congruent. The triangle is ▭ because two sides are congruent. The triangle does not have three congruent angles because it is not ▭.

Answer: The correct answer is ▭.   Ⓓ

Guided Practice Classify the triangle by its angle measures.

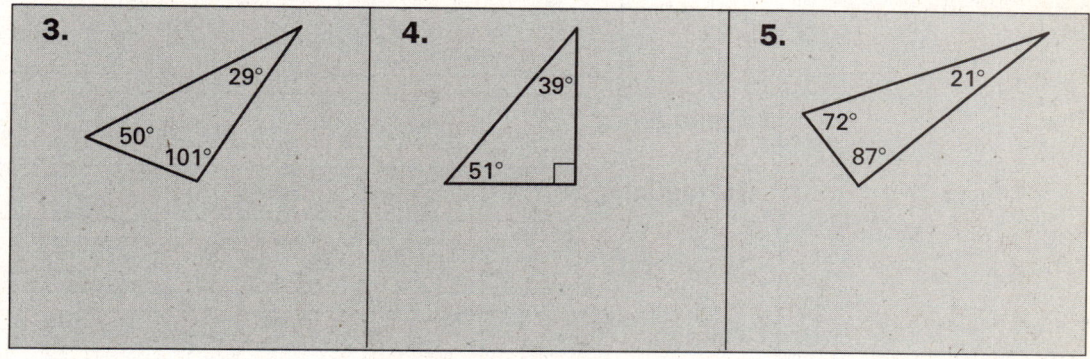

3.

29°
50°
101°

4.

39°
51°

5.

21°
72°
87°

Classify the triangle by the lengths of its sides.

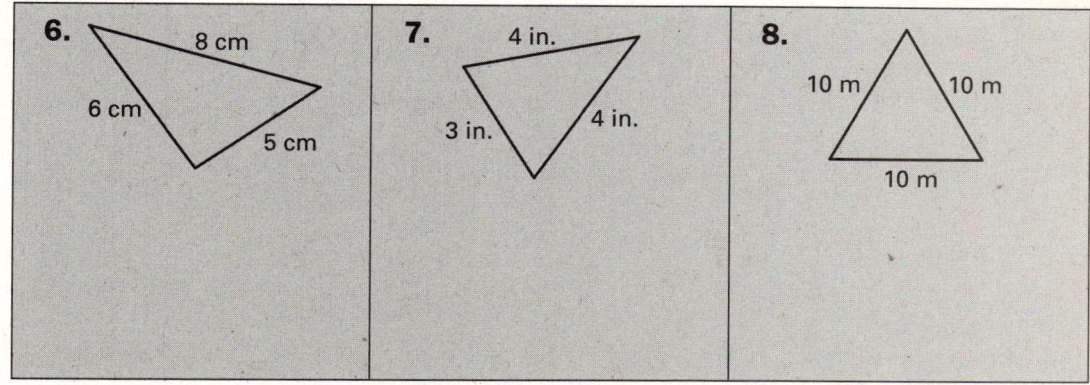

6.

8 cm
6 cm
5 cm

7.

4 in.
3 in.   4 in.

8.

10 m   10 m
10 m

Polygons

Goal: Classify quadrilaterals and other polygons.

Vocabulary

Quadrilateral:

Trapezoid:

Parallelogram:

Rhombus:

Polygon:

Pentagon:

Hexagon:

Heptagon:

Octagon:

EXAMPLE **1** **Classifying a Quadrilateral**

To help you classify quadrilaterals, you could draw a diagram that shows how the special quadrilaterals are related to each other.

Sketch and classify a quadrilateral with opposite sides parallel, and all four sides of length 2 centimeters.

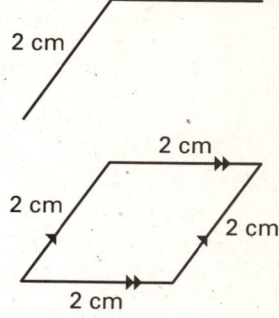

1. Draw two sides with a length of 2 centimeters. The angle between the two sides does not matter, except that it cannot be 0° or 180°.

2. Draw sides parallel to the first two sides to complete the figure.

Answer: The figure is a ⬚ .

Guided Practice **Sketch and classify the quadrilateral described.**

1. A quadrilateral with 4 right angles, 4 congruent sides of length 3 centimeters, and both pairs of opposite sides parallel.

EXAMPLE **2** **Classifying Polygons**

Tell whether the figure is a polygon. If it is, classify it. If it is not, explain why not.

a. 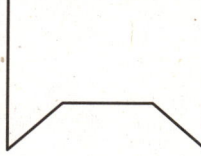   b.

Solution

a.    b. ⬚

Guided Practice Tell whether the figure is a polygon. If it is, classify it. If it is not, explain why not.

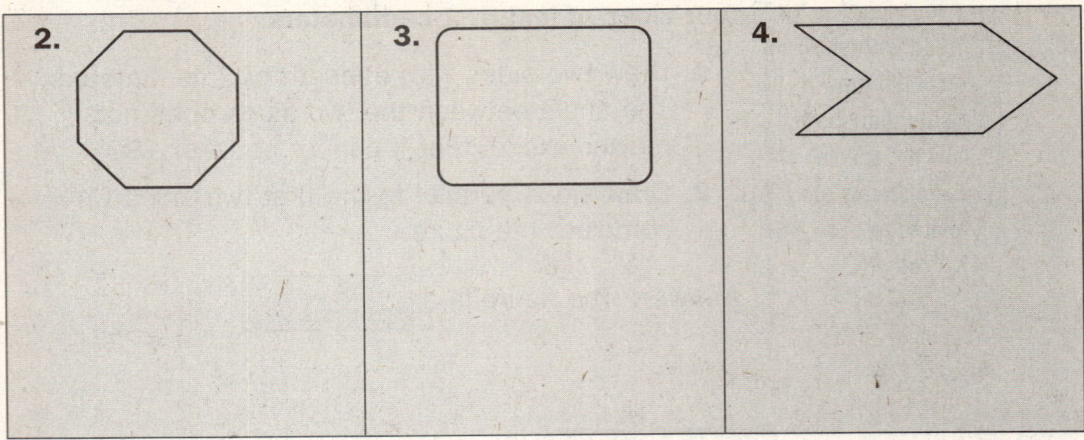

2.

3.

4.

EXAMPLE 3 **Using a Regular Polygon**

The hexagon shown is a regular hexagon. Find the perimeter of the hexagon. Then find the sum of the angle measures of the hexagon.

WATCH OUT!

Just because a polygon has sides that are all congruent does not necessarily mean that it is a regular polygon. All angles must also be congruent.

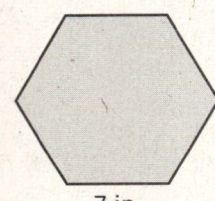

7 in.

1. A regular hexagon has [ ] sides of equal length,

so the perimeter of the hexagon is [ ] ([ ]) = [ ] inches.

2. A hexagon can be divided into [ ] triangles. The sum of the angle

measures in a triangle is [ ] , so the sum of the angle measures

in any hexagon is [ ] + [ ] + [ ] + [ ] = [ ] .

Similar and Congruent Polygons

Goal: Use properties of similar and congruent polygons.

Vocabulary

Similar polygons:

Congruent polygons:

Similar Polygons	**Congruent Polygons**
$\triangle LMN \sim \triangle PQR$	$\triangle ABC \cong \triangle DEF$

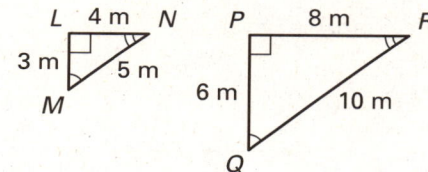

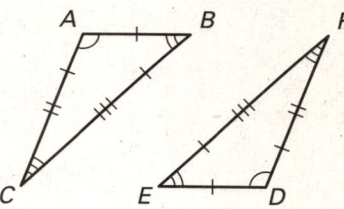

Similar Polygons	**Congruent Polygons**
Angles Corresponding angles are congruent:	**Angles** Corresponding angles are congruent:
$\angle L \cong \angle\ \boxed{}$, $\angle M \cong \angle\ \boxed{}$, and $\angle N \cong \angle\ \boxed{}$	$\angle A \cong \angle\ \boxed{}$, $\angle B \cong \angle\ \boxed{}$, and $\angle C \cong \angle\ \boxed{}$
Sides Ratios of lengths of corresponding sides are equal:	**Sides** Corresponding sides are congruent:
$\dfrac{LM}{\boxed{}} = \dfrac{MN}{\boxed{}} = \dfrac{LN}{\boxed{}}$	$\overline{AB} \cong \boxed{}$, $\overline{AC} \cong \boxed{}$, and $\overline{BC} \cong \boxed{}$

EXAMPLE **1** Finding Measures of Congruent Polygons

WATCH OUT!

When naming congruent or similar polygons, list the letters for the corresponding vertices in the same order. For instance, in Example 1, you cannot write $ABCD \cong XYZW$ because $\angle A$ and $\angle X$ are not corresponding angles.

Given that $ABCD \cong WXYZ$, name the corresponding sides and corresponding angles. Then find XY.

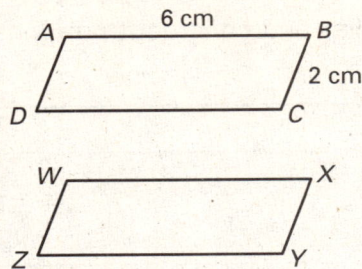

Solution

Corresponding Sides:

$\overline{AB}$ and ☐ , $\overline{BC}$ and ☐ ,

$\overline{CD}$ and ☐ , $\overline{AD}$ and ☐

Corresponding Angles:

$\angle A$ and $\angle$ ☐ , $\angle B$ and $\angle$ ☐ ,

$\angle C$ and $\angle$ ☐ , $\angle D$ and $\angle$ ☐

Because ☐ and $\overline{XY}$ are ☐ sides,

$\overline{XY}$ = ☐ = ☐ centimeters.

Guided Practice Use the fact that $\triangle ABC \cong \triangle LMN$.

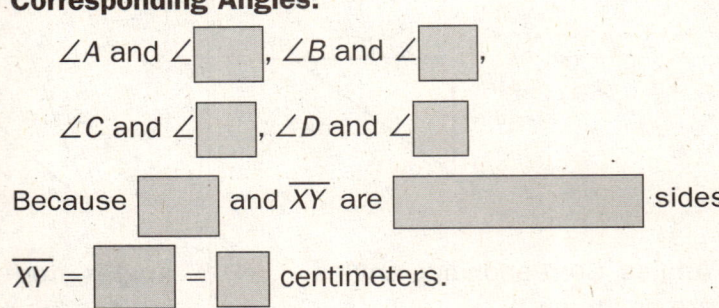

1. Name the corresponding sides and corresponding angles.

Corresponding Sides:

Corresponding Angles:

2. Find the unknown angle measures.

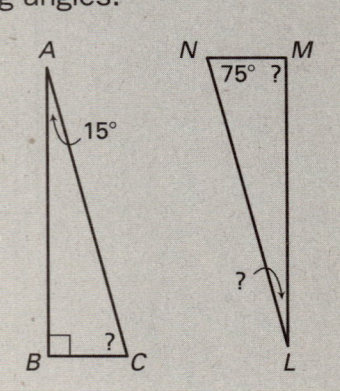

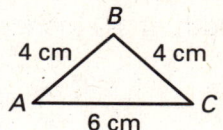

EXAMPLE 2 **Finding a Ratio of Lengths**

Given that △*ABC* ~ △*DEF*, find the ratio of the lengths of the corresponding sides of △*ABC* to △*DEF*.

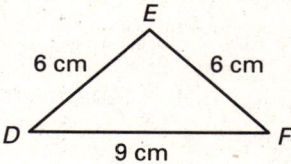

The ratios $\frac{DE}{AB}$, $\frac{EF}{BC}$, and $\frac{DF}{AC}$ are the ratios for the lengths of the corresponding sides of △*DEF* to △*ABC* in Example 2. Using these ratios, the ratio of the lengths of the corresponding sides is $\frac{3}{2}$.

Write the ratio for each pair of corresponding sides. Then substitute the lengths of the sides and simplify each ratio.

$\frac{AB}{DE} =$ ▨ $=$ ▨

$\frac{BC}{EF} =$ ▨ $=$ ▨

$\frac{AC}{DF} =$ ▨ $=$ ▨

Answer: The ratio of the lengths of the corresponding sides is ▨ .

EXAMPLE 3 Checking for Similarity

Landscape Design A landscape architect is planning a memorial garden at a local park. The rectangular garden will have a length of 18 feet and a width of 15 feet. A rectangular blueprint of the garden has a length of 12 inches and a width of 10 inches. Are the garden and the blueprint similar figures?

Solution

Because both figures are rectangles, all angles are [   ] angles, so corresponding angles are [   ]. To determine whether the figures are similar, see if the ratios of the lengths of the corresponding sides are [   ].

$$\frac{\text{Length of garden}}{\text{Length of } [\quad]} \overset{?}{=} \frac{\text{Width of } [\quad]}{\text{Width of } [\quad]}$$
Write ratios for lengths of corresponding sides.

$$\frac{[\quad]}{[\quad]} \overset{?}{=} \frac{[\quad]}{[\quad]}$$
Substitute.

$$\frac{[\quad]}{[\quad]} \overset{?}{=} \frac{[\quad]}{[\quad]}$$
Convert all units to inches.

$$[\quad]$$
Simplify.

Answer: The corresponding angles [   ] and the ratios of the lengths of the corresponding sides [   ], so the figures [   ].

Using Proportions with Similar Polygons

Goal: Use similar triangles to find lengths indirectly.

EXAMPLE 1 Finding an Unknown Length

Quadrilaterals *LMNO* and *PQRS* are similar. Find *MN*.

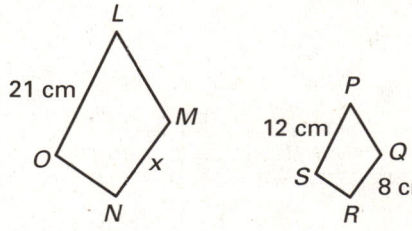

Solution

Use the ratios of the lengths of corresponding sides to write a proportion involving the unknown length.

> Need help writing and solving proportions? See pages 418 and 423 of your textbook.

$$\frac{LO}{\boxed{}} = \frac{MN}{\boxed{}}$$ Write proportion involving *MN*.

$$\frac{\boxed{}}{\boxed{}} = \frac{x}{\boxed{}}$$ Substitute known values.

$$\boxed{} = \boxed{}$$ Cross products property

$$\boxed{} = \boxed{}$$ Divide each side by $\boxed{}$.

Answer: The length of $\overline{MN}$ is $\boxed{}$ centimeters.

Guided Practice Find the unknown length *x* given that the polygons are similar.

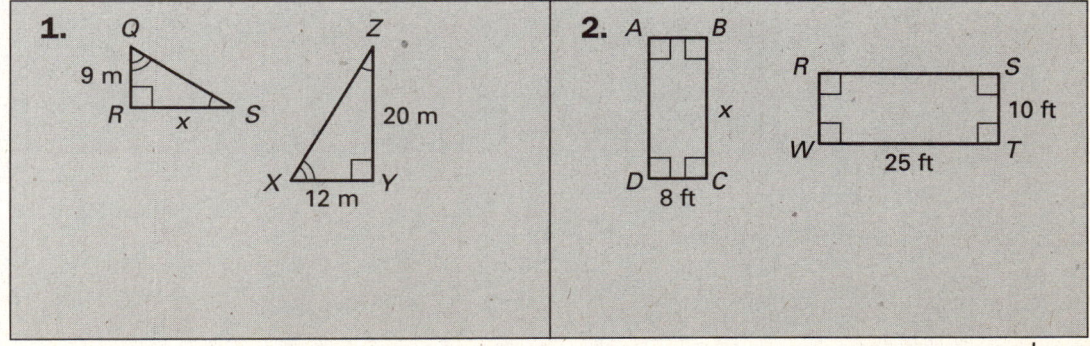

EXAMPLE 2 **Making an Indirect Measurement**

Flagpole A flagpole casts a shadow that is 25 feet long. Joe is 4 feet tall and casts a shadow that is 5 feet long. How tall is the flagpole?

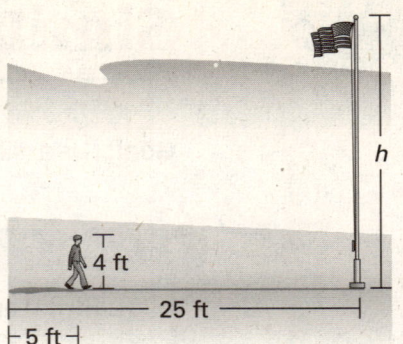

Solution

You can use indirect measurement to find the height of the flagpole. Use the ratios of the lengths of the corresponding parts to write a proportion involving the unknown height *h*.

$$\frac{\text{Height of flagpole}}{\text{Joe's height}} = \frac{\text{Length of flagpole's shadow}}{\text{Length of Joe's shadow}}$$

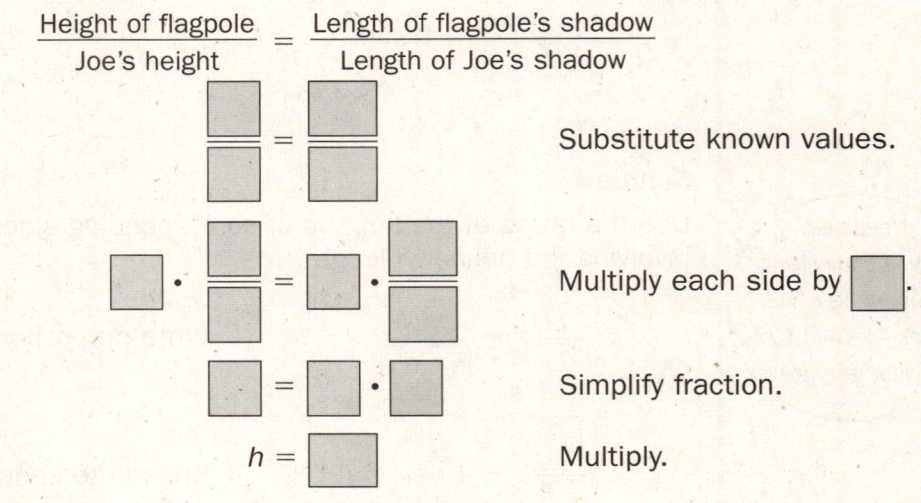

Substitute known values.

Multiply each side by [ ].

Simplify fraction.

$h = $ [ ]   Multiply.

Answer: The flagpole's height is [ ] feet.

Guided Practice Use indirect measurement to solve the problem.

3. The shadow cast by a radio tower is 60 feet long. At the same time, the shadow cast by a 5-foot tall pole is 15 feet long. How tall is the radio tower?

Transformations and Symmetry

Goal: Identify transformations and symmetry in figures.

Vocabulary

Transformation:

Image:

Translation:

Reflection:

Line of reflection:

Rotation:

Center of rotation:

Angle of rotation:

Line symmetry:

Rotational symmetry:

EXAMPLE 1 **Identifying a Translation**

Tell whether the dashed figure is a translation of the solid figure. Explain your reasoning.

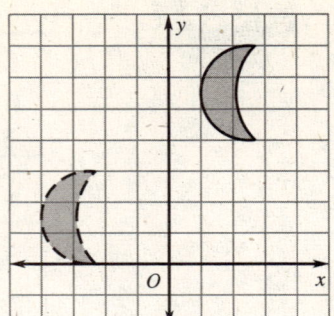

EXAMPLE 2 **Standardized Test Practice**

Which word best describes the transformation shown at the right?

(A) Translation

(B) Reflection in the *x*-axis

(C) Reflection in the *y*-axis

(D) Rotation

Solution

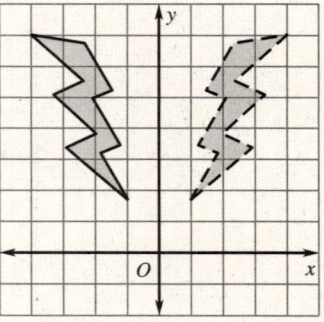

Answer: The correct answer is .

EXAMPLE 3 **Identifying a Rotation**

Tell whether the dashed figure is a rotation of the solid figure. If it is, give the angle and direction of rotation.

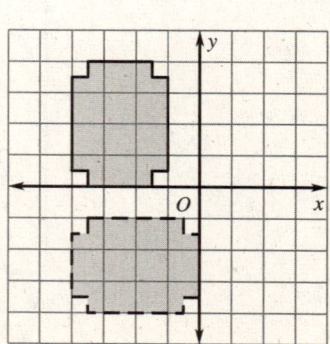

Guided Practice Identify the transformation from the solid figure to the dashed figure. If it is a reflection, identify the line of reflection. If it is a rotation, give the angle and direction of rotation.

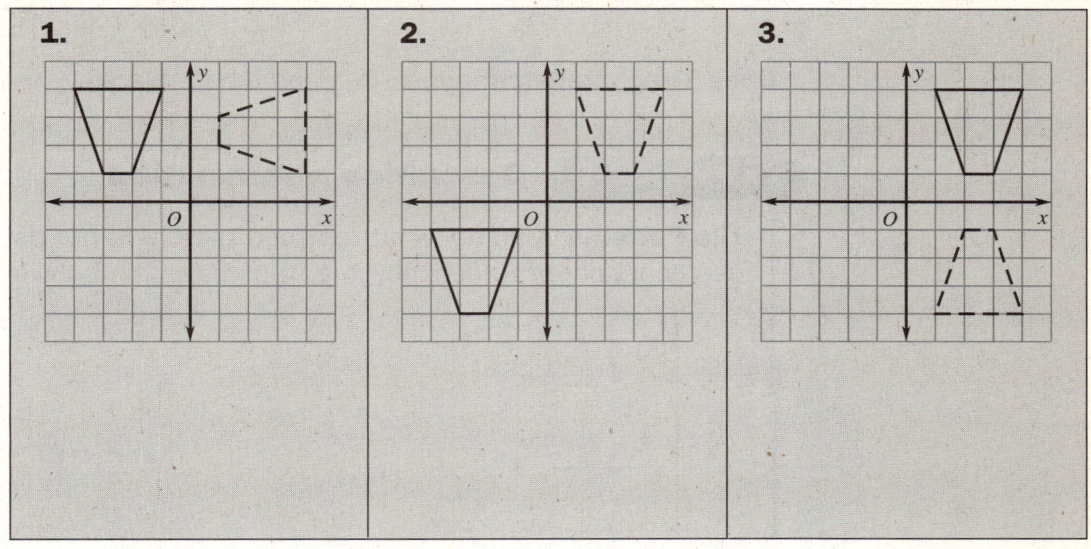

1.
2.
3.

EXAMPLE 4 Identifying Symmetry

Tell whether a regular pentagon has (a) line symmetry and (b) rotational symmetry.

a. A regular pentagon ░░░░░░░░░░. There are ░ lines of symmetry.

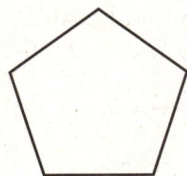

b. A regular pentagon ░░░░░░░░░░░░░. A turn of 72° or 144° clockwise (or counterclockwise) produces an image that fits exactly on the original figure.

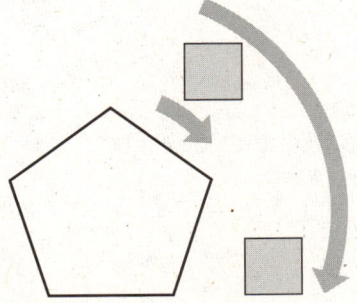

Transformations in the Coordinate Plane

Goal: Graph transformations in a coordinate plane.

EXAMPLE 1 **Describing a Translation**

Tile Patterns A homeowner replaced the tile in her bathroom. How can you use coordinates to describe the transformation shown?

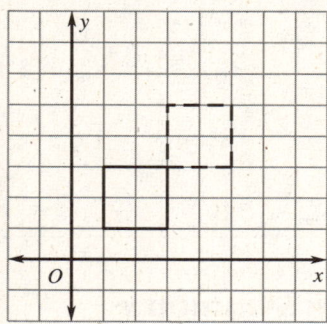

Solution

You can use coordinate notation to describe the translation shown above. Each point on the original figure is moved [   ] and [   ].

Answer: In coordinate notation you write this translation as:

$(x, y) \rightarrow ($ [   ] , [   ] $)$

Guided Practice **Describe the translation using coordinate notation.**

1. A figure is moved 3 units to the left and 1 unit up.

2. A figure is moved 5 units down.

EXAMPLE **2** **Translating a Figure**

Draw triangle *FGH* with vertices F(−4, 4), G(−2, 6), and H(−1, 3). Then find the coordinates of the vertices of the image after the translation (*x*, *y*)→(*x* + 3, *y* − 4), and draw the image.

For each vertex of the original figure, [____] to the *x*-coordinate and

[____] from the *y*-coordinate.

> Each point on an image is labeled with a *prime*. The notation *J′* is read "*J* prime."

Original   **Image**

$F(-4, 4)$ → $F'(\;[\quad]\;,\;[\quad]\;)$

$G(-2, 6)$ → $G'(\;[\quad]\;,\;[\quad]\;)$

$H(-1, 3)$ → $H'(\;[\quad]\;,\;[\quad]\;)$

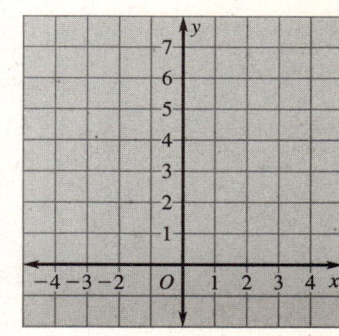

Each point on the original figure is translated [_____] and

[_____]. The graph shows both figures.

Complete the following exercise.

3. Draw quadrilateral *WXYZ* with vertices W(−1, 2), X(1, 2), Y(1, −1), and Z(0, −1). Then find the coordinates of the vertices of the image after the translation (*x*, *y*)→(*x* − 4, *y* + 2), and draw the image.

Original   Image

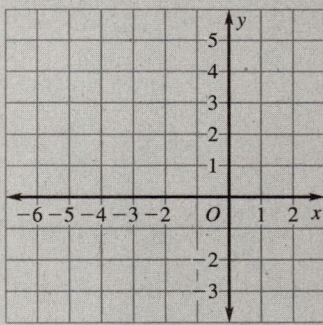

EXAMPLE **3** **Reflecting a Figure**

Draw trapezoid *DEFG* with vertices *D*(3, 3), *E*(1, 4), *F*(1, 1), and *G*(3, 1). Then find the coordinates of the vertices of the image after a reflection in the *y*-axis, and draw the image.

For each vertex of the original figure, multiply the [ ]-coordinate by [ ].

Original		**Image**
D(3, 3)	→	
E(1, 4)	→	
F(1, 1)	→	
G(3, 1)	→	

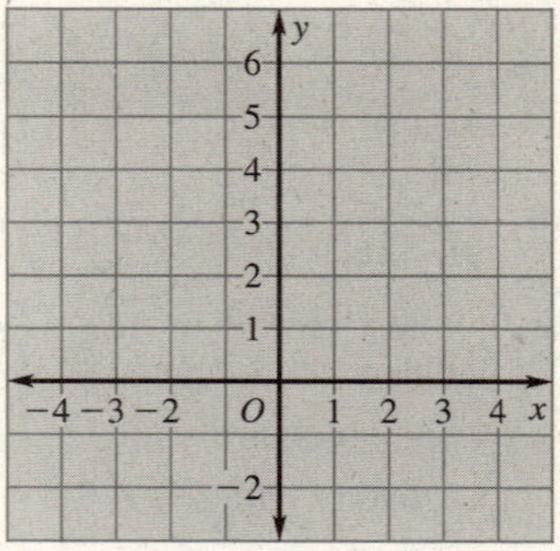

The graph shows both figures.

Words to Review

Give an example of the vocabulary word.

Acute angle

Right angle

Obtuse angle

Straight angle

Complementary

Supplementary

Adjacent angles

Vertical angles

Congruent angles

Parallel lines

Intersecting lines

Perpendicular lines

Corresponding angles

Acute triangle

Right triangle

Obtuse triangle

Congruent sides

Equilateral triangle

Isosceles triangle

Scalene triangle

Quadrilateral

Trapezoid

Parallelogram

Rhombus

Polygon

Pentagon

Hexagon

Heptagon

Octagon

Similar polygons

Congruent polygons

Transformation

Image

Translation

Reflection

Line of reflection

Rotation

Center of rotation

Angle of rotation

Line symmetry

Rotational symmetry

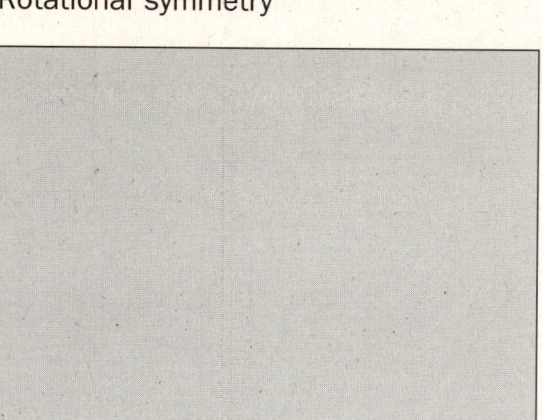

Review your notes and Chapter 10 by using the Chapter Review on pages 564–568 of your textbook.

Square Roots

Goal: Evaluate expressions involving square roots.

Vocabulary

Square root:

Perfect squares
(square numbers):

Radical expression:

The symbol $\sqrt{}$ is called a radical sign.

EXAMPLE 1 **Finding Square Roots**

Find the two square roots of the number.

a. 64 **b.** 100

Solution

a. The square roots of 64 are [ ] and [ ] because [ ] = 64
and [ ] = 64.

b. The square roots of 100 are [ ] and [ ] because [ ] = 100
and [ ] = 100.

EXAMPLE 2 **Evaluating Square Roots**

The expression $\sqrt{25}$ is read "the positive square root of 25."

a. $\sqrt{25}$ = [ ] because [ ] = 25.

b. You know that $\sqrt{4}$ = [ ] because [ ] = 4. So, $-\sqrt{4}$ = [ ].

c. $\sqrt{0}$ = [ ] because [ ] = 0.

EXAMPLE 3 Solving a Square Root Equation

Flooring Pam has enough flooring to cover 196 square feet. If she lays the flooring on a square area, what is the side length of the largest square she can make?

Solution

$s = \sqrt{A}$ ⠀⠀⠀Write equation for side length of a square.

$= \boxed{}$ ⠀⠀Substitute $\boxed{}$ for A.

$= \boxed{}$ ⠀⠀Evaluate square root.

Answer: The side length of the largest square Pam can make is $\boxed{}$.

Guided Practice Find the two square roots of the number.

1. 16	**2.** 81	**3.** 121	**4.** 1

Evaluate the square root.

5. $\sqrt{9}$	**6.** $-\sqrt{9}$	**7.** $-\sqrt{25}$	**8.** $\sqrt{144}$

EXAMPLE 4 Evaluating Radical Expressions

Evaluate the expression when $z = 4$ and $m = -3$.

⠀⠀**a.** $\sqrt{21 + z}$ ⠀⠀⠀⠀⠀⠀⠀⠀⠀**b.** $\sqrt{z^2 + m^2}$

Solution

a. $\sqrt{21 + z} = \boxed{}$ ⠀⠀Substitute $\boxed{}$ for z.

$= \boxed{}$ ⠀⠀Add.

$= \boxed{}$ ⠀⠀Evaluate square root.

Need help with order of operations? See page 17 of your textbook.

b. $\sqrt{z^2 + m^2} = $ [   ]   Substitute [   ] for z and [   ] for m.

$= $ [   ]   Evaluate powers.

$= $ [   ]   Add.

$= $ [   ]   Evaluate square root.

EXAMPLE 5 Solving Equations Using Square Roots

Solve the equation.

a. $x^2 = 100$

b. $g^2 - 4 = 45$

Solution

a. $x^2 = 100$ Write original equation.

[   ] $= \pm$ [   ]   Use definition of square root.

[   ] $=$ [   ]   Evaluate square root.

b. $g^2 - 4 = 45$ Write original equation.

$g^2 - 4$ [   ] $= 45$ [   ]   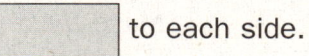 to each side.

[   ] $=$ [   ]   Simplify.

[   ] $=$ [   ]   Use definition of square root.

[   ] $=$ [   ]   Evaluate square root.

Guided Practice Solve the equation.

9. $x^2 = 4$	**10.** $x^2 + 3 = 52$	**11.** $3x^2 = 75$	**12.** $x^2 - 15 = 1$

Approximating Square Roots

Goal: Approximate square roots of numbers.

Vocabulary

Irrational number:

Real number:

EXAMPLE 1 **Approximating to a Whole Number**

Approximate $\sqrt{18}$ to the nearest whole number.

Make a list of whole numbers that are perfect squares:
0, 1, 4, 9, 16, 25, ...

☐ < 18 < ☐   Identify perfect squares closest to 18.

☐ < ☐ < ☐   Take positive square root of each number.

☐ < ☐ < ☐   Evaluate square root of each perfect square.

Answer: Because 18 is closer to ☐ than to ☐, $\sqrt{18}$ is closer to

☐ = ☐. So, to the nearest whole number, $\sqrt{18} \approx$ ☐.

EXAMPLE 2 **Approximating to the Nearest Tenth**

Approximate $\sqrt{18}$ to the nearest tenth.

You know from Example 1 that $\sqrt{18}$ is between ☐ and ☐. Make a list of squares. From the list, you can see that 18 is between ☐ and ☐. So, $\sqrt{18}$ is between ☐ and ☐.

Answer: Because 18 is closer to ☐ than to ☐, $\sqrt{18}$ is closer to ☐ = ☐. So, to the nearest tenth, $\sqrt{18} \approx$ ☐.

$4.0^2 =$ ☐

$4.1^2 =$ ☐

$4.2^2 =$ ☐

$4.3^2 =$ ☐

$4.4^2 =$ ☐

> Once you find the approximation of a square root to the tenths' place, you can use the same method to find the approximation to the hundredths' place, thousandths' place, and so on.

Guided Practice Approximate the square root to the nearest whole number and then to the nearest tenth.

1. $\sqrt{7}$	2. $\sqrt{30}$	3. $\sqrt{52}$	4. $\sqrt{125}$

EXAMPLE 3 **Using Square Roots**

Wolves The formula for an animal's maximum walking speed s, in inches per second, is $s = 19.6\sqrt{\ell}$ where ℓ is the animal's leg length, in inches. A wolf has 18-inch legs. Estimate the maximum walking speed of the wolf.

Solution

You can use the approximation the square root of 18 from Example 2 to estimate the maximum walking speed of the wolf.

$s = 19.6\sqrt{\ell}$ Write maximum walking speed formula.

$= 19.6$ ☐   Substitute ☐ for ℓ.

$\approx 19.6($ ☐ $)$ Use approximation of $\sqrt{18}$ to the nearest tenth.

$\approx$ ☐   Multiply.

Answer: The maximum walking speed is about ☐ inches per second.

Need help with rational numbers? See page 301 of your textbook.

EXAMPLE 4 Identifying Rational and Irrational Numbers

Tell whether the number is *rational* or *irrational*. Explain.

a. $\sqrt{3}$ **b.** $-\dfrac{2}{5}$ **c.** $-\sqrt{225}$ **d.** 2.363663. . .

Solution

a. $\sqrt{3}$ is [   ] because

[   ].

b. $-\dfrac{2}{5}$ is [   ] because

[   ].

c. $-\sqrt{225}$ is [   ] because

[   ].

d. 2.363663. . . is [   ] because

[   ].

The Pythagorean Theorem

Goal: Find the length of a side of a right triangle.

Vocabulary

Hypotenuse:

Leg:

Pythagorean theorem:

Pythagorean Theorem

Words For any right triangle, the ☐ of the

☐ of the lengths of the ☐ equals

the ☐ of the length of the ☐ .

Algebra ☐ = ☐

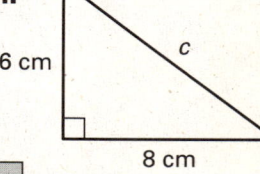

EXAMPLE 1 **Finding the Length of a Hypotenuse**

Find the length of the hypotenuse of the triangle shown.

To find c, the length of the hypotenuse, use the Pythagorean theorem. Let $a = 6$ and $b = 8$.

$a^2 + b^2 = c^2$ Write Pythagorean theorem.

☐ + ☐ $= c^2$ Substitute ☐ for a and ☐ for b.

☐ $= c^2$ Simplify.

☐ = ☐   Take positive square root of each side.

☐ = ☐   Evaluate square root.

Answer: The length of the hypotenuse is ☐ centimeters.

Take the positive square root in Example 1 because length is never negative.

6 cm c

8 cm

EXAMPLE 2 **Approximating the Length of a Hypotenuse**

For the right triangle shown, find the length of
the hypotenuse to the nearest tenth.

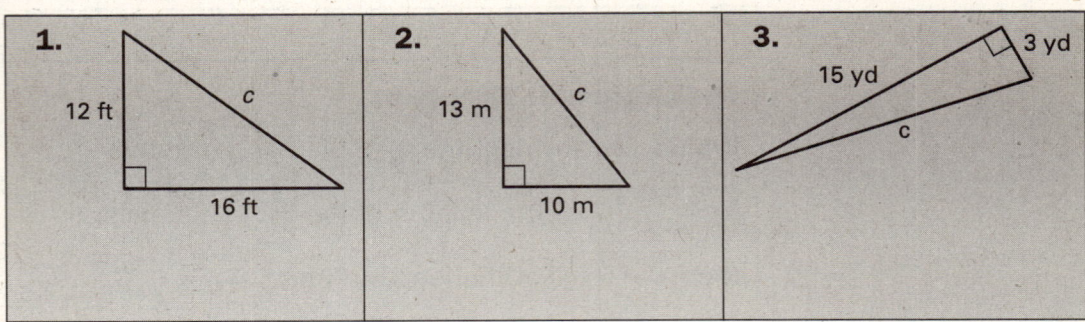

$a^2 + b^2 = c^2$ Write Pythagorean theorem.

$\boxed{} + \boxed{} = c^2$ Substitute $\boxed{}$ for a and $\boxed{}$ for b.

$\boxed{} = c^2$ Simplify.

$\boxed{} = \boxed{}$ Take positive square root of each side.

$\boxed{} \approx \boxed{}$ Approximate square root.

Answer: The length of the hypotenuse is about $\boxed{}$ millimeters.

> Need help with approximating square roots? See page 582 of your textbook.

Guided Practice Find the length of the hypotenuse. Round to the nearest tenth if necessary.

1. 12 ft, c, 16 ft

2. 13 m, c, 10 m

3. 15 yd, 3 yd, c

EXAMPLE 3 **Finding the Length of a Leg**

House Painting A painter sets his 25 foot ladder against
the side of a house. The base of the ladder is 7 feet from
the house. At what height does the ladder touch the house?

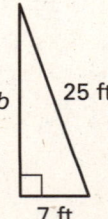

Solution

$a^2 + b^2 = c^2$ Write Pythagorean theorem.

$\boxed{} + b^2 = \boxed{}$ Substitute $\boxed{}$ for a and $\boxed{}$ for c.

$\boxed{} + b^2 = \boxed{}$ Evaluate powers.

$b^2 = \boxed{}$ Subtract $\boxed{}$ from each side.

$\boxed{} = \boxed{}$ Take positive square root of each side.

$\boxed{} = \boxed{}$ Evaluate square root.

Answer: The ladder touches the house $\boxed{}$ feet above the ground.

Area of a Parallelogram

Goal: Find the areas of parallelograms.

Vocabulary

Base of a parallelogram:

Height of a parallelogram:

Area of a Parallelogram

Words The area *A* of a parallelogram is the ____ of a ____ and the corresponding ____.

Algebra ☐ = ☐

height

base

EXAMPLE 1 **Finding the Area of a Parallelogram**

WATCH OUT!
Area is measured in square units, not linear units.

Find the area of the parallelogram.

$A = bh$　Write formula for area.

= ☐(☐)　Substitute ☐ for *b* and ☐ for *h*.

= ☐　Multiply.

6 cm

8 cm

Answer: The area of the parallelogram is ____.

Guided Practice Find the area of the parallelogram with the given base and height.

1. $b = 12$ m, $h = 7$ m	**2.** $b = 7$ mm, $h = 7$ mm	**3.** $b = 10.5$ ft, $h = 8$ ft

EXAMPLE 2 **Finding the Base of a Parallelogram**

Glass Cutting A window in an office building is a parallelogram. The height of the window is 12 inches. The window covers 180 square inches. Find the base of the window.

Solution

$A = bh$ Write formula for area of a parallelogram.

$\boxed{} = b\left(\boxed{}\right)$ Substitute $\boxed{}$ for A and $\boxed{}$ for h.

$\dfrac{\boxed{}}{\boxed{}} = \dfrac{b\left(\boxed{}\right)}{\boxed{}}$ Divide each side by $\boxed{}$.

$\boxed{} = b$ Simplify.

Answer: The base of the window is $\boxed{}$.

Guided Practice Find the unknown base or height or the parallelogram.

4. $A = 96$ m^2	**5.** $A = 153$ cm^2	**6.** $A = 121$ in.^{2}
8 m b	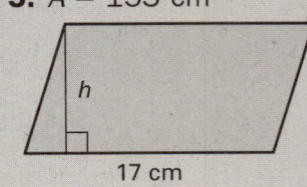17 cm h	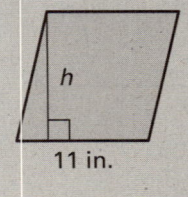11 in. h

Areas of Triangles and Trapezoids

Goal: Find the areas of triangles and trapezoids.

Vocabulary

Base of a triangle:

Height of a triangle:

Bases of a trapezoid:

Height of a trapezoid:

Area of a Triangle

Words The area A of a triangle is [ ] the product of a [ ] and the [ ].

Algebra [ ] = [ ]

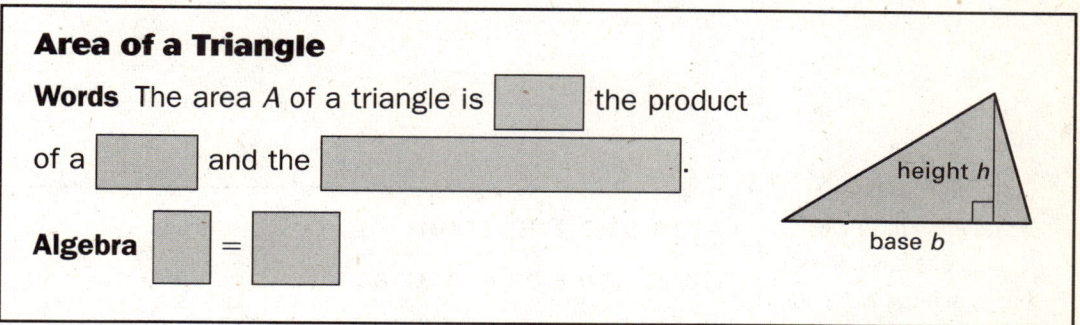

height h

base b

EXAMPLE 1 Finding the Area of a Triangle

Sculpture An artist is creating a sculpture that includes a triangular face that has a base 125 feet long and a height of 84 feet. Find the area of the triangular face.

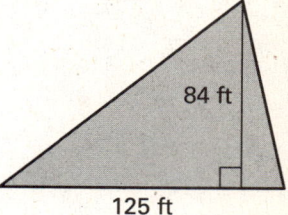

84 ft

125 ft

Solution

$A = \frac{1}{2}bh$ Write formula for area of a triangle.

$= \frac{1}{2}\left(\boxed{} \right)\left(\boxed{} \right)$ Substitute [ ] for b and [ ] for h.

$= \boxed{}$ Multiply.

Answer: The area of the face is [ ].

EXAMPLE 2 **Finding the Base of a Triangle**

A triangle has a height of 15 centimeters and an area of 202.5 square centimeters. Find the base of the triangle.

$A = \frac{1}{2}bh$ Write formula for area of a triangle.

[   ] = [   ]   Substitute [   ] for A and [   ] for h.

[   ] = [   ]   Simplify.

[   ] = b Divide each side by [   ].

Answer: The base of the triangle is [   ].

Guided Practice Find the unknown area or height of the triangle.

1. $A = \underline{\ ?\ }$, $b = 7$ ft, $h = 12$ ft	**2.** $A = 52$ m², $b = 8$ m, $h = \underline{\ ?\ }$

Because a trapezoid has more than one base, the bases of a trapezoid are usually labeled b_1 and b_2. b_1 is read "b sub one."

Area of a Trapezoid

Words The area A of a trapezoid is [   ] the product of the [   ] and the [   ].

Algebra [   ] = [   ]

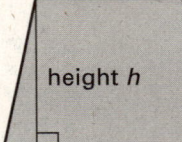

base b_1

height h

base b_2

Finding the Area of a Trapezoid

Find the area of the trapezoid shown.

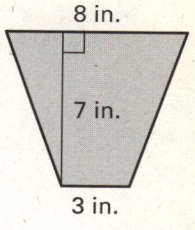

8 in.

7 in.

3 in.

$A = \frac{1}{2}(b_1 + b_2)h$ Write formula for area of a trapezoid.

$= \frac{1}{2}\left(\boxed{} + \boxed{}\right)\left(\boxed{}\right)$ Substitute $\boxed{}$ for b_1, $\boxed{}$ for b_2, and $\boxed{}$ for h.

$= \boxed{}$ Simplify.

Answer: The area of the trapezoid is $\boxed{}$.

EXAMPLE 4 Finding the Height of a Trapezoid

A trapezoid has an area of 82 square meters. The bases are 11 meters and 9 meters. Find the height.

$A = \frac{1}{2}(b_1 + b_2)h$ Write formula for area of a trapezoid.

$\boxed{} = \frac{1}{2}\left(\boxed{} + \boxed{}\right)h$ Substitute $\boxed{}$ for A, $\boxed{}$ for b_1, and $\boxed{}$ for b_2.

$\boxed{} = \frac{1}{2}\left(\boxed{}\right)h$ Add.

$\boxed{} = \boxed{}\,h$ Multiply.

$\boxed{} = h$ Divide each side by $\boxed{}$.

Answer: The height of the trapezoid is $\boxed{}$.

Guided Practice Find the unknown area, base, or height of the trapezoid.

3. $A = \underline{\ ?\ }$, $b_1 = 12$ ft, $b_2 = 8$ ft, $h = 4$ ft

4. $A = 22$ m^2, $b_1 = 7$ m, $b_2 = \underline{\ ?\ }$, $h = 4$ m

5. $A = 15$ cm^2, $b_1 = 3$ cm, $b_2 = 7$ cm, $h = \underline{\ ?\ }$

Circumference of a Circle

Goal: Find the circumferences of circles.

Vocabulary

Circle:

Center:

Radius:

Diameter:

Circumference:

Circumference of a Circle

Words The circumference C of a circle is the product

of [ ] and the [   ], or [   ] the product

of [ ] and the [   ].

Algebra [   ] = [   ]   [   ] = [   ]

diameter d

radius r

EXAMPLE 1   **Finding the Circumference of a Circle**

Find the circumference of the sundial. Use 3.14 for π.

$C = \pi d$ Write formula for circumference.

$\approx$ [   ]([   ])   Substitute [   ] for π and

[   ] for d.

$=$ [   ]   Multiply.

24 in.

Answer: The circumference of the sundial is about [   ].

WATCH OUT!

The circumference of a circle is measured in linear units, not square units.

When the radius or diameter of a circle is divisible by 7, use $\frac{22}{7}$ as the approximation for π.

EXAMPLE 2 **Finding the Circumference of a Circle**

Find the circumference of the circle. Use $\frac{22}{7}$ for π.

$C = 2\pi r$ Write formula for circumference.

$\approx 2\left(\boxed{}\right)\left(\boxed{}\right)$ Substitute $\boxed{}$ for π and $\boxed{}$ for r.

$= \boxed{}$ Multiply.

Answer: The circumference is about $\boxed{}$.

28 cm

Guided Practice Find the circumference of the circle. Use $\frac{22}{7}$ or 3.14 for π.

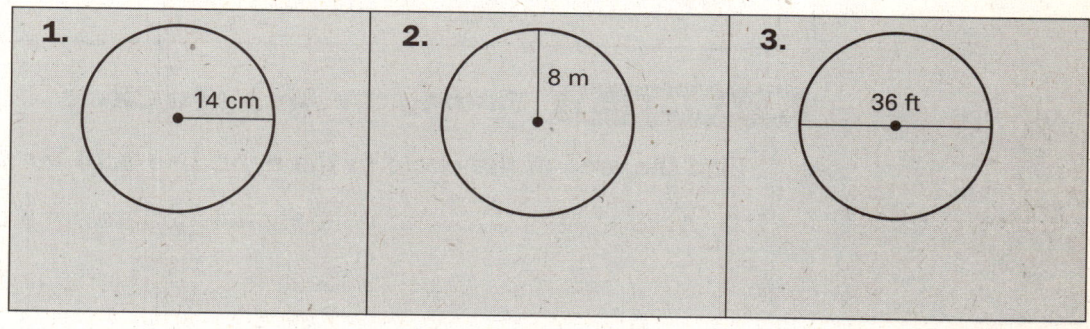

1. 14 cm

2. 8 m

3. 36 ft

EXAMPLE 3 **Finding the Diameter of a Circle**

Needlework Amelia is making a rug for her dining room floor. The rug will have a circumference of 44 feet. What will the diameter of the rug be?

Solution

$C = \pi d$ Write formula for circumference.

$\boxed{} \approx \frac{22}{7}d$ Substitute $\boxed{}$ for C and $\frac{22}{7}$ for π.

$\boxed{}\left(\boxed{}\right) \approx \boxed{}\left(\frac{22}{7}\right)d$ Multiply each side by $\boxed{}$.

$\boxed{} \approx d$ Simplify.

Answer: The diameter of the rug will be about $\boxed{}$.

Guided Practice Solve the following problem.

4. The circumference of a circle is 100.48 meters. Find the circle's diameter.

Area of a Circle

Goal: Find the areas of circles.

Area of a Circle

Words The area A of a circle is the product of [ ]

and [_____].

Algebra [ ] = [ ]

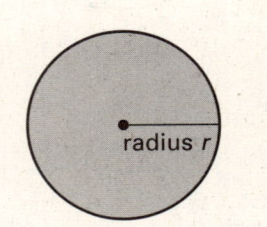

radius r

EXAMPLE 1 Finding the Area of a Circle

Find the area of the circle to the right. Use 3.14 for π.

$A = \pi r^2$ — Write formula for area of a circle.

$\approx \left(\boxed{} \right) \boxed{}$ — Substitute [ ] for π and [ ] for r.

$= \boxed{}$ — Simplify.

Answer: The area of the circle is about [_____].

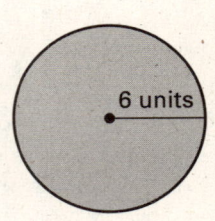

6 units

EXAMPLE 2 Finding the Area of a Circle

Irrigation A farmer uses an irrigation system to water his crops. The diameter of the circle formed by the system is 54 feet. Find the area of the irrigated area.

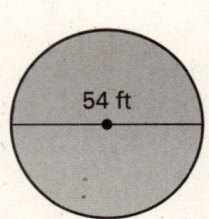

54 ft

Solution

1. Find the radius.

$r = \boxed{} = \boxed{}$ ft

2. Find the area.

$A = \pi r^2$ — Write formula for area of a circle.

$\approx \left(\boxed{} \right) \boxed{}$ — Substitute 3.14 for π and [ ] for r.

$\approx \boxed{}$ — Simplify.

Answer: The area of the irrigated area is about [_____].

Find the area of the circle. Use $\frac{22}{7}$ or 3.14 for π.

1.

12 m

2.

35 yd

3.

13 ft

EXAMPLE 3 **Standardized Test Practice**

Which expression can be evaluated to find the radius of a circle that has an area of 1384.74 square meters.

A $\dfrac{1384.74}{\pi}$

B $\pi(1384.74)^2$

C $\sqrt{\dfrac{1384.74}{\pi}}$

D $\sqrt{1384.74\pi}$

Solution

$A = \pi r^2$ Write formula for area of a circle.

$\boxed{} = \pi r^2$ Substitute $\boxed{}$ for A.

$\dfrac{1384.74}{\pi} = \boxed{}$ Simplify.

$\sqrt{\dfrac{1384.74}{\pi}} = \boxed{}$ Take positive square root of each side.

$\boxed{} \approx \boxed{}$ Evaluate square root.

Answer: The radius of the circle is $\boxed{}$, which is about

. The correct answer is .   **A**   **B**   **C**   **D**

Words to Review

Give an example of the vocabulary word.

Square root

Perfect square (square numbers)

Radical expression

Irrational number

Real number

Hypotenuse

Leg

Pythagorean theorem

Base of a parallelogram

Height of a parallelogram

Base of a triangle

Height of a triangle

Bases of a trapezoid

Height of a trapezoid

Circle

Center

Radius

Diameter

Circumference

Review your notes and Chapter 11 by using the Chapter Review on pages 619–622 of your textbook.

Classifying Solids

Goal: Classify solids and identify their parts.

Vocabulary

Solid:

Prism:

Pyramid:

Cylinder:

Cone:

Sphere:

Face:

Edge:

Vertex:

EXAMPLE 1 **Classifying Solids**

Classify the solid as a *prism*, *pyramid*, *cylinder*, *cone*, or *sphere*.

a.  b.  c.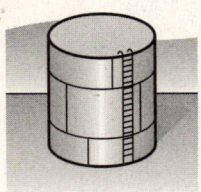

Solution

  a. The baseball is a [   ].

  b. The trunk is a [   ].

  c. The water tower is a [   ].

EXAMPLE 2 **Standardized Test Practice**

Geometry Which solid is made up of two congruent, parallel pentagons and 5 rectangles?

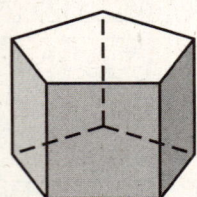

  Ⓐ Pentagonal pyramid   Ⓑ Pentagonal prism

  Ⓒ Rectangular prism   Ⓓ Hexagonal prism

Solution

A prism is a solid made up of polygons with two [   ], [   ]

bases. When its base is a pentagon, a prism is a [   ].

Answer: A [   ] is made up of two [   ],

[   ] pentagons and 5 rectangles. The correct answer is [   ].

  Ⓐ   Ⓑ   Ⓒ   Ⓓ

EXAMPLE 3 **Counting Faces, Edges and Vertices**

Count the number of faces, edges, and vertices in the triangular pyramid.

Dashed lines are used to show hidden edges of a solid.

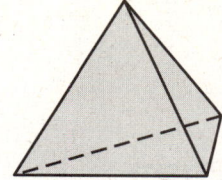 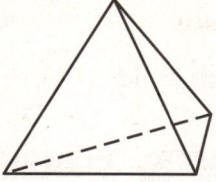 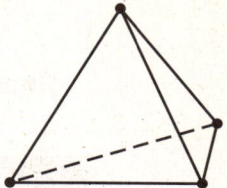

Answer: The pyramid has ⬚ faces, ⬚ edges, and ⬚ vertices.

Guided Practice Classify the solid. Be as specific as possible.

1.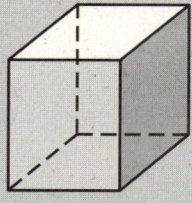

2.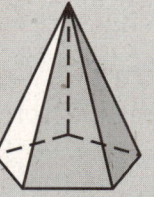

3.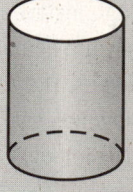

4. Count the number of faces, edges, and vertices in the solid in Exercise 1.

Sketching Solids

Goal: Sketch solids.

EXAMPLE 1 **Sketching a Prism**

Sketch a hexagonal prism.

1. Sketch two congruent hexagons.

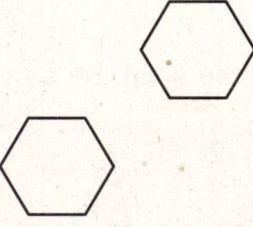

In Example 1, notice that six of the faces appear to be parallelograms even though they are actually rectangles. The parallelograms give the illusion of depth.

2. Connect the corresponding vertices using line segments.

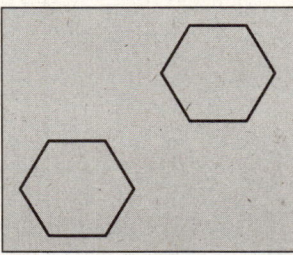

3. Make any "hidden" lines dashed.

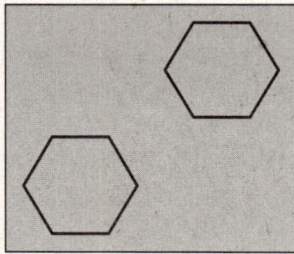

Guided Practice **Sketch the solid.**

1. Rectangular prism	**2.** Pentagonal prism

EXAMPLE 2   **Sketching a Pyramid**

Sketch a triangular pyramid.

1. Sketch a triangle for the base and draw a dot directly above the triangle.

2. Connect the vertices of the triangle to the dot.

3. Make any "hidden" lines dashed.

EXAMPLE 3   **Sketching Three Views of a Solid**

Sketch the top, side, and front views of the cylinder.

Solution

The top view of a cylinder is a ⬚.

The side view of a cylinder is a ⬚.

The front view of a cylinder is a ⬚.

Guided Practice   Complete the following exercises.

3. Sketch a pentagonal pyramid.

4. Sketch the top, side, and front views of the pentagonal pyramid you sketched in Exercise 3.

Surface Area of Rectangular Prisms

Goal: Find the surface area of rectangular prisms.

Vocabulary

Surface Area:

Net:

EXAMPLE 1 **Finding Surface Area Using a Net**

Find the surface area of the rectangular prism.

1. Find the area of each face.

   Area of top or bottom: ☐ = ☐

   Area of front or back: ☐ = ☐

   Area of either side: ☐ = ☐

   8 in.   2 in.   3 in.

   3 in.

   8 in.   2 in.   8 in.   2 in.

2. Add the areas of all six faces.

   ☐ = ☐

Answer: The surface area of the prism is ☐ .

Surface Area of a Rectangular Prism

Words The surface area *S* of a rectangular prism is the ☐ .

h   *w*   *ℓ*

Algebra ☐ = ☐

EXAMPLE 2 Finding Surface Area Using a Formula

Find the surface area of the rectangular prism.

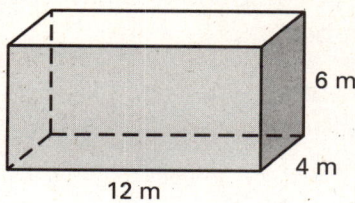

$S = 2\ell w + 2\ell h + 2wh$ Write formula for surface area.

$= 2\left(\boxed{}\right)\left(\boxed{}\right) + 2\left(\boxed{}\right)\left(\boxed{}\right)$ Substitute $\boxed{}$ for ℓ, $\boxed{}$ for

$+ 2\left(\boxed{}\right)\left(\boxed{}\right)$ w, and $\boxed{}$ for h.

$= \boxed{} + \boxed{} + \boxed{}$ Multiply.

$= \boxed{}$ Add.

Answer: The surface area of the prism is $\boxed{}$.

Guided Practice Find the surface area of the rectangular prism. Check your answer by finding the area of the prism's net.

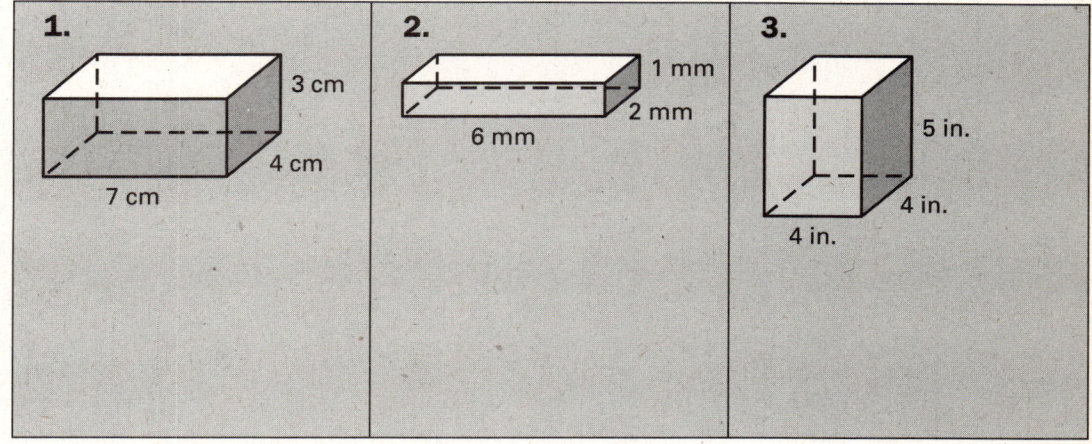

1. 3 cm, 4 cm, 7 cm

2. 1 mm, 2 mm, 6 mm

3. 5 in., 4 in., 4 in.

EXAMPLE 3 **Using Surface Area**

Gift Wrap Leann is wrapping a present for her father. She has 15 square feet of wrapping paper. Does she have enough wrapping paper to cover the box?

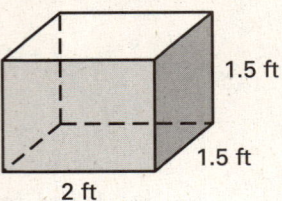

1.5 ft

1.5 ft

2 ft

Solution

1. Find the surface area of the box.

$S = 2\ell w + 2\ell h + 2wh$ Write formula.

$= 2()() + 2()() + 2()()$ Substitute values.

$= $ Simplify.

2. Compare the surface area to the amount of gift wrap Leann has.

Answer: Leann _____ have enough wrapping paper.

Surface Area of Cylinders

Goal: Find the surface area of cylinders.

Surface Area of a Cylinder

Words The surface area S of a cylinder is the [ ] of the area of the [ ] and the areas of the [ ].

Algebra [ ] = [ ]

EXAMPLE 1 **Finding the Surface Area of a Cylinder**

Find the surface area of the cylinder. Use 3.14 for π.

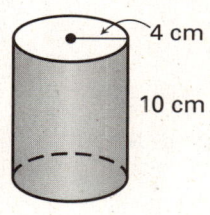

4 cm

10 cm

Solution

$$S = 2\pi rh + 2\pi r^2 \qquad \text{Write formula.}$$

$$\approx 2\big(\ \big)\big(\ \big)\big(\ \big) + 2\big(\ \big)\ \qquad \text{Substitute values.}$$

$$= \boxed{} + \boxed{} \qquad \text{Multiply.}$$

$$\approx \boxed{} \qquad \text{Add.}$$

Answer: The surface area is about [   ].

EXAMPLE **2** **Finding the Height of a Cylinder**

Water Heater A company manufactures covers for cylindrical water heaters to help save energy and retain heat. The water heater has a radius of 1.5 feet. The cover uses 45 square feet of insulated fabric. Find the height of the cylinder. Use 3.14 for π.

Solution

$S = 2\pi rh + 2\pi r^2$ Write formula for surface area.

[ ] $\approx 2($ [ ] $)($ [ ] $)h + 2($ [ ] $)$ [ ]   Substitute values.

[ ] $\approx$ [ ] $+$ [ ]   Multiply.

[ ] $-$ [ ] $\approx$ [ ] $+$ [ ] $-$ [ ]   Subtract [ ] from each side.

[ ] $\approx$ [ ]   Simplify.

$\dfrac{[\ ]}{[\ ]} \approx \dfrac{[\ ]}{[\ ]}$ Divide each side by [ ].

[ ] $\approx h$ Simplify.

Answer: The height of the water heater is about [ ].

Guided Practice **Find the surface area of the cylinder. Use 3.14 for π.**

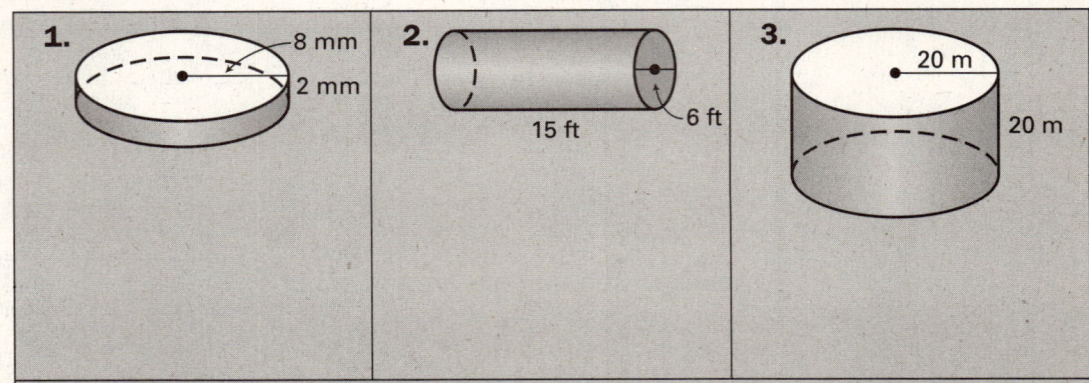

1. 8 mm, 2 mm

2. 15 ft, 6 ft

3. 20 m, 20 m

4. Find the height of a cylinder that has a radius of 9 meters and a surface area of 791 square meters. Use 3.14 for π. Round your answer to the nearest meter.

Volume of Rectangular Prisms

Goal: Find the volume of rectangular prisms.

Vocabulary

Volume: [   ]

Volume of a Rectangular Prism

Words The volume V of a rectangular prism is the

[   ] of the [   ], [   ], and [   ].

Algebra [   ] = [   ]

EXAMPLE 1 **Volume of a Rectangular Prism**

Freezer The Gilbert family has a chest freezer that has a length of 48 inches, a width of 30 inches, and a height of 36 inches. What is the volume of the freezer?

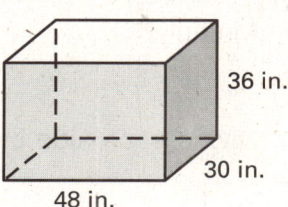

36 in.

30 in.

48 in.

Solution

$V = \ell wh$ Write formula for volume of a rectangular prism.

$= ()()()$ Substitute [   ] for ℓ, [   ] for w, and [   ] for h.

$= $ Multiply.

Answer: The freezer will hold [   ].

Guided Practice Find the volume of the rectangular prism.

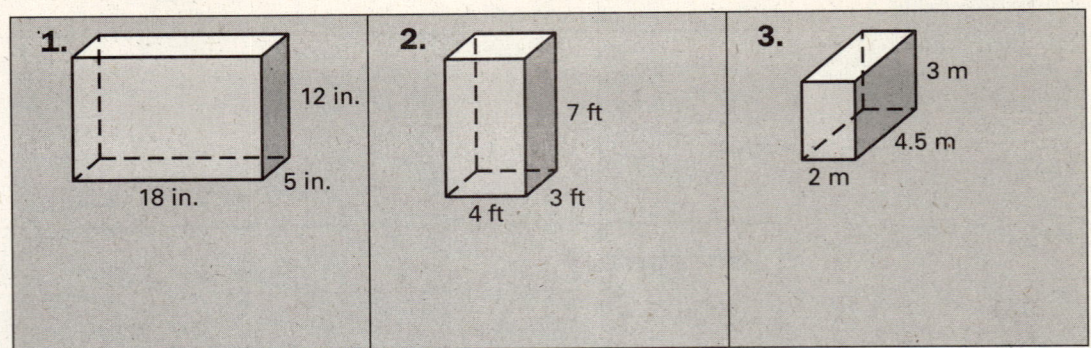

1.	2.	3.
12 in. 18 in. 5 in.	7 ft 4 ft 3 ft	3 m 4.5 m 2 m

EXAMPLE 2 **Finding the Height of a Rectangular Prism**

The rectangular prism shown has a volume of 2052 cubic millimeters. Find the prism's height.

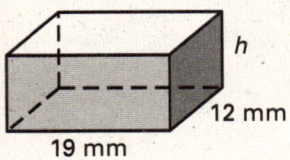

h
12 mm
19 mm

Solution

$V = \ell wh$ Write formula for volume of a rectangular prism.

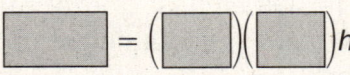   Substitute [　] for V, [　] for ℓ, and [　] for w.

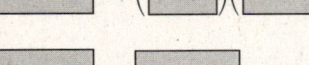   Multiply.

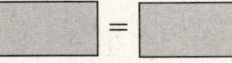   Divide each side by [　].

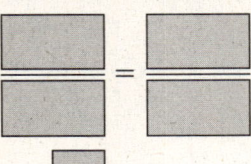

 $= h$ Simplify.

Answer: The height of the prism is [　　　　].

Find the unknown length, width, or height of the rectangular prism.

4. $V = 144$ ft^3, $\ell = \underline{}$, $w = 3$ ft, $h = 6$ ft

5. $V = 308$ cm^3, $\ell = 7$ cm, $w = \underline{}$, $h = 11$ cm

6. $V = 78$ m^3, $\ell = 6.5$ m, $w = 4$ m, $h = \underline{}$

EXAMPLE 3   Using the Volume of a Rectangular Prism

Snack Mix A cereal box is 6 inches long, 10 inches tall, and 1.5 inches wide. Marta is mixing a snack mix in a tin canister that holds 585 cubic inches. How many boxes of cereal will Marta open in order to fill her container?

Solution

1. Find the volume of the cereal box.

$V = \ell wh$

$= ()()()$

$= \boxed{}$ in.^{3}

2. To find the number of cereal boxes Marta will open, divide $\boxed{}$ cubic inches by $\boxed{}$ cubic inches.

$\boxed{}$ in.$^3 \div \boxed{}$ in.$^3 = \boxed{}$

Answer: Because it doesn't make sense to open $\boxed{}$ boxes, Marta must open $\boxed{}$ boxes of cereal to fill the container.

Volume of Cylinders

Goal: Find the volume of cylinders.

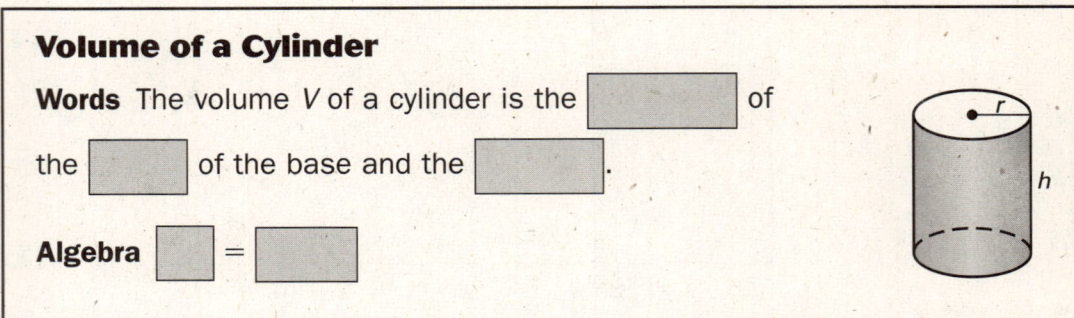

Volume of a Cylinder

Words The volume V of a cylinder is the [ ] of the [ ] of the base and the [ ].

Algebra [ ] = [ ]

EXAMPLE 1 **Standardized Test Practice**

What is the volume of the cylinder? Use 3.14 for π.

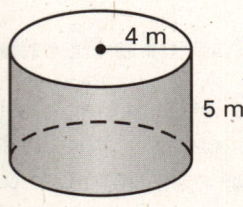

4 m

5 m

A 62.8 m³

B 251.2 m³

C 314 m³

D 1256 m³

You have learned many properties and formulas related to solids. Writing a summary of what you have learned may help you prepare for the chapter test.

Solution

$V = \pi r^2 h$ Write formula for volume of a cylinder.

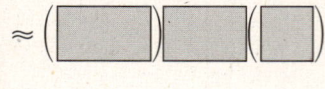 $\approx$ ([ ] [ ] [ ])   Substitute [ ] for π, [ ] for r, and [ ] for h.

 = [ ]   Multiply.

Answer: The volume of the cylinder is about 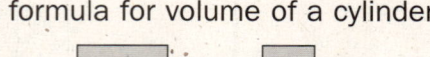.

The correct answer is . **A** **B** **C** **D**

EXAMPLE **2** **Comparing Volumes of Cylinders**

Tomato Sauce Carlos found two cans of tomato sauce in the pantry. One can has a diameter of 4 inches and a height of 5 inches. The second one has a diameter of 3 inches and a height of 6 inches. Which can has the greater volume?

Solution

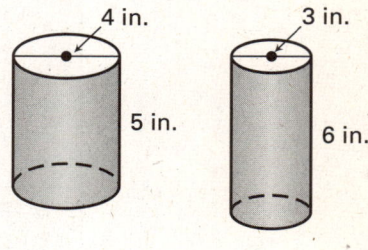

1. Find the radius of each can, which is half of the diameter.

   Can 1: $r = \boxed{} = \boxed{}$ in.

   Can 2: $r = \boxed{} = \boxed{}$ in.

2. Find the volume of each can. Use 3.14 for π.

Can 1:	**Can 2:**
$V = \pi r^2 h$	$V = \pi r^2 h$
$\approx (\boxed{}\ \boxed{})\ \boxed{}$	$\approx (\boxed{}\ \boxed{})\ \boxed{}$
$= \boxed{}$ in.^{3}	$= \boxed{}$ in.^{3}

   Answer: Can $\boxed{}$ has the greater volume.

WATCH OUT!

Make sure to use the radius, not the diameter, in the formula for volume of a cylinder.

EXAMPLE **3** **Finding the Radius of a Cylinder**

A cylinder has a height of 12 feet and a volume of 3768 cubic feet. Find the radius of the cylinder. Use 3.14 for π.

Need help with solving equations using square roots? See page 579 of your textbook.

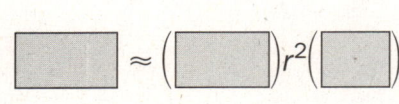

$$V = \pi r^2 h$$

Write formula for volume of a cylinder.

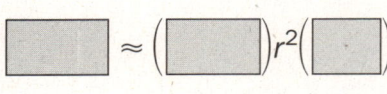

$$\boxed{} \approx (\boxed{})r^2(\boxed{})$$

Substitute $\boxed{}$ for V, $\boxed{}$ for π, and $\boxed{}$ for h.

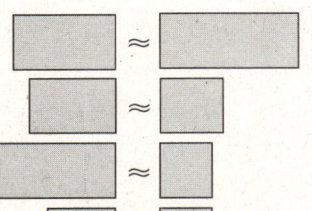

$$\boxed{} \approx \boxed{}$$

Multiply.

$$\boxed{} \approx \boxed{}$$

Divide each side by $\boxed{}$.

$$\boxed{} \approx \boxed{}$$

Take positive square root of each side.

$$\boxed{} \approx \boxed{}$$

Evaluate square root.

Answer: The radius of the cylinder is about $\boxed{}$.

Guided Practice Find the volume of the cylinder. Use 3.14 for π.

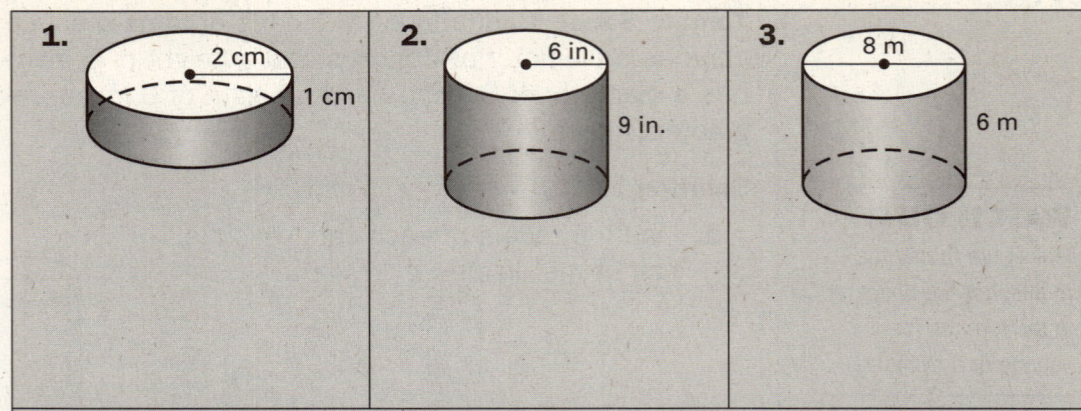

1.
2 cm
1 cm

2.
6 in.
9 in.

3.
8 m
6 m

4. Find the radius of a cylinder that has a height of 7 inches and a volume of 351.68 cubic inches. Use 3.14 of π.

Words to Review

Give an example of the vocabulary word.

Solid

Prism

Pyramid

Cylinder

Cone

Sphere

Face

Edge

Vertex

Surface area

Net

Volume

Review your notes and Chapter 12 by using the Chapter Review on pages 669–672 of your textbook.

Introduction to Probability

Goal: Find probabilities.

Vocabulary

Outcomes:

Event:

Favorable outcomes:

Probability:

Theoretical probability:

Experimental probability:

EXAMPLE 1 **Finding a Probability**

Find the probability of randomly choosing a striped ball from the balls shown at the right.

Solution

$P(\text{striped}) = \dfrac{\boxed{}}{\boxed{}}$ ⟵ There are ☐ striped balls.

⟵ There are ☐ balls in all.

You can write probabilities as fractions, decimals, or percents.

Answer: The probability of randomly choosing a striped ball is ☐ , ☐ , or ☐ .

1. From the balls in Example 1, you randomly choose a spotted ball.

2. You get heads when you flip a coin.

3. You get a multiple of 3 when you roll a number cube.

EXAMPLE 2 **Finding an Experimental Probability**

Guests Robert tracked whether guests knocked on his door or rang his doorbell and wrote his results in the table at the right. Find the probability that the next guest will ring the doorbell.

Doorbell	15
Knock	10

1. Determine the number of successes and the number of trials.

Because a success is [ ], there are [ ] successes.

There are [ ] + [ ] = [ ] trials.

2. Find the probability.

$P(\text{doorbell}) = \dfrac{\boxed{}}{\boxed{}}$ ⟵ There are [ ] successes.

⟵ There are [ ] trials.

$= \dfrac{\boxed{}}{\boxed{}}$

Answer: The probability that the next guest will ring the doorbell

is [ ], [ ], or [ ].

4. In Example 2, what is the probability that the next guest will knock on the door?

5. At an auto dealership, of the last 150 vehicles purchased, 45 were sport utility vehicles. Find the probability that the next purchase will be a sport utility vehicle.

EXAMPLE 3 **Standardized Test Practice**

Cell Phones A survey of 150 twelve to seventeen year olds indicates that 48 of them have a cell phone. Which equation could you use to predict the number of twelve to seventeen year olds out of 1000 who have a cell phone?

Ⓐ $\dfrac{48}{150} = \dfrac{1000}{x}$

Ⓑ $\dfrac{48}{1000} = \dfrac{x}{150}$

Ⓒ $\dfrac{48}{150} = \dfrac{x}{1000}$

Ⓓ $\dfrac{150}{48} = \dfrac{x}{1000}$

Solution

You can solve the problem by using ratios to form a proportion.

$$\boxed{} = \boxed{}$$

$$\boxed{} = \boxed{}$$

Answer: You can solve $\boxed{} = \boxed{}$ to predict that $\boxed{}$ out of 1000

twelve to seventeen year olds have a cell phone. The correct answer is $\boxed{}$.

Ⓐ Ⓑ Ⓒ Ⓓ

Tree Diagrams

Goal: Use a tree diagram to find all possible outcomes.

Vocabulary

Tree diagram:

EXAMPLE 1 Making a Tree Diagram

Sandwich Shop A sandwich shop has a daily special where customers can choose from ham, turkey, or roast beef. Customers can then choose between Swiss cheese and cheddar cheese. Make a tree diagram to find all the possibilities of sandwiches.

Solution

List the meats.   List the choices of cheese for each meat.   List the outcomes.

ham — Swiss
    — cheddar

Answer: There are ☐ different choices of sandwiches.

1. At a children's photography studio, parents can choose from pink, blue, black, or white for the background color and a rocking horse, a truck, or a doll for the prop. How many choices of photographs do parents have?

EXAMPLE 2 **Making a Tree Diagram**

Camp Scheduling You are scheduling your afternoon activities at camp. The activities are at 1:00 P.M. and 3:00 P.M., and the choices are crafts, rappelling, weight lifting, horseback riding, and music. If you must choose two different activities, how many afternoon activity schedules are possible?

Solution

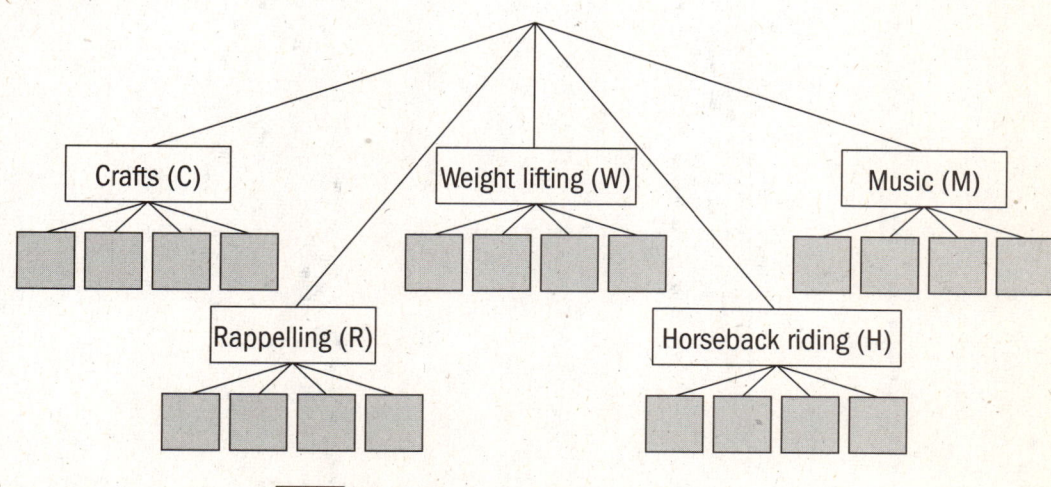

Answer: There are ⬜ possible schedules.

EXAMPLE 3 **Using a Tree Diagram**

A sack has three chips in it: a red chip, a blue chip, and a green chip. To find the probability of randomly drawing the same chip when drawing a chip from the sack, replacing it, and drawing again, make a tree diagram to find the outcomes.

Solution

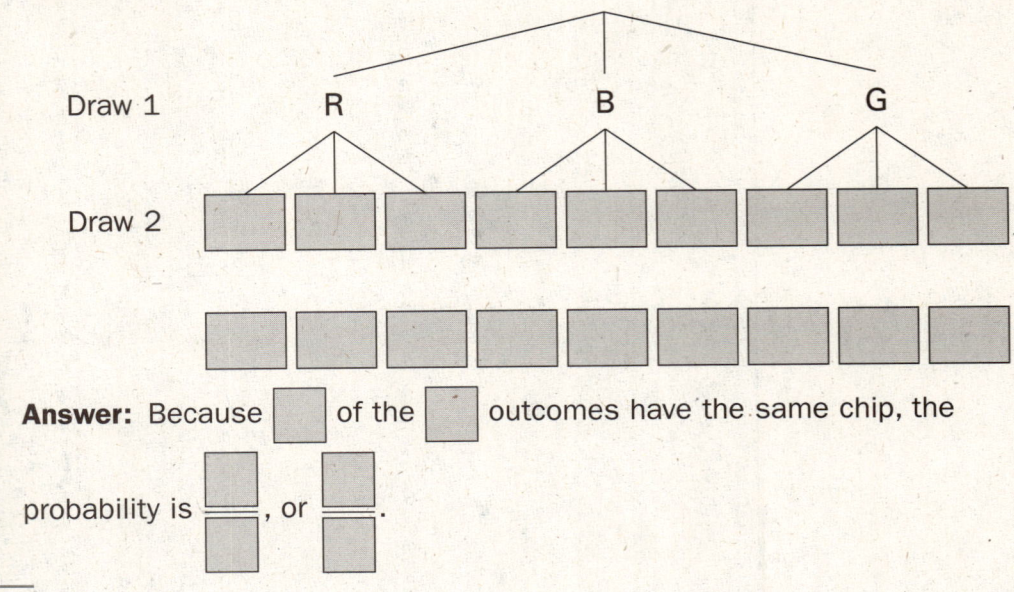

Draw 1   R   B   G

Draw 2

Answer: Because ☐ of the ☐ outcomes have the same chip, the

probability is $\dfrac{☐}{☐}$, or $\dfrac{☐}{☐}$.

Guided Practice **Use a tree diagram to find the probability.**

2. You roll a number cube and flip a coin. What is the probability that you roll a number greater than 4 and heads?

The Counting Principle

LESSON 13.3

Goal: Use the counting principle to find outcomes.

> ### The Counting Principle
>
> If one event can occur in *m* ways, and for each of these a second event can occur is *n* ways, then the number of ways that the two events can occur together is [ ].
>
> The counting principle can be extended to three or more events.

EXAMPLE 1 Using the Counting Principle

Dance Toward the end of a school dance, the disc jockey has three ballads, five pop songs, and two jazz songs to choose from. How many different choices does the disc jockey have if one ballad, one pop song, and one jazz song are to be played?

Number of ballads	×	Number of pop songs	×	Number of jazz songs	=	Number of choices
[ ]	×	[ ]	×	[ ]	=	[ ]

Answer: The disc jockey has [ ] choices.

EXAMPLE 2 Using the Counting Principle

License Plates How many different 6 character license plates are possible, if each character can be a digit or a letter and can be repeated?

Solution

Use the counting principle to find the number of different license plates.

There are [ ] + [ ] = [ ] choices for each character.

[ ] × [ ] × [ ] × [ ] × [ ] × [ ] = [ ]

Answer: There are [ ] possible license plates.

EXAMPLE 3 Finding a Probability

Student Identification Numbers Students at a small college are assigned student identification numbers. The IDs are made up of five digits. If the digits can be repeated, what is the probability that a randomly chosen student will be assigned the ID number 12345?

Solution

1. Find the number of different ID numbers.

$$\boxed{} \times \boxed{} \times \boxed{} \times \boxed{} \times \boxed{} = \boxed{}$$

Use the counting principle.

2. Find the probability that the ID number is 12345.

$P(12345) = \boxed{}$ Only $\boxed{}$ of the outcomes is 12345.

Answer: The probability that a randomly chosen student will be assigned the

ID number 12345 is $\boxed{}$.

WATCH OUT!

In both Example 2 and Example 3, notice that the digits 0 through 9 represent 10 digits, not 9 digits.

Guided Practice Use the counting principle to solve the problem.

1. You have 36 baseball cards, 20 from American League teams and 16 from National League teams. How many outcomes are possible if you randomly choose 1 American League card and 1 National League card?

2. You spin a spinner with 6 different numbers (1 through 6) and another spinner with 8 different numbers (1 through 8). How many different outcomes are possible?

3. In Exercise 2, what is the probability that the first spinner lands on 3 and the second spinner lands on 7?

Permutations and Combinations

Goal: Use permutations and combinations.

Vocabulary

Permutation:

Combination:

EXAMPLE 1 **Counting Permutations**

Basketball Five players are introduced as the starting players of a basketball team. How many ways can the five players be introduced?

Solution

Use the counting principle.

Choices for first player	×	Choices for second player	×	Choices for third player	×	Choices for fourth player	×	Choices for fifth player	=	Ways to introduce players
☐	×	☐	×	☐	×	☐	×	☐	=	☐

Answer: There are ☐ different ways to introduce the players.

EXAMPLE 2 **Counting Permutations**

Spelling Bee There were 47 children entered in this year's city-wide spelling bee. In how many ways could the first, second, and third places be awarded?

Solution

Choices for first place	×	Choices for second place	×	Choices for third place	=	Ways to award first, second, and third place
☐	×	☐	×	☐	=	☐

Answer: There were ☐ ways to award first, second, and third place.

1. In how many ways can you arrange the letters in the word HOLIDAY?

2. There are 10 runners in a long distance race. In how many ways can the runners place first, second, and third?

EXAMPLE 3 **Listing Combinations**

Errands Maurice's mom asks him to choose two errands to run. He can pick from the grocery store (GS), the dry cleaners (DC), the car wash (CW), the post office (PO), and City Hall (CH). How many different choices does Maurice have if the order in which the errands are done does not matter?

In Example 3, you can use a tree diagram to find the permutations of 2 errands. Then cross out one of any pair of permutations that lists the same two errands.

Solution

Start by listing all of the permutations of 2 errands. Because the order in which Maurice chooses the errands does not matter, cross out one of any pair of permutations that lists the same two errands.

Answer: Maurice has [ ] different choices for running two errands.

EXAMPLE 4 **Relating Combinations and Permutations**

Vacation Allison is packing for a vacation. She owns 16 pairs of shoes, and plans on taking 3 pairs with her. How many choices does she have?

Solution

Because the order in which the pairs of shoes are chosen does not matter, you need to find the number of combinations.

1. Find the number of permutations when choosing 3 pairs from 16.

$$\boxed{} = \boxed{}$$

2. Find the number of permutations when arranging 3 objects.

$$\boxed{} = \boxed{}$$

3. Divide the number of permutations when choosing 3 pairs of shoes from 16 by the number of permutations when arranging 3 objects.

$$\boxed{} = \boxed{}$$

Answer: Allison has $\boxed{}$ choices.

Guided Practice **Find the number of combinations.**

3. You want to see 6 different movies over spring break, but only have money to see 3. How many choices do you have if the order in which you see them is not important?

4. Your city is offering Museum Day, where you can visit any of the 12 museums for free. You have time to visit 4 museums. How many ways can you choose 4 museums if the order in which you visit them is not important?

Disjoint Events

Goal: Find the probability that either of two events occurs.

Vocabulary

Disjoint events:

Overlapping events:

Complementary events:

EXAMPLE 1 **Disjoint and Overlapping Events**

Tell whether the events involving the spinner are **disjoint** *or* **overlapping**.

Event P: Get a number greater than 4.

Event Q: Get an even number.

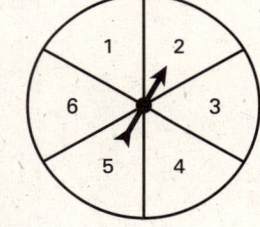

Solution

Make a list of the outcomes for each event.
Then determine whether the events have any
outcomes in common.

Event P: [   ]   List the numbers greater than 4.

Event Q: [   ]   List the even numbers.

Answer: There [   ] in common, so the events [   ].

> To help you understand the difference between disjoint and overlapping events, you can make a concept grid for each term.

Tell whether the events involving the spinner in Example 1 are *disjoint* or *overlapping*.

1. Event J: Get a prime number.
Event K: Get a number greater than 5.

Probability of Disjoint Events

Words For two disjoint events, the probability that either of the events occurs is the [ ] of the probabilities of the events.

Algebra If A and B are disjoint events, then $P(\text{A or B}) =$ [ ] .

EXAMPLE 2 **Probability of Disjoint Events**

Television Viewing The table shows the types of television shows viewed by a family in a month. What is the probability that a randomly chosen show watched by the family that month is a sitcom or a news program?

Solution

The events are disjoint because a news program is not a sitcom.

$P(\text{sitcom}) + P(\text{news}) =$ [ ] % $+$ [ ] %

$=$ [ ] %

Answer: The probability that the show is either a sitcom or a news program is [ ] %.

Show type	Percent
Cartoon	31%
Sitcom	28%
Drama	17%
News	13%
Reality	11%

2. What is the probability that a randomly chosen program is a reality program or a cartoon?

EXAMPLE 3 **Probability of Complementary Events**

Day Care Of the workers at Kids Kingdom Day Care Center, 78% of the employees have professional certifications. What is the probability that a randomly chosen employee at the center is *not* certified?

Solution

$$P(\text{not certified}) = \boxed{} - P(\text{certified}) \qquad \text{Write verbal model.}$$

$$= \boxed{} - \boxed{} \qquad \text{Substitute } \boxed{}\%, \text{ or } \boxed{},$$

$$P(\text{certified}).$$

$$= \boxed{} \qquad \text{Subtract.}$$

Answer: The probability that a randomly chosen employee is not certified is $\boxed{}$, or $\boxed{}$%.

Independent and Dependent Events

Goal: Find the probability of dependent events.

Vocabulary

Independent events:

Dependent events:

EXAMPLE 1 **Independent and Dependent Events**

A drawer contains 15 socks, 7 blue and 8 white. You close your eyes and pull out a blue sock first, then a white sock, without replacing the blue sock. Are these events independent or dependent?

Whether or not you choose a blue sock first ⬚ affect the likelihood that you choose a white sock second. This is because the ratio of blue to white socks in the drawer ⬚ after the first sock is pulled from the drawer and not put back.

Answer: The events are ⬚.

Guided Practice **A jar contains 8 red and 12 blue marbles.**

1. You randomly choose a marble, put it back, then randomly choose another marble. Are the events "choose a red marble first" and "choose a blue marble second" *independent* or *dependent*?

Probability of Independent Events

Words For two independent events, the probability that both events occur is the [____] of the probabilities of the events.

Algebra If A and B are independent events, the $P(A \text{ and } B) =$ [____].

EXAMPLE 2 **Probability of Independent Events**

Carnival Tara is playing a game at a carnival where she picks a rubber duck from a pond. There are 12 ducks in the pond for which there is no prize and 4 ducks that will award a prize. What is the probability that Tara picks a prize-winning duck, replaces the duck in the pond, then picks another prize-winning duck?

Solution

1. Find the probability of each event.

$P(\text{win}) = \dfrac{\boxed{}}{\boxed{}} = \boxed{}$ There are [____] ducks in all.

$P(\text{win}) = \dfrac{\boxed{}}{\boxed{}} = \boxed{}$ Because Tara replaces the first duck, there are [__] winning ducks for the second pick.

2. Because the events are independent, multiply the probabilities.

$P(\text{win and win}) = \boxed{}$

$= \boxed{}$

$= \boxed{}$

Answer: The probability that Tara selects 2 winning ducks from the pond in a row is [____], or [____]%.

> In common usage, being independent means being free from the control of others. This may help you remember the meaning of independent events.

Probability of Dependent Events

Words For two dependent events, the probability that both events occur is the [____] of the probability of the first event and the probability of the second event [____].

Algebra If A and B are dependent events, then $P(A \text{ and } B) =$ [____].

EXAMPLE 3 **Probability of Dependent Events**

Beverages Jeffrey's mother has 10 orange juice boxes, 7 grape juice boxes, and 3 lemonade juice boxes in the cooler for Jeffrey and his friends. Jeffrey randomly takes a juice box from the cooler, then randomly chooses another juice box without replacing the first. Find the probability that both juice boxes are grape.

Solution

Find the probability of the first event and the probability of the second event given the first. Then multiply the probabilities.

1. P(grape) = ☐   Out of ☐ juice boxes, ☐ are grape.

2. P(grape given grape) = ☐   Of the remaining ☐ juice boxes, ☐ are grape.

3. P(grape and grape) = ☐   Multiply probabilities.

        = ☐   Divide out common factor.

        = ☐   Multiply.

Answer: The probability that both juice boxes are grape is ☐.

Guided Practice **Refer to Example 3.**

2. Find the probability that both juice boxes are lemonade when the first juice box chosen is not replaced.

Words to Review

Give an example of the vocabulary word.

Outcomes

Event

Favorable outcomes

Probability

Theoretical probability

Experimental probability

Tree diagram

Permutation

Combination

Disjoint events

Overlapping events

Complementary events

Independent events

Dependent events

Review your notes and Chapter 13 by using the Chapter Review on pages 723–726 of your textbook.

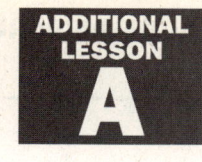

Estimation and Precision of Measurement

Goal • Use estimation strategies reasonably and fluently.

Your Notes

VOCABULARY

Estimation

When to Estimate

Precision:

Calculation of Error

Example 1 — Estimate a reasonable solution

Estimate: $\sqrt{53}$

Find the perfect square just less than 53 and the perfect square just greater than 53.

The perfect squares on either side of 53 are 49 . . . 53 . . . 64. Therefore $\sqrt{53}$ is between $\sqrt{49}$ and $\sqrt{64}$ which means the $\sqrt{53}$ is between 7 and 8.

The difference between 49 and 53 is 4, the difference between 49 and 64 is 15, the difference between 7 and $\sqrt{53}$ is "x" and the difference between 7 and 8 is 1. Solve the following proportion.

$$\frac{4}{15} = \frac{x}{1}$$

$$15x = 4$$

$$x = \frac{4}{15}$$

$$x = .266$$

Therefore $\sqrt{53} = 7.3$, with accuracy to the tenths place.

Copyright © by McDougal Littell, a division of Houghton Mifflin Company.

Example 2   **Estimate and determine a reasonable amount of error**

Estimate the measure of ∠*ABC* and ∠*FBC* in the drawing.

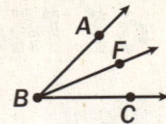

Compare ∠*ABC* with an angle of known measure such as a right angle or a straight angle.

If ∠*DBC* is a right angle, and ∠*ABC* appears to be approximately $\frac{1}{2}$ of ∠*DBC*, then ∠*ABC* is approximately 45°.

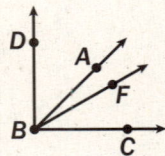

∠*FBC* is approximately $\frac{1}{3}$ of the right angle ∠*DBC*, or approximately 30°. Depending on your estimation skills, the error of the measure of the angle could be as much as 10° on either side of 30°.

Example 3   **Using tools to measure line segments and angles**

What is the measure of line segment $\overline{AB}$?

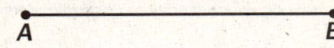

If the ruler being used has increments of eighths of an inch, the measure is approximately $1\frac{5}{8}$ inches with an error of $\frac{1}{8}$ of an inch in either direction. If the ruler is incremented in sixteenths of an inch, the measure is $1\frac{11}{16}$ inches with an error of $\frac{1}{16}$ of an inch in either direction.

What is the measure of ∠*CAB*?

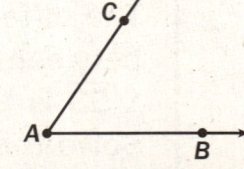

If the protractor that is being used has increments in degrees, the measure of the angle is approximately 56° with an error of 1° greater or less than 56°.

If the protractor is incremented every 5°, the angle is still approximately 56° with an error range of 5° greater or less than 56°.

Copyright © by McDougal Littell, a division of Houghton Mifflin Company.

Copyright © by McDougal Littell, a division of Houghton Mifflin Company.

Your Notes

✔ Checkpoint **Complete the following exercises.**

1. Estimate the $\sqrt{94}$.

2. Estimate the measure of $\angle CAT$.

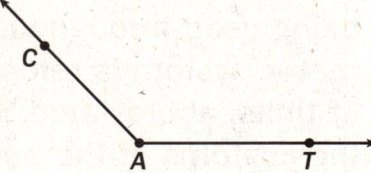

3. Measure $\angle CAT$.

4. Measure line segment $\overline{ME}$.

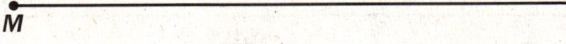

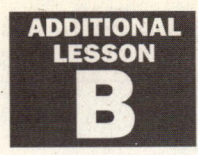

Metric/Customary Conversions

Goal • Use the Metric to Customary Converstion Tables to understand how one unit of measure relates to the other.

Your Notes

HISTORY

The metric system was developed in France in the late 18th century to replace the various systems that were being used throughout the world at that time. Today, the metric system is referred to as the International System of Units, abbreviated SI. Customary Systems grew out of the customs of the area. The system presently used in the United States is the English System and the United States is the only industrial nation using it.

ABBREVIATIONS

Customary
inch = in.
foot = ft.
mile = mi.
quart = qt.
gallon = gal.
Fahrenheit = F

Metric
centimeter = cm
meter = m
kilometer = km
liter = l or L
Celsius = C

CONVERSION TABLES

Into Metric **Into Customary**

Length						
From	multiply by	To		From	multiply by	To
in.	2.54	cm		m	39.36	in.
ft.	30.48	cm		cm	0.39	in.
mi.	1.61	km		km	0.62	mi.
Mass (Weight)						
From	multiply by	To		From	multiply by	To
qt.	.95	L		L	1.06	qt.
gal.	3.79	L		L	0.26	gal.
Temperature						
From		To		From		To
F	subtract 32 then multiply by $\frac{5}{9}$	C		C	multiply by $\frac{9}{5}$ then add 32	F

Copyright © by McDougal Littell, a division of Houghton Mifflin Company.

Example 1 Convert from Customary into Metric Units

Convert 4.56 in. to centimeters.

$$4.56 \times 2.54 = 11.58 \text{ cm}$$

Convert 5 miles to kilometers

$$5 \times 1.61 = 8.05 \text{ km}$$

Example 2 Convert from Metric into Customary Units

The Smith family is driving a rental car in Europe. They stop and put 52 liters of gas into the car. They are surprised at such a large number for the amount of gas. Determine the number of gallons they used.

$$52 \times 0.26 = 13.52 \text{ gallons}$$

Example 3 Convert from Celsius (C) to Fahrenheit (F)

As they were driving through a small town, they noticed a sign at the bank indicating that the temperature was 10°. Knowing that Celsius is the unit used in Europe for temperature, what is the Fahrenheit equivalent?

$$10 \times \frac{9}{5} = 18.0, \ 18.0 + 32 = 50.0°F$$

Copyright © by McDougal Littell, a division of Houghton Mifflin Company.

You are planning on taking a trip to Canada and driving through the country for two weeks. In order to budget enough money for the trip, you need to determine the cost of gas. You have found out that the average cost of gas in Canada is $0.78 per liter (Canadian Dollars). What is the cost of gas in gallons (in Canadian dollars)? You have also calculated that you will be driving approximately 1890 kilometers on your trip. How many miles will you be driving?

The average temperature in Canada at the time of your trip is 23°C. Are you going to dress for warm or cold weather? Determine the temperature in Fahrenheit.

Copyright © by McDougal Littell, a division of Houghton Mifflin Company.

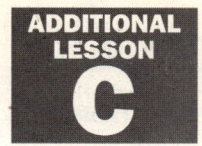

Rules of Exponents

Goal • Use laws of exponents to simplify.

Product of Powers Property

Words To multiply powers with the same base, add their exponents.

Algebra $a^m \cdot a^n = a^{m+n}$

Numbers $4^5 \cdot 4^3 = 4^{5+3} = 4^8$

Example 1   Using the Product of Powers Property

$x^2 \cdot x^8 = x^{2+8}$ Product of powers property

$ = x^{10}$ Add exponents.

Example 2   Using the Product of Powers Property

$2^4 x^3 \cdot 2x^4 = (2^4 \cdot 2) \cdot (x^3 \cdot x^4)$ Use properties of multiplication.

$ = 2^{4+1} \cdot x^{3+4}$ Product of powers property

$ = 2^5 x^7$ Add exponents.

$ = 32x^7$ Evaluate the power.

Quotient of Powers Property

Words To divide two powers with the same nonzero base, subtract the exponent of the denominator from the exponent of the numerator.

Algebra $\dfrac{a^m}{a^n} = a^{m-n}$ **Numbers** $\dfrac{6^8}{6^6} = 6^{8-6} = 6^2$

Copyright © by McDougal Littell, a division of Houghton Mifflin Company.

Example 3 — Using the Quotient of Powers Property

Simplify the expression. Write your answer as a power.

a. $\dfrac{x^{11}}{x^3} = x^{11-3}$ Quotient of powers property

      $= x^8$ Subtract exponents.

b. $\dfrac{7^9}{7^6} = 7^{9-6}$ Quotient of powers property

      $= 7^3$ Subtract exponents.

Your Notes

✔ **Checkpoint** Complete the following exercises.

Simplify the expression. Write your answer as a power.

1. $m^{10} \cdot m^5$

2. $3^7 \cdot 3^2$

3. $\dfrac{x^{12}}{x^4}$

4. $\dfrac{8^9}{8^8}$

Example 4 — Simplifying Fractions with Powers

a. $\dfrac{t^6 \cdot t^2}{t} = \dfrac{t^8}{t}$ Simplify numerator using product of powers property.

      $= t^{8-1}$ Quotient of powers property

      $= t^7$ Subtract exponents.

b. $\dfrac{m^3 n^5}{n^4} = m^3 n^{5-4}$ Quotient of powers property

      $= m^3 n$ Subtract exponents.

Your Notes

✔ **Checkpoint** Complete the following exercises.

Simplify the expression. Write your answer as a power.

5. $\dfrac{a \cdot a^7}{a^4}$

6. $\dfrac{5^8 \cdot 5^5}{5^{10}}$

7. $\dfrac{q^9}{pq^3}$

8. $\dfrac{x^{12} y^{12}}{y^5}$

Copyright © by McDougal Littell, a division of Houghton Mifflin Company.

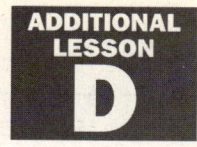

Introduction to Recursive Functions for Sequences

Goal • Evaluate problems using basic recursive formulas.

Your Notes

VOCABULARY

Sequence

Recursive

Recursive formula

Term notation

Example 1 **Write terms of sequences**

a. Write the first 6 terms of the sequence 1, 4, 7, . . . where $t_n = t_{n-1} + 3$, that is, any term is determined by adding 3 to the previous term.

$t_4 = t_3 + 3 \qquad t_4 = 7 + 3 = 10$

$t_5 = t_4 + 3 \qquad t_5 = 10 + 3 = 13$

$t_6 = t_5 + 3 \qquad t_6 = 13 + 3 = 16$

Thus the first 6 terms are 1, 4, 7, 10, 13, 16

b. Write the first 5 terms of the sequence 1, 2, 5, . . . where $t_n = (t_{n-1})^2 + 1$, that is, 1 is added to the previous term squared .

$t_4 = (t_3)^2 + 1 \qquad t_4 = 5^2 + 1 = 25 + 1 = 26$

$t_5 = (t_4)^2 + 1 \qquad t_5 = 26^2 + 1 = 676 + 1 = 677$

Thus the first 5 terms are 1, 2, 5, 26, 677

Copyright © by McDougal Littell, a division of Houghton Mifflin Company.

✔ *Checkpoint* **Complete the following exercises.**

1. Write the first 6 terms of the sequence 1, 5, . . . where
$t_n = t_{n-1} + 4$

2. The *Fibonacci numbers* are shown below. Use the Fibonacci numbers to answer the following questions.

$$1, 1, 2, 3, 5, 8, 13, 21, 34, 55, 89 \ldots$$

a. Copy and complete: After the first two numbers, each number is the _____ of the _____ previous numbers.

b. Write the next three numbers in the pattern.

| **Example 2** | **Write a rule for the *n*th term of a sequence** |

Find the *n*th term, that is, the formula or rule that is used to determine the next term in the sequence 1, 3, 7, 15, 31, 63 . . .

Examine each term. How do you get the second term from the first? How do you get the third term from the second? And so on.

$1 \times 2 + 1 = 3$

$3 \times 2 + 1 = 7$

$7 \times 2 + 1 = 15$

$15 \times 2 + 1 = 31$

$31 \times 2 + 1 = 63$

The previous term is multiplied by 2 and 1 is added to it.

The *n*th term $t_n = 2(t_{n-1}) + 1$

Copyright © by McDougal Littell, a division of Houghton Mifflin Company.

Checkpoint **Complete the following exercise.**

1. Find the *n*th term, that is, the formula for determining the next term for the sequence 1, 6, 11, 16, 21, 26 . . .

Copyright © by McDougal Littell, a division of Houghton Mifflin Company.

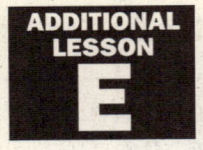

Vertex-Edge Graphs, Circuits, Networks, and Routing

Your Notes

Goal • Use vertex-edge graphs to represent and find solutions to practical problems.

VOCABULARY

Graph

Vertex

Edge

Adjacent Vertices

Adjacent Edges

Degree of a vertex

Path

Circuit

Ordinal

Subscript

Route

Network

Copyright © by McDougal Littell, a division of Houghton Mifflin Company.

If a graph has any odd vertices, then it cannot be a circuit (starting and ending at the same point and traveling over each edge only once). If a graph has more than two odd vertices, then it cannot have a path.

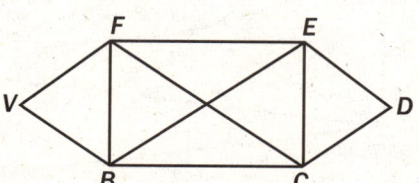

Degree of each vertex

$A = 2$ Since all of the vertices
$B = 4$ are even, the figure can
$C = 4$ be traced starting at
$D = 2$ one vertex returning to
       the same vertex without
$E = 4$ tracing over one edge
$F = 4$ more than once.

Copyright © by McDougal Littell, a division of Houghton Mifflin Company.

Your Notes

✔ *Checkpoint* **Complete the following exercises.**

Find the degree of each vertex and determine if the graph is a circuit. Trace the graph and show that it forms a circuit or a path.

1. 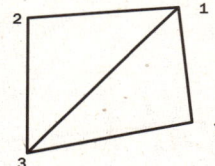   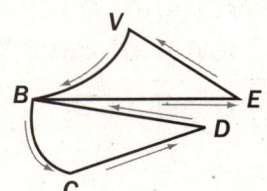

2. Place appropriate letters on this graph using subscript notation. Find the degree of each vertex and determine if the graph is a circuit. Trace the graph and show that it forms a circuit or a path.

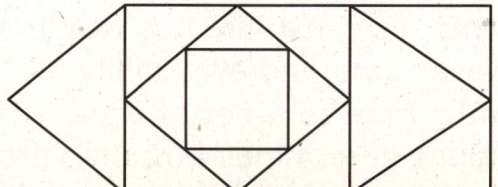

Example 2

Determine if a network presents the best route basing the solution on the number of vertices and edges

The following network shows several cities and the paths connecting them. The vertices represent cities and the edges indicate nonstop airline routes between them.

Drawing 1

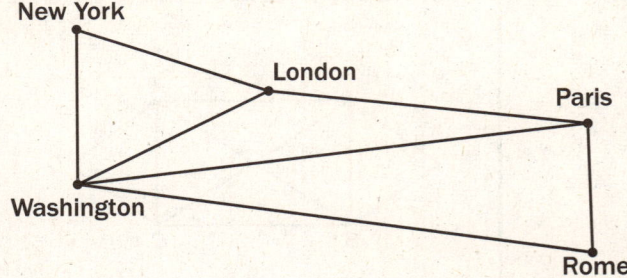

An alternate method is to mark the graph using subscripts.

Drawing 2

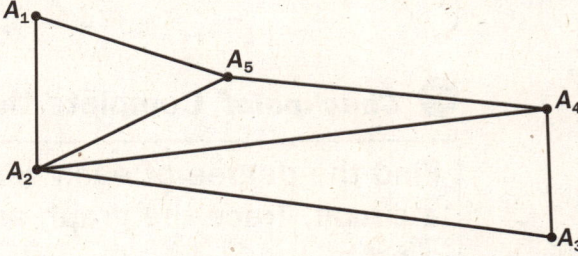

Another alternate method is to mark the graph using the first letter of each city.

Drawing 3

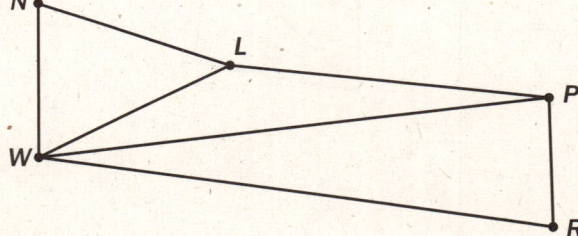

According to this particular airlines network, there are direct flights between New York and London, between Washington and London, between Washington and Paris, and between Washington and Rome. There are no direct flights between New York and Paris and New York and Rome.

There are several paths that describe a trip from New York to Paris, using drawing 2; $A_1A_5A_4$, $A_1A_2A_4$, $A_1A_2A_5A_4$, and $A_1A_2A_3A_4$ or using drawing 3; NLP, NWP NWLP, and NWRP. The path that seems the most direct is NLP however, depending on cost, layover time and availability (see chart 1) one of the other paths may be a better choice. The consideration of these values determines a routing problem.

(continued)

Copyright © by McDougal Littell, a division of Houghton Mifflin Company.

Example 2 (continued)

Chart 1: The prices and times are listed below.

New York to London	$1414.00	6 hr. 50 min.
London to Paris	$147.00	1 hr. 15 min.
Layover		2 hr. 25 min.
New York to Washington	$142.00	1 hr. 15 min.
Washington to Paris	$1370.00	6 hr. 57 min.
Layover		2 hr. 47 min.
New York to Washington	$142.00	1 hr. 15 min.
Washington to Rome	$2321.00	11 hr. 20 min.
Rome to Paris	$393.00	2 hr. 10 min.
2 Layovers		4 hr. 25 min.

Your Notes

✔ **Checkpoint** **Complete the following exercise.**

Place the numbers on the graph and compare the different routes with respect to total cost and total time of each trip. Use the chart above for the total prices and time. Which route would you take and why?

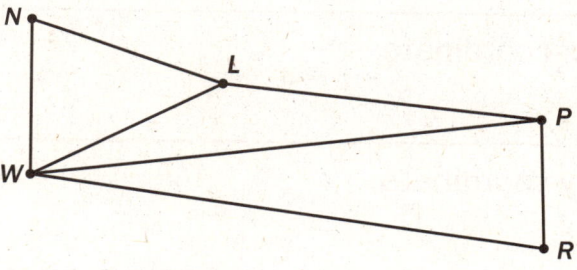

Copyright © by McDougal Littell, a division of Houghton Mifflin Company.

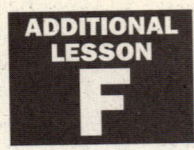

Coordinate Geometry and Geometric Figures

Goal • Given ordered pairs, identify geometric shapes in the coordinate plane using their properties.

Your Notes

VOCABULARY

Coordinate Plane:

Axes:

Ordered Pair:

Coordinates:

x-coordinate:

y-coordinate:

Origin:

Quadrant:

Geometric Shapes:

Copyright © by McDougal Littell, a division of Houghton Mifflin Company.

Example 1 | **Use coordinate geometry to construct geometric shapes**

Plot the given ordered pairs on graph paper. Then, connect them to form a geometric figure. Finally, identify what type of figure is formed.

a. $A(1, 3)$, $B(4, 1)$, $C(2, 0)$

The figure formed is a triangle.

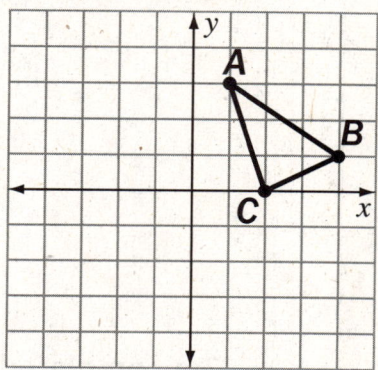

b. $A(-5, -1)$, $B-5, -3)$, $C(-2, -1)$, $D(-2, -3)$

The figure formed is a rectangle.

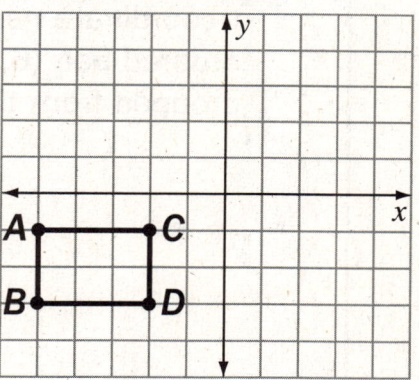

c. $A(-4,3)$, $B(-1, 4)$, $C(3,3)$, $D(0, 2)$

The figure formed is a parallelogram.

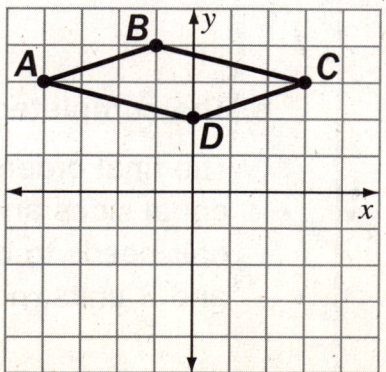

Copyright © by McDougal Littell, a division of Houghton Mifflin Company.

Example 2

State the missing coordinate of a given geometric figure based on its properties

When complete, the graphs below will form geometric shapes. Determine the remaining coordinates of the figure based on its geometric type and then complete the drawing. Explain how you determined the final ordered pair.

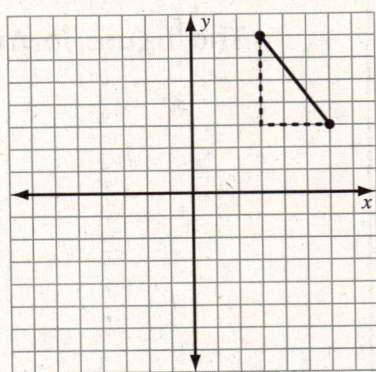

a. The completed figure will form a right triangle.

The final ordered pair is (3, 3). Because a right triangle must contain one right angle, the *x*-coordinate needs to be in line with the 3 from the ordered pair (3, 7) and the *y*-coordinate needs to be in line with the 3 from the ordered pair (6, 3). The intersection of the two lines dropped from the given ordered pairs meet at (3, 3).

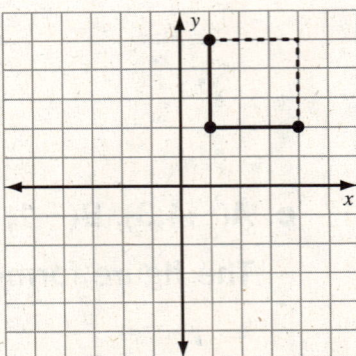

b. The completed figure will form a square.

The final ordered pair is (4, 5). Because a square has four equal sides and the opposite sides are parallel, the ordered pair needs to be in line with (4, 2) for the *x*-coordinate (4) and 3 units more for the *y*-coordinate (2 + 3).

Copyright © by McDougal Littell, a division of Houghton Mifflin Company.

Copyright © by McDougal Littell, a division of Houghton Mifflin Company.

Your Notes

✔ *Checkpoint* Complete the following exercises.

1. Plot the given ordered pairs on the graph paper. Connect them to form a geometric figure. Name the type of figure that has been formed.

   a. A(−2, 2), B(−6, 2), C(−6, 5), D(−2,5)

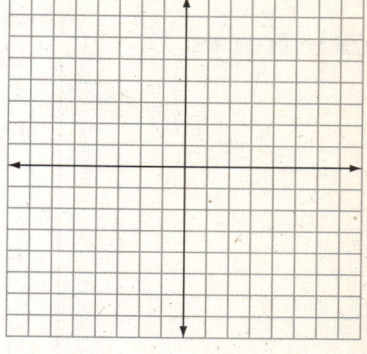

   b. A(−4, −3), B(−1, −6), C(−4, −6),

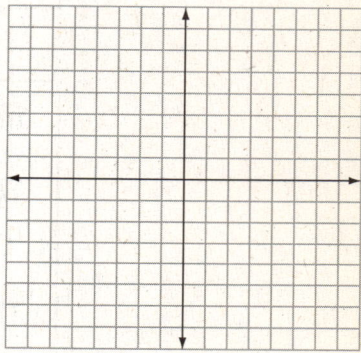

2. Based on the figure drawn, what would be the coordinates of point *D*? Explain how you determined your answer.

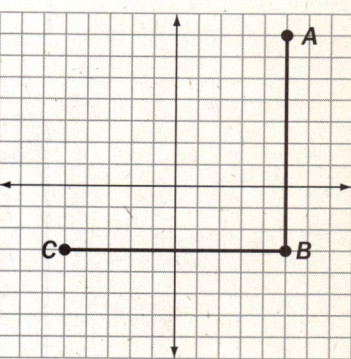

3. Determine what the new coordinates would be for a second rectangle, if you were to *fold* the graph on the *y*-axis. The new rectangle would be in the first quadrant.

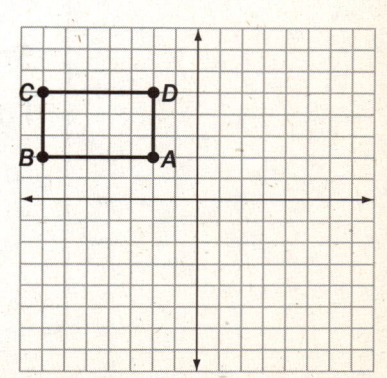

Angles and Polygons

Goal • Find measures of interior and exterior angles.

Your Notes

VOCABULARY

Interior angle:

Exterior angle:

Measures of Interior Angles of a Convex Polygon

The sum of the measures of the interior angles of a convex n-gon is given by the formula $(n - 2) \cdot 180°$.

The measure of an interior angle of a regular n-gon is given by the formula $\frac{(n - 2) \cdot 180°}{n}$.

Example 1 **Finding the Sum of a Polygon's Interior Angles**

Find the sum of the measures of the interior angles of the polygon.

Solution

For a convex hexagon, $n = 6$.

$(n - 2) \cdot 180° = (6 - 2) \cdot 180°$

$= 4 \cdot 180°$

$= 720°$

Copyright © by McDougal Littell, a division of Houghton Mifflin Company.

Copyright © by McDougal Littell, a division of Houghton Mifflin Company.

Example 2 Finding the Measure of an Interior Angle

Find the measure of an interior angle of a regular octagon.

Solution

For a regular octagon, $n = 8$.

Measure of an
interior angle $= \dfrac{(n - 2) \cdot 180°}{n}$ Write formula.

$= \dfrac{(8 - 2) \cdot 180°}{8}$ Substitute for n.

$= 135°$ Simplify.

Your Notes

✔ **Checkpoint** Complete the following exercises.

1. Find the sum of the measures of the interior angles of a convex 9-gon.

2. Find the measure of an interior angle of a regular 18-gon.

Example 3 Finding the Measure of an Exterior Angle

An interior angle and an exterior angle at the same vertex form a straight angle.

Find $m\angle 1$ in the diagram.

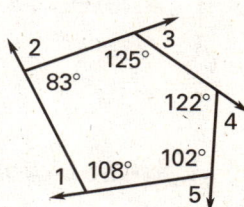

Solution

The angle that measures 108° forms a straight angle with $\angle 1$, which is the exterior angle at the same vertex.

$m\angle 1 + 108° = 180°$ Angles are supplementary.

$m\angle 1 = 72°$ Subtract 108° from each side.

✅ **Checkpoint** Complete the following exercise.

3. In Example 3, find $m\angle 2$, $m\angle 3$, $m\angle 4$, and $m\angle 5$.

Example 4   **Using the Sum of Measures of Exterior Angles**

Each vertex of a convex polygon has two exterior angles. If you draw one exterior angle at each vertex, then the sum of the measures of these angles is 360°.

Find the unknown angle measure in the diagram.

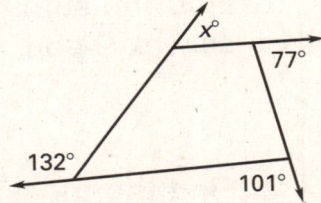

Solution

$x° + 77° + 101° + 132° = 360°$

$\qquad\qquad\qquad x + 310 = 360$ Add.

$\qquad\qquad\qquad\qquad x = 50$ Subtract 310 from each side.

Answer: The angle measure is 50°.

✅ **Checkpoint** Complete the following exercise.

4. Five exterior angles of a convex hexagon have measures 42°, 78°, 60°, 55°, and 62°. Find the measure of the sixth exterior angle.

Copyright © by McDougal Littell, a division of Houghton Mifflin Company.

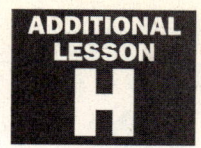

Volumes of Pyramids and Cones

Goal • Find the volumes of pyramids and cones.

Volume of a Pyramid

Words The volume of a pyramid is one third the product of the area of the base and the height.

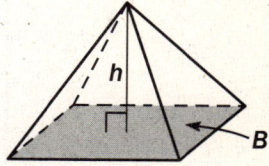

Algebra $V = \frac{1}{3} Bh$

Remember that the height of a pyramid is different from the slant height of a regular pyramid.

Example 1   Finding the Volume of a Pyramid

Paperweight A paperweight has the shape of a square pyramid. It has a height of 7 centimeters, and each side of its base measures 12 centimeters. What is the volume of the paperweight?

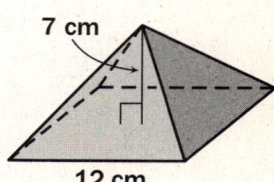

Solution

$$V = \frac{1}{3} Bh \qquad \text{Write formula for volume of a pyramid.}$$

$$= \frac{1}{3}(12^2)(7) \qquad \text{The base is square, so } B = s^2.$$

$$= 336 \qquad \text{Evaluate using a calculator.}$$

Answer: The paperweight has a volume of 336 cubic centimeters.

Copyright © by McDougal Littell, a division of Houghton Mifflin Company.

Example 2 **Finding the Volume of a Pyramid**

Find the volume of the pyramid.

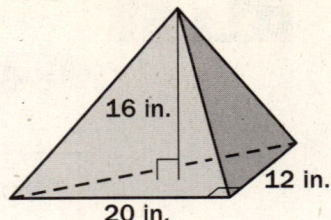

16 in.

12 in.

20 in.

$V = \frac{1}{3} Bh$ Write formula for volume of a pyramid.

$= \frac{1}{3}\left(\frac{1}{2} \cdot 20 \cdot 12\right)(16)$ The base is a triangle, so $B = \frac{1}{2} bh$.

$= 640$ Multiply.

Answer: The pyramid has a volume of 640 cubic inches.

Your Notes

✓ **Checkpoint** Complete the following exercise.

Find the volume of the pyramids.

1.

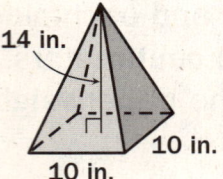

14 in.

10 in.

10 in.

2.

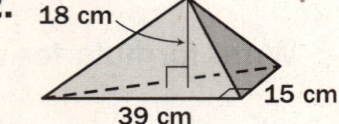

18 cm

15 cm

39 cm

3.

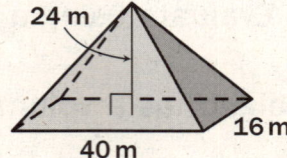

24 m

16 m

40 m

4. Critical Thinking A square pyramid has a volume of 750 cubic inches. Each side length of the base is 15 inches. What is the height of the pyramid?

Copyright © by McDougal Littell, a division of Houghton Mifflin Company.

Volume of a Cone

Words The volume of a cone is one third the product of the area of the base and the height.

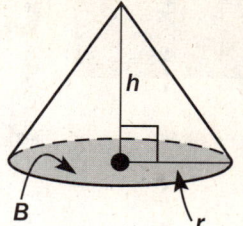

Algebra $V = \dfrac{1}{3} Bh = \dfrac{1}{3} \pi r^2 h$

Example 3   Finding the Volume of a Cone

Paper Cups A paper cup has the shape of a cone. The cup has a height of 7 centimeters and a base diameter of 6 centimeters. What is the capacity of the cup?

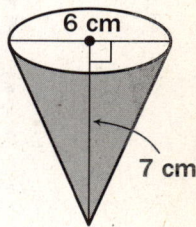

Solution

The radius is one-half the diameter, so $r = 3$ cm.

$V = \dfrac{1}{3} \pi r^2 h$	Write formula for volume of a cone.
$= \dfrac{1}{3} \pi (3)^2 (7)$	Substitute 3 for r and 7 for h.
$= 21\pi$	Simplify.
≈ 65.97	Evaluate using a calculator.

Answer: The capacity of the paper cup is about 66 cubic centimeters.

Your Notes

✔ *Checkpoint* Complete the following exercise.

Find the volume of the cone with radius r and height h. Round to the nearest tenth.

5. $r = 2$ in., $h = 10$ in.

6. $r = 8$ cm, $h = 8$ cm

7. $r = 20$ ft, $h = 6$ ft

Copyright © by McDougal Littell, a division of Houghton Mifflin Company.

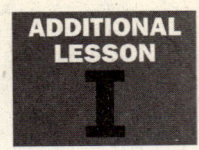

Circles and Sectors

Goal • Identify parts of a circle and calculate the area of a sector of a circle.

Your Notes

VOCABULARY

Chord:

Central angle of a circle:

Sector of a circle:

Area of a sector:

Example 1   **Identify Parts of a Circle**

Tell whether the indicated segment is best described as a *radius*, *diameter*, or *chord* of the circle.

a. $\overline{BF}$ **b.** $\overline{BD}$ **c.** $\overline{BC}$

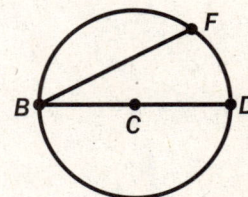

Solution

a. $\overline{BF}$ is a chord because it is a segment whose endpoints are on the circle.

b. $\overline{BD}$ is a diameter because it is a chord with the center C as one of its points.

c. $\overline{BC}$ is a radius because B is a point on the circle and C is the center.

Copyright © by McDougal Littell, a division of Houghton Mifflin Company.

Example 2 **Find the Area of a Sector**

Find the area of the sector formed by $\angle PQR$.

Write and solve a proportion to find the area of the sector.

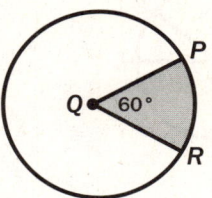

Solution

$$\frac{\text{Area of sector}}{\text{Area of entire circle}} = \frac{\text{Measure of central angle}}{\text{Measure of entire circle}}$$

$$\frac{a}{25\pi} = \frac{60°}{360°} \qquad \text{Substitute.}$$

$$a \cdot 360 = 25\pi \cdot 60 \qquad \text{Find cross products.}$$

$$360a \approx 4710 \qquad \text{Simplify. Use 3.14 for } \pi.$$

$$a \approx 13.0833 \qquad \text{Divide both sides by 360.}$$

Answer: Rounded to tenths, the area is 13.1 square yards.

Copyright © by McDougal Littell, a division of Houghton Mifflin Company.

Checkpoint Complete the following exercises.

Tell whether the indicated segment or angle is best described as a radius, diameter, chord, angle, or central angle.

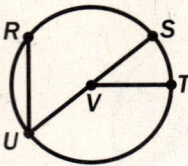

1. ∠SVT

2. $\overline{VT}$

3. $\overline{RU}$

4. ∠RUS

5. $\overline{SU}$

6. $\overline{BC}$

7. ∠ADC

8. ∠CAD

9. $\overline{AD}$

10. $\overline{AC}$

Find the area of the sector formed by ∠XYZ to the nearest tenth. Use 3.14 for π.

11.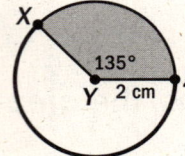

12.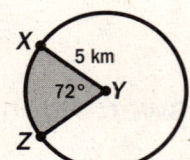

13.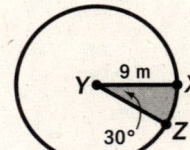

14.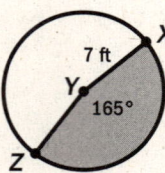

15.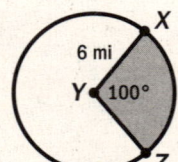

16.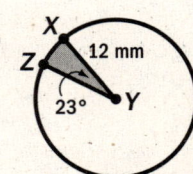

(continued)

Copyright © by McDougal Littell, a division of Houghton Mifflin Company.

17.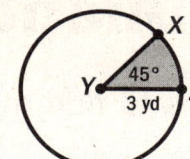

18.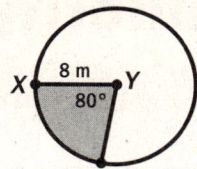

19.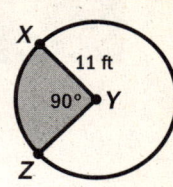

20. In each part, give your answer to the nearest 0.1 square unit. Use 3.14 for π.

a. What is the area of $\odot C$?

b. What is the area of the square?

c. What is the area of the overlapping region?

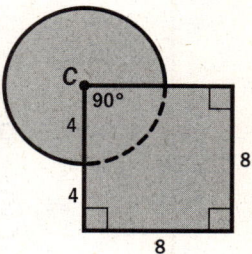

d. What is the area of the part of $\odot C$ that does not overlap the square?

e. What is the area of the square that does not overlap $\odot C$?

f. What is the area of the shaded figure?

Copyright © by McDougal Littell, a division of Houghton Mifflin Company.

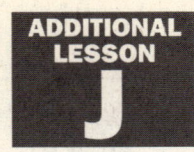

ADDITIONAL LESSON J

Similarity and Dilations

Goal • Use similar polygons to find missing measures.

Your Notes

VOCABULARY

Similar polygons:

Dilation:

Scale factor:

Similar Polygons

$\triangle ABC \sim \triangle XYZ$

Corresponding angles are conguent.

$\angle A \cong \angle X$ $\angle B \cong \angle Y$ $\angle C \cong \angle Z$

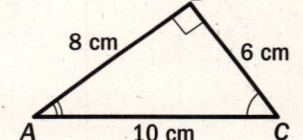

Corresponding side lengths
are proportional.

$$\frac{AB}{XY} = \frac{BC}{YZ} \qquad \frac{BC}{YZ} = \frac{AC}{XZ} \qquad \frac{AC}{XZ} = \frac{AB}{XY}$$

Copyright © by McDougal Littell, a division of Houghton Mifflin Company.

Example 1 Identifying Similar Polygons

Photography Two photographs are different sizes but have the same shape. Tell whether the photographs are similar.

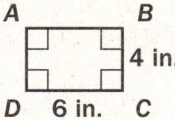 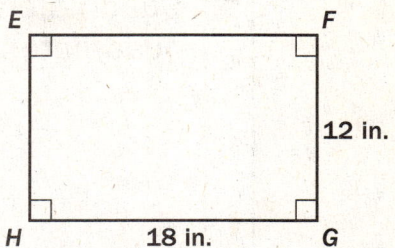

1. Corresponding angles are congruent.
   Each angle measures 90°.

   $\angle A \cong \angle E$ $\angle B \cong \angle F$ $\angle C \cong \angle G$ $\angle D \cong \angle H$

2. Corresponding side lengths are proportional.

   $$\frac{18 \text{ inches}}{6 \text{ inches}} = \frac{12 \text{ inches}}{4 \text{ inches}}$$

   $$3 = 3$$

Notice that when naming similar polygons, the corresponding vertices are listed in the same order.

Answer: Yes, quadrilateral *ABCD* ~ quadrilateral *EFGH*

Example 2 Standardized Test Practice

In the diagram, $\triangle PQR \sim \triangle STU$.
What is the value of *y*?

Ⓐ 6 ft   Ⓑ 12 ft

Ⓒ 13 ft   Ⓓ 13.5 ft

Corresponding side lengths are proportional.

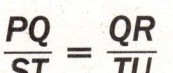

$\dfrac{PQ}{ST} = \dfrac{QR}{TU}$ Write a proportion.

$\dfrac{y}{9} = \dfrac{9}{6}$ Substitute given values.

$y = 13.5$ Solve the proportion.

Answer: The value of *y* is 13.5 feet. The correct answer is D.

Copyright © by McDougal Littell, a division of Houghton Mifflin Company.

Your Notes

✔ **Checkpoint** Complete the following exercise.

Find the value of *x*.

1. Quadrilateral *PQRS* ~ quadrilateral *WXYZ*

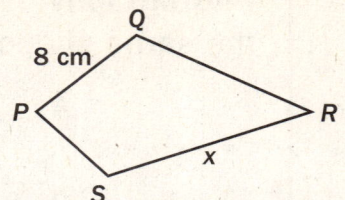
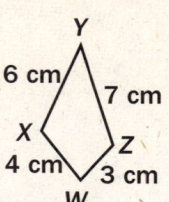

Example 3 **Using Indirect Measurement**

Height A building is 25 feet tall and casts a 10 foot shadow. At the same time, a fence casts a 6 foot shadow. The triangles formed are similar. Find the height of the fence.

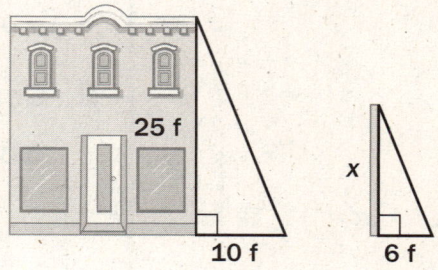

Solution

You can use a proportion to find the height of the fence.

$$\frac{\text{Fence's height}}{\text{Building's height}} = \frac{\text{Length of fence's shadow}}{\text{Length of building's shadow}}$$ Write a proportion.

$$\frac{x}{25 \text{ feet}} = \frac{6 \text{ feet}}{10 \text{ feet}}$$ Substitute given values.

$$x = 15$$ Solve the proportion.

ANSWER The fence is 15 feet tall.

Dilation

Words To dilate a polygon, multiply the coordinates of each vertex by the scale factor *k* and connect the vertices.

Numbers $P(3, 2) \rightarrow P'(6, 4)$

Algebra $P(x, y) \rightarrow P'(kx, ky)$

Copyright © by McDougal Littell, a division of Houghton Mifflin Company.

Example 4   **Dilating a Polygon**

Quadrilateral *ABCD* has vertices *A*(−3, 0), *B*(−2, 3), *C*(1, 1), and *D*(0, −1). Dilate using a scale factor of 2. Then graph its image.

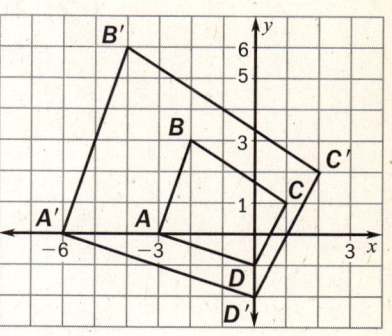

Original		**Image**
(*x*, *y*)	$\longrightarrow$	(2*x*, 2*y*)
A(−3, 0)	$\longrightarrow$	*A*′(−6, 0)
B(−2, 3)	$\longrightarrow$	*B*′(−4, 6)
C(1, 1)	$\longrightarrow$	*C*′(2, 2)
D(0, −1)	$\longrightarrow$	*D*′(0, −2)

The scale factor is the ratio of corresponding side lengths:

$$\frac{\text{after dilation}}{\text{before dilation}}$$

Copyright © by McDougal Littell, a division of Houghton Mifflin Company.

✔ *Checkpoint* Complete the following exercises.

Graph the polygon with the given vertices. Then graph its image after dilation by the scale factor *k*.

2. Triangle *LMN* has vertices *L*(2, −1), *M*(3, 2), and *N*(4, 1); *k* = 4.

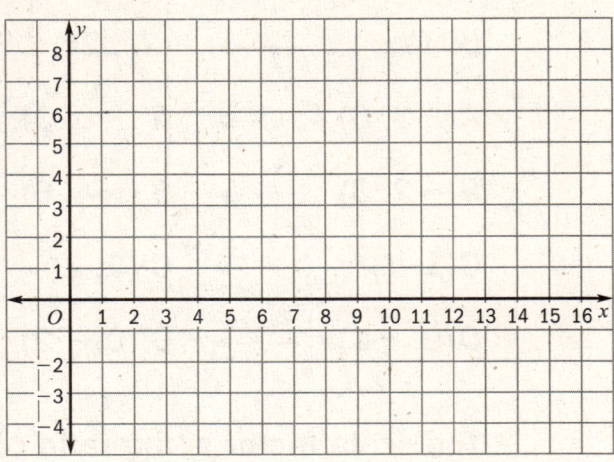

3. Quadrilateral *RSTU* has vertices *R*(−10, −4), *S*(−6, 4), *T*(−2, −2), *U*(−8, −6); $k = \frac{1}{2}$.

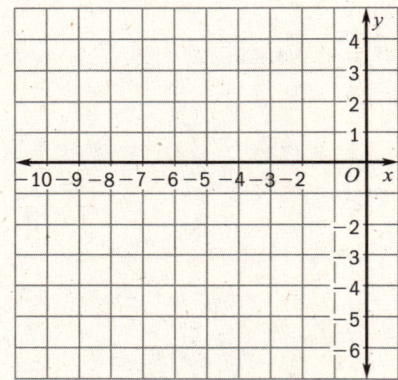

4. Triangle *DEF* has vertices *D*(−3, 6), *E*(3, 12), and *F*(6, 0); $k = \frac{1}{3}$.

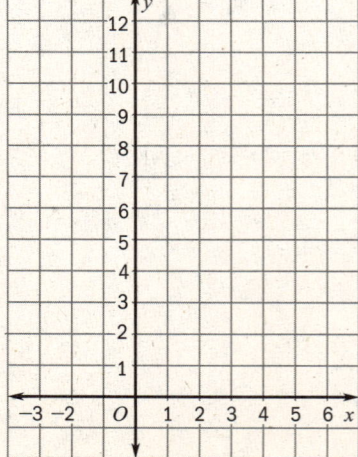

Copyright © by McDougal Littell, a division of Houghton Mifflin Company.

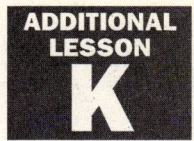

Stem-and-Leaf Plots

Goal • Make and interpret stem-and-leaf plots.

Your Notes

VOCABULARY

Stem-and-leaf plot:

Example 1   **Making a Stem-and-Leaf Plot**

Snowboarding The scores of the top 15 finishers of a snowboard half pipe competition are shown below. How can the data be displayed to show the distribution of the scores?

38.4, 40.6, 37.8, 38.9, 41.7, 39.2, 37.1, 41.4, 40.5, 38.8, 40.9, 39.3, 41.2, 38.3, 37.1

Solution

You can display the scores in a stem-and-leaf plot.

1. Identify the stems and leaves. The scores range from 37.1 through 41.7. Let the stems be the digits in the tens' and ones' places. Let the leaves be the tenths' digits.

2. Write the stems first. Then record each score by writing its tenths' digit on the same line as its corresponding stem. Include a key that shows what the stems and leaves represent.

3. Make an ordered stem-and-leaf plot. The leaves for each stem are listed in order from least to greatest.

Unordered Plot					Ordered Plot			
37	8	1	1		37	1	1	8
38	4	9	8	3	38	3	4	8	9
39	2	3			39	2	3	
40	6	5	9		40	5	6	9
41	7	4	2		41	2	4	7

Key: 38 | 4 = 38.4   Key: 38 | 4 = 38.4

Copyright © by McDougal Littell, a division of Houghton Mifflin Company.

Checkpoint Complete the following exercise.

Make an ordered stem-and-leaf plot of the data.

1. Baseball pitch speeds (mi/h): 86, 83, 74, 95, 89, 97, 68, 88, 72, 97, 94, 85, 70, 89, 80, 93, 91, 84

Example 2 **Interpreting a Stem-and-Leaf Plot**

In a stem-and-leaf plot, a stem can be one or more digits. A leaf is usually a single digit.

Movies The stem-and-leaf plot below shows the ages of people in a movie theater. Use the stem-and-leaf plot to describe the data. What interval includes the most ages?

```
0 | 5  6  7  7  8  8  8  9  9
1 | 0  0  0  1  1  2  2  2  3  3  4  5  6
2 | 0  2  8  9
3 | 3  7
4 | 8
5 | 1
```
Key: 2 | 0 = 20

Solution

The oldest person is 51 years old and the youngest person is 5 years old. So the range of ages is 46 years. Most of the ages are in the 10–19 interval.

Copyright © by McDougal Littell, a division of Houghton Mifflin Company.

Example 3 **Making a Double Stem-and-Leaf Plot**

Swimming The data below show the number of laps swum during practice by swimmers on two different swim teams. Overall, which team swam more laps?

Dolphins: 19, 25, 31, 26, 17, 25, 26, 18, 23, 19, 25, 24

Sharks: 18, 25, 9, 15, 30, 24, 17, 18, 22, 16, 28, 19

Solution

You can use a double stem-and-leaf plot to compare the number of laps swum.

				Dolphins				Sharks				
					0	9						
	9	9	8	7	1	5	6	7	8	8	9	
6	6	5	5	5	4	3	2	2	4	5	8	
					1	3	0					

Key: 1 | 3 | 0 represents 31 and 30.

Answer: The dolphins swim team swam more laps because it had more swimmers swim a number of laps in the twenties.

Your Notes

✔ **Checkpoint** Complete the following exercise.

2. Make an ordered double stem-and-leaf plot to compare the times, in minutes, that two friends spent online in the last week.

Omar: 35, 26, 30, 48, 55, 13, 38
Joseph: 46, 15, 68, 0, 44, 49, 32

3. In general, who spent the most time online in the last week, Omar or Joseph?

Copyright © by McDougal Littell, a division of Houghton Mifflin Company.

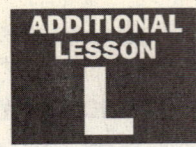

Misleading Data Displays

Goal • Determine if the data displayed is giving a misleading impression.

Your Notes

VOCABULARY

Data

Display

Scale

Interval

Range

Misleading Displays

Copyright © by McDougal Littell, a division of Houghton Mifflin Company.

Copyright © by McDougal Littell, a division of Houghton Mifflin Company.

Example 1 Analyze a graph to determine how an incorrect conclusion may be drawn

The graph on the left displays the number of calories burned walking **down** a set of stairs while the graph on the right displays the number of calories burned walking **up** a set of stairs.

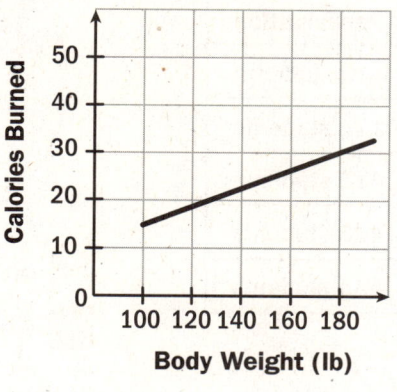 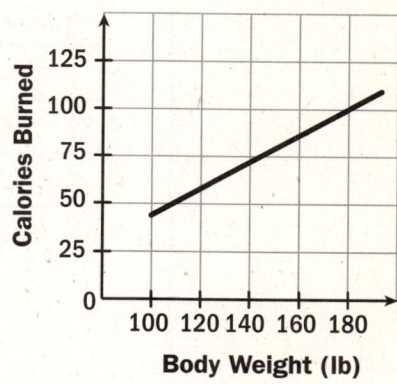

The two graphs appear to be very similar, therefore implying that walking up or down the stairs burn the same amount of calories. This is an incorrect conclusion since the scales on the vertical axis are different. The choice of interval affects the slope of the lines.

Example 2 Analyze a set of data to determine if the display is appropriate

The following data indicates the number of families with zero, one, two, or three pets.

From the display, the number having zero, one, two, or three pets is difficult to determine. The upper level on the scale used for the vertical axis is too large and the size of the intervals is also too large to make an accurate estimate.

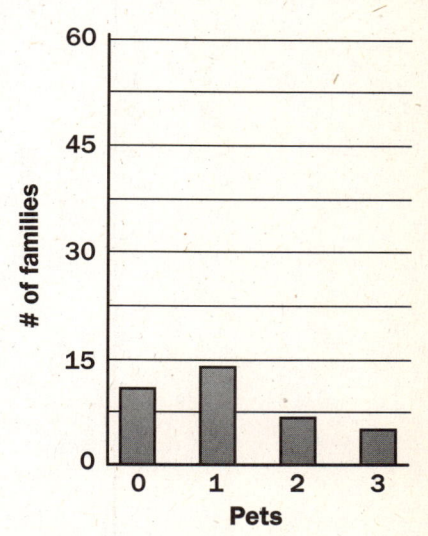

✔ **Checkpoint** Complete the following exercises.

1. The table and the circle graph show the same data about student participation in a school district's sports program. Explain how the graph could be misleading.

Grade Level	Participation
–	440 students
9	172 students
10	412 students
11	433 students
12	444 students

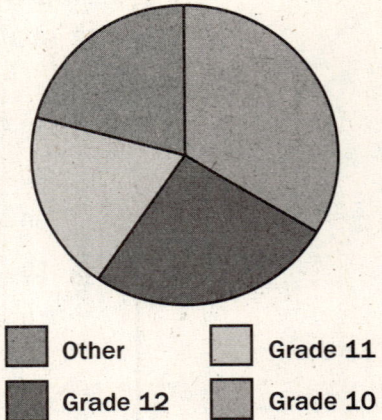

☐ Other   ☐ Grade 11
☐ Grade 12   ☐ Grade 10

2. The scores of a student's last 10 math tests are given below. Explain how the display could be misleading.

Test Scores: 90, 62, 65, 75, 83, 80, 61, 82, 85, 68

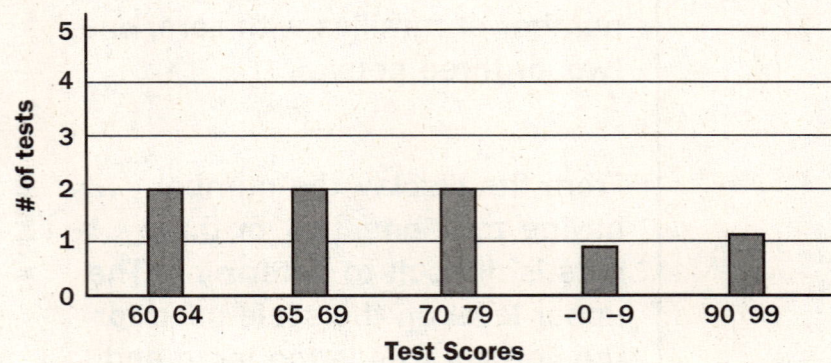

Copyright © by McDougal Littell, a division of Houghton Mifflin Company.

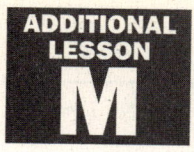

ADDITIONAL LESSON

M

Designing and Conducting an Investigation

Goal • Use statistical methods to analyze and communicate data.

Your Notes

VOCABULARY

Descriptive Statistics:

Inferential Statistics:

Sample:

Mean:

Median:

---

continued

Copyright © by McDougal Littell, a division of Houghton Mifflin Company.

Mode:

Standard Deviation:

Formula for Standard Deviation:

Copyright © by McDougal Littell, a division of Houghton Mifflin Company.

Example 1

Analyze data to determine how an incorrect conclusion may be drawn

In a particular factory, two machines package popcorn kernels into 1.25-pound containers. To test the packaging process, a quality control worker weighs a random sample of 20 containers from each machine. Find the mean, median, and mode. Use the results to make conclusions about the machines. The weight of the 20 containers from the two machines is listed below.

Container #	Machine #1	Machine #2
1	1.250	1.254
2	1.252	1.245
3	1.248	1.253
4	1.252	1.250
5	1.251	1.261
6	1.256	1.253
7	1.253	1.254
8	1.248	1.244
9	1.246	1.250
10	1.257	1.252
11	1.250	1.260
12	1.251	1.257
13	1.250	1.248
14	1.255	1.242
15	1.251	1.253
16	1.253	1.243
17	1.249	1.260
18	1.249	1.248
19	1.245	1.251
20	1.251	1.259
Mean	1.25085	1.25185
Median	1.251	1.2525
Mode	1.251 (4 times)	1.253 (3 times)
Standard Deviation	.00304	.00575

The means are almost equal, therefore no conclusion can be drawn from that data. However, the standard deviation of machine #1 (.00304) is less than the standard deviation of machine #2 (.00575). Machine #1 has less variability and will produce closer to the desired weight more often than machine #2.

Copyright © by McDougal Littell, a division of Houghton Mifflin Company.

✓ **Checkpoint** Complete the following exercise.

Design your own survey of interest to you or use the following data.

Mr. Smith commutes to Chicago daily. There are two possible routes, Hwy 90 or Hwy 290. One route is a diagonal line and the other is "L" shaped, however, both routes start at the same point in the suburbs and ends at the same point in Chicago. One week he traveled Hwy 90 and the other Hwy 290. The times for the trips are listed below. Determine the mean, median, mode, and standard deviation to determine the route that is more consistent.

Minutes per trip

	M	T	W	Th	F
Route 290	40	56	76	42	53
Route 90	54	45	64	53	51

Copyright © by McDougal Littell, a division of Houghton Mifflin Company.

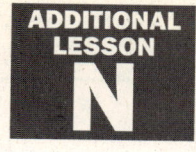

Experimental vs. Observational Study

Goal • Differentiate between an experiment and an observational study.

Your Notes

Copyright © by McDougal Littell, a division of Houghton Mifflin Company.

VOCABULARY

Descriptive Statistics:

Inferential Statistics:

Population:

Sample:

  a) **Simple Random:**

  b) **Systematic:**

  c) **Stratified:**

  d) **Convenience:**

  e) **Self-Selected:**

continued

VOCABULARY *continued*

Biased Sample:

    a) **Underrepresented:**

    b) **Overrepresented:**

Parameter:

Statistic:

Example 1   **Classifying samples and determining if the sample is biased**

1. The officials of the National Football League (NFL) want to know how the players feel about some proposed changes to the NFL rules. They decide to ask a sample of about 100 players. Classify the sample.

   a. The official choose the first 100 players that volunteer their opinions.

   Self-selected

   b. The officials randomly choose 3 players from each of the 32 teams in the NFL.

   Stratified

   c. The officials have a computer generate a list of 100 players from a database that includes all of the players in the NFL.

   Simple Random

continued

Copyright © by McDougal Littell, a division of Houghton Mifflin Company.

Example 1 (continued)

2. Administrators at your school want to know if more vegetarian items should be added to the lunch menu. Decide whether the sampling method could result in a biased sample. Explain your reasoning.

   a. Survey every 10th student waiting in line to purchase lunch.

      This method could result in a biased sample because it underrepresents the students who do not purchase lunch. Some of these students may not purchase lunch because there are not enough vegetarian items on the lunch menu.

   b. Survey every 25th student who enters the cafeteria during the lunch period.

      This method is not likely to result in a biased sample because a wide range of students will be surveyed.

Your Notes

✔ **Checkpoint** Complete the following exercises.

Identify the population and the sample.

1. A quality control inspector needs to estimate the number of defective computers in a group of 250 computers. He tests 25 randomly chosen computers.

2. The manager of the human resources department at a company wants to know if any of the company's 281 employees would take advantage of a reduced membership to a health club. The manager asks a sample of 70 randomly chosen employees.

---

continued

Copyright © by McDougal Littell, a division of Houghton Mifflin Company.

In Exercises 3–5, classify the sample related to the following situation.

The principal of a school wants to know if the students at the school would like to have the morning announcements posted on the school's Web site.

3. Survey the first 30 students who enter the cafeteria during the lunch period.

4. Survey every 10th female student and every 10th male student who enters the cafeteria during the lunch period.

5. Survey every 20th student who enters the cafeteria during the lunch period.

In Exercises 6–8, classify the sample.

6. The manager of a movie theater wants to know how the movie viewers feel about the new stadium seating at the theater. She asks every 30th person who exits the theater each Saturday night for a month.

7. The manager of a credit union wants to know whether its members utilize the on-line services offered on their Web site. He decided to call members who have been randomly chosen from a database of all of the members of the credit union.

continued

Copyright © by McDougal Littell, a division of Houghton Mifflin Company.

8. The owner of a bakery wants to know if its customers are satisfied with its selection of baked goods. She asks the first 20 people who make a purchase on a Saturday morning.

Decide whether the sampling method could result in a biased sample. Explain your reasoning.

9. On the first day of school, all of the incoming freshmen attend an orientation program. The principal wants to learn the opinions of the freshmen regarding the orientation program. He decides to ask the first 25 freshmen that he sees.

10. The manager of an apartment building wants to know if the residents are satisfied with his service. He writes each apartment number on a piece of paper and places the pieces of paper in a hat. Then he randomly chooses 10 apartment numbers. He decides to ask the residents of the 10 apartments about his service.

11. The members of the school drama club want to know how much students are willing to pay for a ticket to one of their productions. They decide that each member of the drama club should ask 5 of his or her friends what they are willing to pay.

Copyright © by McDougal Littell, a division of Houghton Mifflin Company.

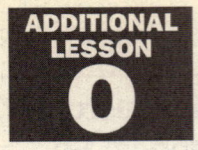
Inductive and Deductive Reasoning

 **Goal** • Solve simple logic problems using inductive and deductive reasoning.

Your Notes

VOCABULARY

Inductive reasoning:

Deductive reasoning:

Law of Detachment:

Law of Syllogism:

Example 1 **Use the Law of Detachment**

Use the Law of Detachment to make a valid conclusion in the true situation

If two angles have the same measure, then they are congruent. You know that $m\angle A = m\angle B$.

Solution

First, identify the hypothesis and the conclusion of the first statement. The hypothesis is "If two angles have the same measure." The conclusion is "then they are congruent."

Because $m\angle A = m\angle B$ satisfies the hypothesis of a true conditional statement, the conclusion is also true.
So, $m\angle A \cong m\angle B$.

Copyright © by McDougal Littell, a division of Houghton Mifflin Company.

Example 2   **Use the Law of Syllogism**

If possible, use the Law of Syllogism to write the conditional statement that follows from the pair of true statements.

a. If the electric power is off, then the refrigerator does not run. If the refrigerator does not run, then the food will spoil.

b. If $2x > 10$, then $2x > 7$.
   If $x > 5$, then $2x > 10$.

Solution

a. The conclusion of the first statement is the hypothesis of the second statement, so you can write the following statement.
   If the electric power is off, then the food will spoil.

b. Notice that the conclusion of the second statement is the hypothesis of the first statement.
   If $x > 5$, then $2x > 7$.

Your Notes

 **Checkpoint** Complete the following exercises.

Complete the following exercises for Examples 1 and 2.

1. If A is acute, then $0° < m\angle A < 90°$. Angle B is an acute angle. Using the Law of Detachment, what conclusion can you make?

2. If B is between A and C, then $AB + BC = AC$. E is between D and F. Using the Law of Detachment, what conclusion can you make?

3. If you study hard, you will pass all of your classes. If you pass all of your classes, you will graduate. Using the Law of Syllogism, what statement can you make?

4. If $x^2 > 9$, then $x^2 > 8$. If $x > 4$, then $x^2 > 9$. Using the Law of Syllogism, what statement can you make?

Copyright © by McDougal Littell, a division of Houghton Mifflin Company.

Example 3 | **Use inductive and deductive reasoning**

What conclusion can you make about the sum of two even integers?

Solution

Step 1 Look for a pattern in several examples. Use inductive reasoning to make a conjecture.

$-2 + 4 = 2, -4 + 10 = 6, 6 + 8 = 14,$
$12 + 6 = 18, -20 + 14 = -6, -12 + 2 = -10,$
$-6 + 2 = -4, -2 + (-6) = -8$

Conjecture: Even integer + Even integer = Even integer

Step 2 Let n and m be any integer. Use deductive reasoning to show the conjecture is true.

$2n$ and $2m$ are even integers because any integer multiplied by 2 is even.

$2n + 2m$ represents the sum of two even integers.

$2n + 2m$ can be written as $2(n + m)$.

The sum of two integers $(n + m)$ is an integer and any integer multiplied by 2 is even.

The sum of two even integers is an even integer

Your Notes

✔ **Checkpoint** Complete the following exercises.

Complete the following exercise for Example 3.

5. What conclusion can you make about the sum of two odd integers? (Hint: An odd integer can be written as $2n + 1$, where n is any integer.)

Copyright © by McDougal Littell, a division of Houghton Mifflin Company.

ADDITIONAL LESSON

P

Triangle Inequalities

Goal • Use triangle measurements to decide which side is longest and which angle is largest.

Your Notes

Words If one side of a triangle is longer than another side, then the angle opposite the longer side is ___larger___ than the angle opposite the shorter side.

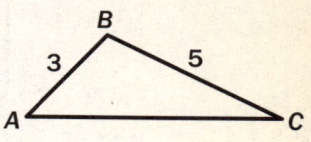

Symbols If $BC > AB$, then $m\angle A$ __>__ $m\angle C$.

Words If one angle of a triangle is larger than another angle, then the side opposite the larger angle is ___longer___ than the side opposite the smaller angle.

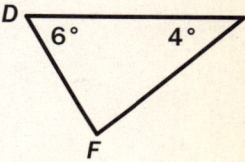

Symbols If $m\angle D > m\angle E$, then EF __>__ DF.

Example 1 **Order Angle Measures**

Name the angles from largest to smallest.

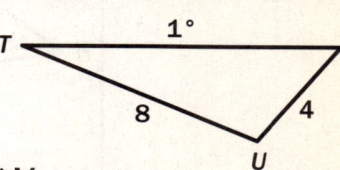

Solution

TV __>__ TU, so $m\angle U$ __>__ $m\angle V$.

TU __>__ UV, so $m\angle V$ __>__ $m\angle T$.

The order of the angles from largest to smallest is __∠U__, __∠V__, __∠T__

Copyright © by McDougal Littell, a division of Houghton Mifflin Company.

Example 2   **Order Side Lengths**

Name the sides from longest to shortest.

Solution

$m\angle E$ ___>___ $m\angle D$, so DF ___>___ FE.

$m\angle D$ ___>___ $m\angle F$, so FE ___>___ DE.

The order of the sides from longest to shortest is ___$\overline{DF}$___,
___$\overline{FE}$___, ___$\overline{DE}$___

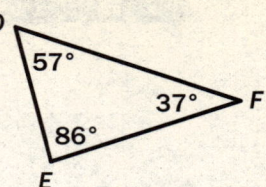

Your Notes   ✔ **Checkpoint** Name the angles from largest to smallest.

1.	2.	3.
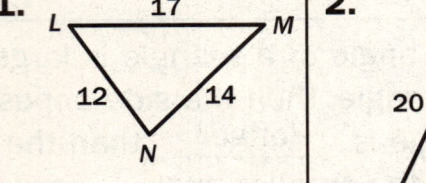		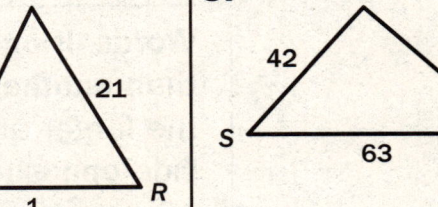

Name the sides from longest to shortest.

4.	5.	6.
	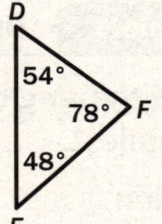	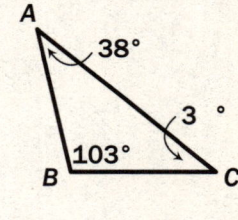

Copyright © by McDougal Littell, a division of Houghton Mifflin Company.

Words The sum of the lengths of any two sides of a triangle
is ___greater___ than the length of the third side.

Symbols

$CA + AB$ __>__ BC

$AB + BC$ __>__ CA

$BC + CA$ __>__ AB

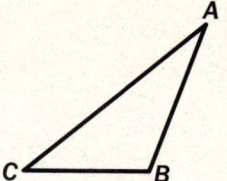

Example 3   **Use the Triangle Inequality**

Can the side lengths form a triangle? Explain.

a. 3, 5, 9   **b.** 3, 5, 8   **c.** 3, 5, 7

Solution

a.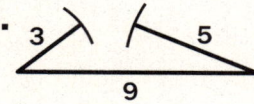

These lengths
do not form a
triangle, because
$3 + 5$ __<__ 9.

b.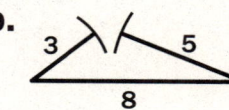

These lengths
do not form a
triangle, because
$3 + 5$ __=__ 8.

c.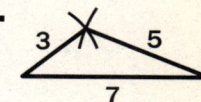

These lengths
do form a
triangle, because
$3 + 5$ __>__ 7,

$3 + 7$ __>__ 5,

and $5 + 7$ __>__ 3.

Your Notes

 Checkpoint Can the side lengths form a triangle? Explain.

7. 5, 7, 13	**8.** 6, 9, 12	**9.** 10, 15, 25

Copyright © by McDougal Littell, a division of Houghton Mifflin Company.